MICHELLE BOUDREAU'S

DEBT
RE$CUE

What The Credit Industry Doesn't Want You To Know!

Published by HG Publishing, LLC

Published by: HG Publishing, LLC
PRINTED IN THE UNITED STATES OF AMERICA
FOR WORLDWIDE DISTRIBUTION

© 2008 Debt Rescue, LLC

ISBN 978-1-934959-01-5

Mission Statement

My Mission and Intention for Debt Rescue is to increase financial awareness across America. My focus and passion is to use knowledge to help people raise their confidence with personal finances. When people are more financially savvy our economy will inevitably benefit. It is my life's purpose to always convey hope.

May the divine that resides in all of us give us wisdom to grow.

Acknowledgement...

This book has been a true labor of love from a multitude of people contributing to the success of the final outcome. I certainly could not have accomplished the completion of this book without everyone's help. With full heart I thank each and every one of you for your contribution.

TABLE OF CONTENTS

A Message from Michelle..13

Introduction: Financial Success: Your Key To Security..................17

Chapter 1: The History of Credit: A Look at
          Our Country's Credit Card History...............................21

Chapter 2: Ducks in a Row: Organization.......................................29

Chapter 3: Debt, A Good Thing?: Examples of Good Debt...........41

Chapter 4: Plastic Jungle: Credit Cards 59

Chapter 5: Taming the Beast: Collection Agencies.........................77

Chapter 6: Alter Ego: Your Credit Identity 97

Chapter 7: Suit of Armor: Protection and
          Rectifying Identity Theft 113

Chapter 8: A Piece of American Pie: Mortgages...........................127

Chapter 9: The Great Escape: Foreclosure 141

Chapter 10: To Claim or Not To Claim: Bankruptcy....................157

Chapter 11: Get Your Head Out of the Sand: Tax Debt 175

Chapter 12: Good Bedside Manner: Medical Debt........................187

Chapter 13: The Young and the Reckless: Student Loans.............201

Chapter 14: 1, 2, 3 Qualify Me: Grants 217

Chapter 15: The Future So Bright: Investing and Saving 267

A message from Michelle...

I can sincerely convey to you that I have experienced what you are going through in one way or another. I have either personally experienced it or witnessed a family member or clients go through this hardship. I have felt the fear, the pain and the financial stress, either directly or indirectly.

We have so much to be grateful for in this country. We have electricity, running water, air conditioning, heating and grocery stores full of food. The current employment rate is at 93.5%, and a large majority of our teens own cell phones and computers. Americans are some of the most blessed people in the world. Please do not misunderstand, as I do have empathy for what people are going through. In fact, in the past I have gone through it myself. Faced with job loss and the possibility of losing my house, I had to move out of a beautiful house on the water in Florida and into a 1 bedroom apartment. At another point in my life, after my divorce, I was faced with having to sleep on my sister's couch. I never lost my faith and I rarely felt sorry for myself. I learned to move on and up!

The point is many wealthy people have had to face adversity at some point in their lives. In fact if you talk to any successful person I am sure they have a story or two about living through it and coming out on the other side of adversity. This type of struggle can build character and lead to great things in life. Many of my greatest successes have evolved from the ashes of adversity.

How I became a financial authority....

I am now an accomplished businesswoman and real estate investor who has had my share of financial success and I'm thrilled to share what I have learned from my years of experience and investigation into the credit industry. Many of you will gain confidence with the knowledge and experiences that I am about to share with you. The good news is, inside this book are great solutions that can help you.

Several years ago my friends, family, and business associates started coming to me for financial and business advice. As they were becoming more financially responsible, they were concerned about their financial future. Some of them were going through a life-altering situation, such as divorce, change of career, loss of job, relocation, illness, etc., and they were concerned about their monetary situation. Money happens to be the number one reason for conflicts in relationships and is known to be one of the largest contributors of stress.

People around me saw how I was managing my money and credit and they watched my various real estate investments, retirement plan, and the businesses I built from the ground up grow into a great success. I also had started my non-profit charitable foundation to help children and animals. Today I live in a state of constant gratitude for my financial success.

However, it wasn't always like that for me. Like many people, I started out growing up in a typical middle-class family in the Midwest. Then, when I was 16, everything changed. After my parent's divorce there was a lot of financial stress in our household, and it had a big impact on me. I hurried to get my first job at 16 so I could afford the things I wanted. When I turned 18, I qualified for my first credit card. I didn't realize at the time how significant this milestone was. It marked the starting point to my lifelong journey of building and managing credit. To this day most of my wealth has been established with good credit. Being responsible with money and having business success has always been a big priority in my life. I even worked my way through college, paying for it myself.

As you can imagine, my financial journey caught people's attention and they wanted to know how I achieved it. I found myself advising people on what I had learned about financial success from years of reading, studying and from my hands-on experience. Also, having been employed by multi-billion dollar enterprises and business entities, I focused on modeling successful business plans and acquiring financial expertise from some of the most successful companies in the world, as well as being mentored by wealthy individuals. I have used a multitude of knowledge from several different arenas.

Anyone can experience this prosperity too. You can learn the techniques and secrets that got me where I am today in my series of books, CDs and programs. It didn't take long before we all saw this real world advice working and making money for others, as well!

Today more and more people keep coming to me for advice and everyday I see how they are reaching greater heights after working with my techniques. I wish you the same success.

Introduction

FINANCIAL SUCCESS: YOUR KEY TO SECURITY

Happiness
Security
Peace of Mind
Financial Freedom

Do any of these words or phrases resonate with you? When you think about the life you would like to lead, is happiness, security, peace of mind and financial freedom at the top of your list? If so, you are amongst the majority who strive to obtain the American dream. When people are asked what they want most out of life, their unanimous answer is, "to be happy."

Happiness means different things to different people. Most will agree that a key factor in happiness is having enough money to spend. People desire financial security and the peace of mind that it brings.

Unfortunately, the average person does not understand money, credit and finance. We're not all CPA's or accountants. I outlined this book to make it an easy step-by-step process that anyone can follow. If you follow this book you can eliminate your debt quickly. In some cases you can do this in as little as five minutes. I want to share with you the peace of mind I gained when I achieved financial security, and empower you on your individual path out of debt and into wealth. With this knowledge you will hone the skills necessary to secure financial freedom and live a debt free life.

The path towards reaching your financial goals will be slightly different for each of you. However, the knowledge of how it can be obtained is universal. With a proper education about where and how to obtain money and eliminate debt, YOU can be financially successful. All that is needed is a willingness to learn and follow-through in applying the simple steps outlined in this book. These are steps that have worked for me and I know they will also work for you.

Each money principle I practice I learned by studying, working with experts, and having a desire to make a financial change in my life. If you have the desire and actually take action steps towards making a change, you are guaranteed results! The level of results you wish to achieve are up to you. Everyone can do this! The only way to create financial change in your life is by your own choice, and taking action.

Regardless of where you are on your path towards financial freedom and independence, the key is to move forward at a pace that is comfortable for you. It is time to stop being complacent about your debt and push yourself beyond your comfort zone.

By using the tips and suggestions outlined in this book, I am confident that YOU can achieve independent financial security, eliminate debt, and bring the financial happiness you seek into your life.

In order to achieve financial independence and security, you must be free from financial worry. When all of your bills are paid and you are able to support yourself without depending on anyone else, that is financial security. With the knowledge and the application of these techniques, you will come to understand why people who make sound, educated decisions are financially secure. They are free from financial worry. You can be too.

The word "secure" comes from the Latin words: se=without and cure=care. By living "without care," you will always be free from anxiety -- especially about money. It is time to leave your financial woes behind you and pick up and move towards your bright financial future. Ralph Waldo Emerson said it best with, "What lies behind us, and what lies before us are tiny matters compared to what lies within us."

By reading this book you have taken the first important step. It shows that you are at least curious about the necessity of being financially savvy. In the financial world, sticking your head in the sand and hoping that nothing bad happens is not realistic and no way to live. This type of behavior is what has contributed to the outrageous state of debt in America.

The second step in preparation for wealth is in your attitude towards money. You have to believe that becoming wealthy or financially secure is an absolute possibility for you! Trust that you have the knowledge and skills to make your own fortune and become the wealthy person that you've always dreamed of becoming.

Belief that you can become financially secure is the key to making this happen. I will give you the information necessary to help you feel confident in financial matters. You can then position yourself with the realistic goals you would like to achieve. People who succeed in life are those who embrace and welcome change. They seek out what is new and gather the information and skills necessary to move forward. They have an open mind and are willing to try new things that lead to greater success. This can be you. Trust in your ability and it will be your greatest ally.

My shift in life occurred years ago when I left my marriage and had $20,000 in credit card debt. Devastated, and in a financial hole, I knew this was not where I wanted to be. I completely changed my thoughts about money, saving, spending and investing, and managed to pay off all of my debt in less than a year. The experience gave me motivation to take action steps towards change. No matter what kind of financial stress you are experiencing, remember, it could be a gift in disguise and the catalyst to getting you to take action! In the beginning, sometimes it takes baby steps, and that is okay. There is a great expression by Napoleon Hill that states, "What the mind of man can conceive and believe, it can achieve."

The knowledge you gain will be a great help on your journey to success, and most importantly, you need to believe that you can do it. You absolutely can have every opportunity to go from **Debt Elimination to Wealth Creation**. If you truly have the desire, no matter who you are, you can do it. You deserve it!

Before we get down to the task of planning for your future, think about what you would have today if you had started saving $100 a month when you were just eighteen. Let's say you are thirty-three years old now. That would mean, that since the age of eighteen, fifteen years have gone by. In that time you could have saved $1,200 each year ($100 x 12 months a year) for a total of $18,000 dollars. If you were forty-four, you would have $31,200. In most states, that's almost enough for a down payment on a house. And that's without interest and without investing! Now imagine if you had invested and collected interest. You could have $100,000 or even half of a million dollars, just from saving a $100 a month.

Realize that saving and having $18,000 or $31,200 is a good indication of how little effort it takes to get started! This is a quote by Anthony Robbins that I have lived by, "If you do what you've always done, you'll get what you've always gotten." So, now is the time for you to move forward and make a change! You will be amazed at how easy it is to shift your financial future.

"Concentrate on where you want to go, not on what you fear."
- Anthony Robbins

It is a proven fact that 80% of the things you worry about never happen.

If you want the lifelong feeling of self-satisfaction, you will make the decision to assume personal responsibility for your financial security. It is time to stop standing on the sidelines and waiting for life to happen to you. Take charge of your future. With belief, the proper education, training and the right attitude, you can live debt free and start building your wealth. Answer that inner part of you that says, "Yes!" to a financially free life. Make the move towards building financial security and gain peace of mind for your future.

Now let's get started on your road from Debt Elimination to Wealth Creation.

Chapter

The History of Credit

A LOOK AT OUR COUNTRY'S CREDIT CARD HISTORY

According to David Evans and Richard Schmalensee, authors of the book, "Paying with Plastic: The Digital Revolution in Buying and Borrowing," the history of credit goes back 3,000 years to ancient Babylon and Egypt. If customers did not have the financial means to pay for needed items, they would make an agreement with merchants to pay them at a later date. The debt would be recorded and the customer would either pay it off in installments, or the full amount would be paid over a certain period of time.

Credit tokens were another method used to purchase items. These tokens were much like the credit cards of today, but instead of being made out of plastic they were made out of metal plates and coins. During the eighteenth century in the U.S. and Great Britain, merchants used the assistance of Tallymen to keep track of customers' purchases and the amount owed. Long wooden sticks with notches represented purchases made by customers. The notch on the stick on one side would represent the money paid, and on the other side, the notch represented what was still owed.

Back in 1730, Christopher Thornton was the first to advertise a credit-related purchase. He advertised the sale of furniture that could be paid off in weekly installments. In 1877, "credit card" was a term coined by lawyer and socialist, Edward Bellamy. In his book, "Looking Backward 2000-1887," Bellamy stated that there would be a time when everyone was issued a credit card. With this credit card, people could purchase anything that they needed. His vision was that the credit card would have a specific dollar amount labeled on the front of the card, representing the individual's share of the government money.

Hotels in the early 1900's issued credit cards to their most elite customers. The strategy behind this was to get the customer to stay in their hotel several times a month, while only being billed once a month.

In 1958, Joseph P. Williams, a Bank of America executive, created the revolutionary "revolving" credit card. Up until this time, credit cards had allowed people to purchase items without cash but they had to be paid off within 30 days. Another type of credit card allowed the balance to be paid off in installments, and was limited to local areas. Mr. Williams and BankAmericard were the first to combine these two ideas together. If the balance of the card was paid off within the month, no interest was charged. But if it were only partially paid, interest charges would be added. With the middle class wanting to live like the rich, they jumped at the chance to use this paperless loan.

In order for Bank of America to reach out to more customers, they mailed 60,000 BankAmericards to the residents of Fresno, California. A few months later they sent out over two million cards all over the state of California. These new cards offered pre-approved credit on a much wider scale than ever before. The cards that became widely accepted by merchants gave people the freedom to travel the world with nothing in their pockets except plastic. With the bank's cards now in more people's wallets, it gave them a chance to profit in this $1 trillion a year industry.

At that time with not yet hitting their stride, the credit industry created sheer chaos. There was merchant resentment, cardholder delinquencies, and the company lost $8.8 million in the first 15 months after its introduction.

By the 1960's, "the credit card drops" were still under performing with little profit, while creating a lot of chaos. In 1966, a bunch of Midwestern bankers decided to take advantage of the untapped Chicago market during the holiday season. The incident that followed was later dubbed, "The Chicago Debacle." The banks sent out five million cards to everyone, including, toddlers, convicted felons and even dogs. Corrupt postal workers were feeding the cards to organized crime rings. Suburban housewives were discovering that thousands of dollars were being charged in their name from cards they had never received. The backlash from the credit cards left people feeling like a bull was let loose in a china shop. A Congressional hearing followed and some critics demanded that credit cards be outlawed.

After this debacle in the 1970's, the banks that survived began to get their footing. Technological innovation brought automation to the companies, and Visa and MasterCard were able to link nationwide networks of merchants. Fraud began to recede and after sending out over 100 million credit cards, the banks were starting to see a profit. By 1978, paper money was beginning to seem a way of the past, and the dawn of the modern-day credit card was born.

During the 1980's, Citibank was experiencing financial struggles. Between being squeezed by New York state usury laws and double-digit inflation rates, they were looking at a $1 billion loss. Citibank tried to barter the fact that they employed 3,000 citizens to help buy them some relief from New York's political leaders. Thinking that Citibank would not make good on their threat to leave, they ignored their requested relief.

Chairman of Citibank, Walter Wriston found a loophole, and in 1978 there was a Supreme Court ruling permitting national banks to export interest rates on consumer loans. Now Citibank had to search for a new home.

Bill Janklow, governor of South Dakota, was attempting to lower the state usury laws in order to stimulate economic growth. Mr. Wriston decided to court Mr. Janklow with an offer. In exchange for an invitation to allow Citibank to set up shop in South Dakota, Mr. Wriston offered to create 400 new jobs for local citizens. This seemed inviting to Mr. Janklow, where the economy of South Dakota was suffering. With the support of South Dakota's banking association, Mr. Janklow passed an "emergency bill." This eventually brought in other banks from around the country, which created 3,000 high-paying jobs, creating the source of most jobs for the state of South Dakota. Other states were quick to catch on, and Delaware passed similar legislation the following year.

With the elimination of usury laws, banks could now profit with double-digit interest. Cardholders were willing to pay 18% interest rates while the Federal Reserve lowered the interest rates it charged banks. From 1980 to 1990 credit card usage doubled. Spending increased five-times and the average household credit card debt increased from $518 to $2,700. With interest rates increasing along with the average balances, profits began to soar. According to Elizabeth Warren, a professor at Harvard Law School, as of June 2007 the average American household had $9,200 in credit card debt.

In 1980 with inflation swelling, President Carter tried to implement a freeze on new credit card account solicitation. This standstill only lasted a few months and gave card companies time to introduce a new concept – the $20 annual fees. The annual fees became a new vital source of revenue. This helped replace the pesky problem of reduced revenue from customers who avoided interest fees by paying their credit card balance on time.

In 1991, came what some bankers refer to as, "the Big Scare." In an effort to stimulate the consumer and get consumer confidence back up, Senator Alfonse D. Amato proposed a national legislation to cap credit card interest at 14%. This sent the banking industry into a panic. The economists predicted bank failures and the stock market plunged. In order to cool the public, Vice President Dan Quayle made an announcement that the cap would in all likelihood, be vetoed.

Andrew S. Kahr, a follower of financial behavior, was key in evolving a system to effectively target profitable consumers, because people who paid their credit card in full every month were not profitable to the banks. By using a series of formulas and scoring systems, Mr. Kahr built a system to find the most lucrative consumers who routinely carried high balances, but were unlikely to default. Soon after, major credit card companies used credit scores and financial data to help develop sophisticated pricing and credit strategies. Instead of a generic rate they began basing the limits on the consumer's risk of default. The higher the risk, the higher the rate would be set.

With research, they found that higher credit lines appealed to consumers. By lowering the required minimum monthly payment and increasing the credit line, the credit card companies increased revenue in two ways. Since it took longer to pay off the balance, this increased the amount that would be earned in interest on each dollar. The principal of the card would also increase since customers could take on more debt while making the same monthly payment.

With minimum monthly payments of credit cards lowered from five percent to two percent, analysts acknowledged this lowered the consumer's awareness of their debt. This is considered dangerous leveraging when you consider that since 1990, household credit card debt has more than tripled from $2,700 to $9,200.

In recent years, credit card companies began implementing high penalty fees, creating a whole new stream of revenue. Last year, penalty fees generated $12 billion in revenue. Robert B. McKinley, founder and chairman of CardWeb and Ram Research, a payment credit card research firm said, "Banks are raising interest rates, adding new fees, making the due date for your payment a holiday or on a Sunday in the hopes that maybe you'll trip up and get a payment in late." Most customers, thinking that they will always make their payments on time, so they do not shop around for better late fees. But in the course of a year, most cardholders will average at least one late fee.

Going over the credit card limit or even making a late payment with another creditor is enough to make the card companies consider the consumer high risk. Along with penalties they also may increase your interest rate. Some customers have had their rate increased five times just because of one late payment. In 2003, the industry generated $12 billion in revenue in penalty fees alone.

Millions of Americans are being charged excessive fees and high APR rates, while the credit card industry profits. Mr. Kahr does not apologize for this, saying, "If someone is riskier, he should be paying a higher rate. If there was a demand for a credit card product that never changed its terms and rates and stuck with the customer no matter what, I'd be running around telling people 'Let's market this wonderful fairness card.' "

In my opinion the credit and debt crisis sweeping America is absolutely getting worse. Americans are being taken advantage of to the tune of billions of dollars... and what will surprise you is that this involves some of the largest, most respected financial institutions, banks, credit card companies and mortgage companies in the world.

Why should billions of dollars be going into the big corporations' bank accounts and costing each and every American, thousands, tens of thousands and even hundreds of thousands of dollars in unwanted debt? Years ago when I started researching my book, what I discovered was so upsetting that I had to make it public. In my opinion, what these companies are doing is predatory, and the worst part is that the average person doesn't even have a clue how badly they are being taken advantage of and that's why I say, in many cases debt is not your fault.

It may surprise you that all of these high interest rates and fees are legal which seems hard to believe considering most states do have usury laws which are made to protect people from excessive interest rates. Even more surprising is that in the 1980's the Federal Government changed the federal banking laws and made national banks exempt from those laws. So, now national banks can charge interest rates well above the legal state usury law levels and trust me, they do.

The major credit card companies also figured out how to get past the usury laws by setting up their company headquarters in state's with weak usury laws. If you've ever looked at the return address on your credit card bill, you may notice your credit card company is probably located in South Dakota or Delaware. That's because these are the states that have either the weakest or no usury laws" meaning, there is no limit on the interest rate that credit card companies can charge consumers.

In addition to that, most consumers have credit cards that allow fees to be charged. Most people end up paying all kinds of fees with all kinds of names like monthly, annual and quarterly maintenance fees, over the limit fees, late fees, check deposit fees, application fees and credit verification fees. What I want people to know is that you don't necessarily have to pay all, or any, of these fees. There are "NO APPLICATION AND NO ANNUAL FEE CARDS." Plus, with the information in this book, you'll be able to outsmart those fees and avoid having to pay them.

Chapter

Ducks in a Row

ORGANIZATION

Being organized is the most important step towards getting out of debt and gaining wealth! Getting your ducks in a row and organizing, I know, sounds too easy of a solution to be true. But it works! I can tell you, wholeheartedly, that this step creates a huge impact for 90% of my clients. If you want to see instant money and your debt go away, this is one of your answers. When using this step, my clients learn about the money they are wasting, and money they forgot they had. In many cases, they eliminate debt completely.

Now is the time to take action and to know what is happening with your money! For this to be most effective, you need to know exactly how much money you presently have coming in, as well as potential income in the future. It is also important to know how much money is going out, where the money is going, and to keep track of potential future expenses. Once you know this, you can begin to shift the way you are using money and start setting your goals.

Albert Einstein once said, "It takes a genius to see the obvious." Sometimes the simple things in life are the most powerful. Since they are so simple, sometimes we tend to ignore them and not let them work for us.

This seems like such an easy formula to follow in life, yet most people get caught up in the vicious cycle of living paycheck to paycheck. They are barely getting by and making ends meet. Trying to maintain their checking account balance with enough to scrape by consumes their life. What they're missing is the big picture of their finances.

The state of the modern economy is, spend more, pay later — people living beyond their means. When their finances get to be too much, typically they stick their heads in the sand, ignoring the problem they find too scary to face. This is not serving you or your future by avoiding or denying this is happening. The situation is real and will not just go away. In all likelihood, it will get worse by ignoring it. "If you do what you've always done, you'll get what you've always gotten." When you muster the courage to face the reality of your financial situation, it's usually not as bad as it seems. Fear of the unknown is always worse than the fear of something you understand. Taking action is the only way to create a meaningful shift in the direction of your financial life. You must take action! Step out of your fear and into financial freedom.

In the following pages you will learn that debt is not always your fault. I will teach you Action Steps that in many cases give instant results. So, buckle your seat belts and get ready for the wealth ride of your life.

DEBT ELIMINATION ACTION STEP

Every month, be conscious of what is happening with your money. Start by gathering all of your financial information. Whether it's records in your files, in Quicken, QuickBooks, or that pile of bills that have been sitting on the kitchen counter — collect them all. Create an area where you can access all of your financial records at once. Get down and dirty and dig it all up. On my website there is a great tool for organizing your finances. It is user-friendly and will equip you with everything you need to make this process easier.

Now that you have chosen your space, CREATE A SYSTEM TO KEEP YOU ORGANIZED AND CLEAN OUT THE CLUTTER! You need your financial information to be available to you at a glance. It is important, that at any given moment, you know where you stand with your investments, savings, income, expenses and debt.

Create a weekly, monthly, and yearly system that keeps track of every aspect of your finances. Include your income, assets, expenses, investments and your debt. Commit to using this system faithfully, and stay on top of the financial game. By following this simple rule you will not fall behind again and you will alleviate unnecessary stress from your life.

Okay, let's get to work. Are you more comfortable writing out your finances or using a computer? If you like writing, get a notepad and start by making a list of all your debts. List out all of your monthly payments and the total debts associated with them. Many people, who have financial problems when they get to this step, get frustrated, and give up. This process can be time consuming and requires sustained concentration, especially if you are organizing your finances after a long period of neglect. This initial process is key, so, just take baby steps and go at a pace that you feel comfortable with. DO NOT overwhelm yourself. Realize that there is a light at the end of the tunnel — getting out of debt. So, commit yourself to this process and stick with it. You'll be surprised at how, once you dive in and commit to organizing your finances, and knowing that there is a way out of debt, you'll be debt free before you know it.

I have a great story from one of my clients. Sara thought she was very organized with her money. I asked her to revisit her financial system, and when she did she found a great surprise! She found money! She found a 401k that she had completely forgotten about. She rolled that over into a new account and started making more money, instantly. Now, that is a quick return on her investment! By using one of the most basic steps from my techniques, Sara made a profit. It is not uncommon for me to hear stories like this. My techniques help people save money, and these can do the same for you.

Let go of your fear and face the music. Move forward with organization. This step alone will create amazing shifts in your financial world! You will free up the space to allow more income to come into your life, along with more investments and wealth. If you are a person who is already very organized, I invite you to revisit your system. Go over everything again. Doing this on a regular basis is a **Habit of Wealthy People**, and something I suggest you start implementing into your own life. When you create wealth it is important for you to know what your money is doing and how to manage it on a daily basis. It's a good feeling to make this change and to see the positive shifts that take place. And you will! I can promise you, if you have the desire and you take action, you will see a positive shift in your financial life!

With the financial awareness you gain from staying on top of your money, the next natural process will be to start setting goals and looking at the big picture of your future. Don't be afraid to dream big and make plans that represent an ideal vision of your financial future. Once you know where you want to go, you can figure out how to manage your finances, in order to get you there.

Next, you will fill out your **Debt Elimination Chart** and your **Wealth Creation Chart** (samples are on my website), you will be ready to make a shift for the better in your life. I urge you to stay with me here. I know some people feel so hopeless and discouraged by their financial situation that looking at the numbers will only make them depressed. In actuality, getting organized and understanding your entire financial world is the first crucial step toward empowering yourself to take ownership of your future. The only way to move past your current financial challenge is to dig in and crawl through the trenches. Uncover the good, the bad and the ugly, and face them for what they are. The good news is we have solutions that will work for most people quickly.

Now lets look at expenses. Pull out this list from your **Debt Eliminator Chart**. Here are some examples:

> Home or Office Rent
> Phone
> Cable
> Cell Phone
> Insurance
> Groceries
> Education/Tuition
> Memberships

Start taking a look at where you can move money and reduce these expenses. Can you lower your rent for your home or office??? This could save you money right away. Look at all of your options for downsizing or lowering your costs. Always do a pro's and con's list to see if you are really going to save money. As you are working on your lists, make clear detailed decisions. Can you get a lower phone or cell phone plan? Call your phone company today and find out. Check your insurance rates. They can be very competitive and better offers are always available. Can you lower your monthly grocery bill and membership fees? You may have to make a cut in some areas now, but remember that it's not forever! Can you trade a temporary change or slight discomfort for long-term reward? It is well worth it. Ask anyone who is debt free, and they will tell you that the rewards are well worth the temporary cutbacks.

We are now going to create a plan to reduce or eliminate your debt. First, let's take a look at each category of your finances and see how you can possibly get instant results. Once you organize your debt and expenses, and follow the outline with the **Debt Eliminator Chart**, you will know when your due dates are, when your promotion rates expire, which cards or loans have the highest interest, and which ones have the lowest interest rates. We are going to look at shifting your payments and money around to best serve you. Also, we are going to look at transferring debt to lower interest possibilities. You may even have options available to you that you didn't even know were available. So, let's find out about all the options, and get moving with debt reduction and start building wealth.

One **Healthy Habit of Wealthy People** is that they build relationships with people and communicate well. When you build relationships, you have bargaining power! When you build a good payment history, you also have bargaining power. I have countless stories where my clients were able to get their late fees or other types of fees removed, deleted or waived. When you communicate in a productive manner and you have a great payment history, you get good results. Don't be discouraged if you don't have a good payment history. Try anyway. If you are savvy enough and have a good story, most institutions will work with you. They would rather focus on the millions of people who never pay attention to their credit card rates and fees. Remember that this is where they make their billion dollar profits. But they are not going to get that extra money from you, because you now have the tools to keep your hard earned money in your bank account and/or your investments.

No matter what your financial situation is right now, even if you have bad credit, your payments are late, etc…you can start changing that habit now. It all starts with you **wanting to change!** You bought this book because it caught your attention and you want to get out of debt; or maybe it was a gift. In whatever manner you got here, this is a great start, and a change will happen for you if you follow my advice. I want you to know there is hope for any situation. Again, all you need is the desire for change and to take action towards your goals. Right now your goal is to get your ducks in a row and to get out of debt.

Now, I suggest you take action to lower any interest rates you can. Most of my clients are able to save money instantly by lowering their credit card interest rates. Did you know you can lower your interest rates with your credit cards, sometimes in as little as five minutes, over the phone? I will go into more detail about how to do this in the chapter, "Plastic Jungle." I tell you who to call and how to handle the call. Be ready with all of your credit card statements in hand, to make some phone calls and to start saving yourself money. Most people are throwing away their hard earned money when they don't have to. Quite often you have bargaining power with the credit card companies, especially if you have a long history with them. Even if you don't have a long history with them, you will still have bargaining power. As the customer, all you have to do is be nice, yet assertive, and get to the right people. You will be surprised at the instant response you get when credit card companies think they will lose your business and your hard earned money. Remember, your money is part of the 12 billion dollar business for them. Many times, rather than lose your business they will give you better rates or offers. Some that you did not even know were available to you! All too often, we forget that we are the one who is the customer, and they need to keep our business so we don't take it somewhere else.

The next step is to call your creditors and talk to the credit analyst or credit specialist. Every company has their own titles for the person who handles rates and new business; you just need to get to the right person. I have a client, Dawn, who had to get through five different people to get her rates lowered. She did not give up, and as a result, she got her interest rate lowered to 9.95%. In the long run, this is saving her thousands of dollars. In just a very short period of time, Dawn managed to have great success in getting nine of her credit card interest rates lowered. This was all done by using the simple technique of calling her creditors and telling them her situation.

Dawn is a manicurist who severely injured her thumb, impairing her from work. In one year, due to lack of income, Dawn managed to rack up a sizeable amount of debt. Dawn used her personal story to her advantage with the creditors by going into detail, and have that representative befriend her. She was unable to work for a period of time and she was doing her best to catch up. It has been difficult for her, but she always stays in communication with her creditors.

Your next action step will be lowering the interest on mortgages, HELOC's (home equity line of credit), or any other debt you have. Call your bank and any competitors to see what they can do for you with a better rate or with refinancing. Consider opening a HELOC to pay off your credit card debt; it usually has a tax benefit. In many cases, it really is a good financial decision. I will get more into detail about mortgages and HELOC's in the chapter, "A Piece of the American Pie."

Look at your auto loans to see if you have the best rate available. You can also refinance your car, which could save you thousands of dollars.

STUDENT LOANS, TAX DEBT, PERSONAL LOANS

Lower interest rates now!!! This is the fastest way to save money, instantly. If you have family members, friends, or even business associates that have money, they may be interested in giving you a loan. You can make it a situation that is a win/win for all involved. You will save money and your friends can make more money than if their money is left sitting in the bank collecting 1-3% interest (not to mention the fees they are possibly paying on the account). Let's say you are paying 14% on your auto loan (one of my clients is paying this outrageous amount), if she could to her brother and say, would you be interested in a business deal that could make you more interest than you are currently receiving? If he has the money, I am sure he would be interested. Who doesn't want to make extra money? She would suggest that he buy her car outright and that she make payments to him, somewhere in the range of 5%-10%. This would save her money while putting extra money in her brother's pocket. What a deal! When doing these types of transactions, I suggest having an agreement drawn up for both of you. Make sure that all details are covered in that agreement so there will be no misunderstandings, as far as payment schedule, pay off date, etc. It is in your best interest to make good on all of these types of loans. Down the road, this same person could possibly give you another loan or recommend you to another person who will give you a loan. Next time the loan could be for a house, or something you thought would normally be out of your range. Now that you have built a good payment history with this person, they will trust you and be more willing to help you again. In some cases friends or family members will even be willing to lend you money to pay off your debt without any interest attached if you can present them with a strong plan of action to pay them back in a short amount of time.

There are so many ways to get rid of your debt, you just have to think outside of the box. Take a minute and see if you can think of anyone who would give you a loan and not charge you any interest!!! In an instant, high or out of control interest would be eliminated. My client, Gary, had a no-interest loan from his grandfather, for his house. They had an agreement drawn up that protects the grandfather in case Gary defaults on his loan, in which his grandfather would then legally own the house. When you have something, like a house or a car that is a secured debt or collateral, it has value to the lender. They can recoup any loss and it is a less risky loan for someone to enter into, which then makes it easier to get people to help you with these types of loans.

If you are experiencing financial trouble with your debt, and you are just hanging on....please, keep hanging in there. Remember, "This too shall pass." If you have faith and the desire, you will get to the other side! If you are in survival mode right now, relax. Don't panic. Here I will provide you with a general rule of thumb of which debts to pay first.

Secured debt is a debt that is secured by collateral (home, car, property, etc). It is debt backed by collateral to reduce the risks associated with lending. If you were to stop making payments and default on the repayment of the loan, they could take away the collateral.

Unsecured debt is debt that has nothing attached to it (no collateral) so there is nothing they can take away. The one drawback is they can become a nuisance and harm your credit score or credit history.

Types of Debt to Pay Off First:

1. Property or Tax Debt – it's best not to have the United States government as your partner in an investment. They can attach liens to your income and on anything you own, not including mortgages.

2. Secured Debt - mortgages, cars, anything that falls under the secure debt description.

3. Utility Bills – gas, phone, electricity, etc.

4. Unsecured debt – credit cards, anything they can't take away from you but that could still come back to haunt you later. Prioritize your debt based on what could hurt or help your credit score. For example, first attend to your credit cards with the highest interest rates, then focus on the cards with lower interest rates.

My Suggestion for the Next Step: KEEP A SPENDING LOG. One of the very simple and most powerful money saving ideas is to keep a daily spending log. Include everything you spend for one month or longer. And I mean everything. Write down the fifty cents you spend to buy a daily paper; the candy bar you bought for your child's school fund raiser. EVERYTHING! You may be surprised by how much you spend each month that does not normally register in your mind as, "money spent."

If you keep this log, I assure you that in just a few weeks you will find something magical happening in your financial life. There is something incredibly powerful about writing down ALL of your expenditures. It makes the flow of money in your life more real and exact. It shows you a clear and exact picture of where you are spending and what your money is going towards. Once you are aware of where your money is going it becomes much easier to control your spending. I would be surprised if you are not saving at least an extra $50 a month with this simple tip.

All it takes to get started on your daily spending log is a ballpoint pen and a 75-cent notebook. That's right, the only thing standing between you having a life of financial struggle or a life of financial freedom is a couple dollars and a few minutes of your time each day. Look at this example: If you made a salary of $25,000 a year, and spent $5.50 per day on soft drinks, fast food or coffee, what percent of your total income would be going towards this? $5.50 is actually a small amount when you consider swinging through the drive-thru to grab a medium-size soft drink which will cost you nearly $2. But for now, let's work with $5.50. If you total up that amount, in one year's time you will have spent nearly $2,000 on JUNK FOOD. That's 8% of your TOTAL income! Are you starting to see how much money slips out of people's pockets on frivolous things they can't afford?

If you were to just save the money spent on snacks, soft drinks, and coffee, the following year, you could go on a fantastic vacation. Doesn't a vacation sound like a better alternative than adding twenty pounds to your waistline? And wouldn't it be more rewarding to go on a vacation that you saved for instead of one that puts you into debt? If YOU had a choice between your daily snacks or a much-needed vacation, which would you choose?

The point I am trying to make here is that just knowing where your money goes could help you achieve the clarity needed to take control of your finances. That's what a spending record will do for YOU. It will give you control over your spending and help you on your way to starting a better financial life. I am not saying you need to cut back your spending, cold turkey. I know that over time you have built up certain habits, and habits don't change overnight. What I want is for you to examine where your money is going. I am sure that once you do this, you will discover things about your spending habits that will surprise you. You do not need me to create a budget for you for it to become clear what in your life should go and what can stay. It is all about prioritizing, and that is what your daily spending log does. It will allow you to make priorities for yourself, like spending money on snacks, or on a great vacation!

TAKE CHARGE OF YOUR MONEY AND INVESTMENTS

You are in charge of your finances! You are the CEO of your life. Be a good CEO. You don't want to have to fire yourself. It could be very costly! The whole interview process to replace yourself could be devastating. Keep close watch over your finances so that once you get them under control, you never end up in the debt doghouse again.

If you are managing your money properly, things will be going very smoothly. Rather than a source of stress or worry, your finances will be the key to doing and having the things you want in life. And best of all, you'll be having fun! After all, the CEO always gets the best rewards and the biggest payoff.

I have a dear friend who doesn't like dealing with her finances or spending any in-depth time to learn about them. I suggested to her that she at least learn enough to hire the best planners, strategists, investors and brokers to handle her finances. When going in that direction, there will be costs involved. However, she feels it is worth it. She understands that the people that are handling her money need to make educated decisions. Therefore, the hiring of these people is an important part of her financial future.

No matter what level you're at in your financial education and development, whether you have twenty-five dollars invested in a single CD or 401k, or it's three hundred thousand you've invested in real estate or the stock market, you must be a good CEO who's committed to taking charge of your money. If you're not, your money will be taking charge of you and running your life. And how does it feel to have someone or something run your life? Not good.

Always oversee all the investment opportunities you're involved in. Don't be naive and trust anyone with this important decision just because you don't want to invest the time to learn.

If you are hiring people to manage your money, make sure you have a strict interviewing process. You need to be sure that your financial advisors are making decisions that are in your best interest rather than theirs. It's important that you be proactive with them. This will ensure you the best results. If you address all of the financial steps I have already laid out for you, you should already feel more confident. You have what it takes to make solid financial decisions and a fantastic financial future.

Solution Summary

2: DUCKS IN A ROW: ORGANIZATION

- Collect all your statements, bills, etc.
- Organize your finances.
- Know where your money is going at all times.
- Create a system that tracks your income and expenses. Use my website to help you.
- Go through your expenses seeking ways to save money.
- Create a budget and spending log.
- Set goals, take action, and commit to the process.
- Seek better interest rates.
- Seek potential loans with lower interest rates from friends or family members.
- Leverage your bargaining power.

Debt, A Good Thing?

EXAMPLES OF GOOD DEBT

This chapter is called "Debt, a good thing?" It has a question mark after it because most people reading this ask, "How is debt a good thing?" It truly can be good in some cases. I am an advocate of having some debt! Good debt for assets and building wealth. When I originally started writing this book, this chapter was intended to be towards the end of the book. My thought process in doing so was that this subject is on the up swing towards the building of wealth and savings, as you are eliminating unwanted debt. I considered this chapter to be one of the chapters teaching you how to acquire more wealth, and to build assets and savings for yourself. As the book unfolded and I came closer to finishing, I realized I had to move this chapter closer to the beginning. I give you information and advice on how to eliminate your debt in different arenas, whether it's the banks, the credit card companies, the mortgage companies, the medical industry, student loans etc. I also give you different opportunities that are available to you to save more money and learn how to avoid being overcharged. My goal is to make sure you keep more money in your bank account, while building wealth. And part of wealth building is knowing what is considered "good debt."

The reason why I moved this chapter closer to the front is because after all of the talk on the news about the country's debt and financial crisis, knowing that you bought this book to reduce your debt, can all seem so overwhelming. Most likely, many of you that are reading this book are consumed with some type of debt and are feeling under pressure. This chapter is designed to put you at ease because there IS good debt. Some of you out there may already have good debt. With the forecast of the economy in the news, people are starting to feel depressed and hopeless, and on a spiral downward. This worry may be unnecessary for people with good debt. In our country our economy and our wealth is built on good debt. People just need to be able to determine the difference between "good debt" and "bad debt," and how to take precautions to make sure their "good debt" does not turn into "bad debt."

After completing this chapter you will have a better understanding of good debt, and you can make better decisions on building your financial future, all while utilizing debt and credit. My advice, if you are acquiring or accumulating good debt, is NOT to use this as an excuse to overspend. Do NOT use the categories on the list of good debt as an excuse to get yourself in over your head, thinking I gave you my blessing. If you do, your good debt can possibly turn into bad debt. Always use good judgment, research, and whenever possible hire experts to advise you in making your decisions.

Many of you have heard the term ROI (return on investment). When you are considering acquiring or accumulating debt, before doing so, do your research. I know I say this quite often, and I can't stress this point enough, as lack of research is at the top of the list of why people fail financially. To create less of a risk, weigh the factors. Will you receive a great ROI on what you invest? Is it worth the debt? In many cases, with good debt the answer is yes. However, you may find it is too high of a risk for a good ROI and you are not willing to take the risk. What are the risk factors? The way to calculate your ROI on good debt, after doing your due diligence and research, is to establish the amount you are investing in the debt, along with any interest and fees, then look at the projected numbers on the return for your investment. A good business plan and a professional advisor can help with this decision. Remember to calculate the time it will take to pay back the debt, as well as the time it will take to receive the return. After you calculate the numbers you can then make your decision whether to move forward with the debt or to decline. I am going to give you some examples of possible good debt.

EDUCATION AND CONTINUED EDUCATION GOOD DEBT

Most people do have a good understanding that education can be good debt. Education or continued education is one of the best types of debt a person can have, and the reason why is because you can have a higher chance of getting a return on your investment. Education can set you up to have a higher earning potential. Whether you're just starting out as an 18-year-old college student, right out of high school, or if you are going back to school, at any age, education is a good thing. If you are considering taking out a student loan, take a close look at your new career and the education you are seeking to acquire. Will you get a high return on your investment? Here again, do all the research and due diligence to find out what income levels are available in that particular arena. You want to go in depth with this task. I suggest getting very specific when researching and be sure to look at the numbers across the country, not just in your local area. You may want to consider relocating or you may have to relocate at some point. If that is the case, you will be ready. The reason why people get in over their heads with education debt is that they never ran the numbers and did not do their research. They may later find out that the market is saturated, the starting income is not what they thought it would be, or the area they live in does not have any opportunity for their chosen profession. It is one thing to get a good education and it is another to be able to use it to bring you the financial lifestyle that you desire. It is optimum to have both!

For example, if you live in New York City and you are engaged and planning on moving to Ohio, where your fiancé lives, you don't want to do your research only in New York City for the starting salary in that career. You will want to research Ohio and the national average. I am going to use for this example the career of a dentist. If you are going to school to become a dentist, quite possibly, New York City may have a higher salary base than the rest of the country. You also want to find out the national average for the starting salary, not just the cap. There will usually be a range. It is easy to find information on your chosen profession through Internet research and through counseling at the college of your choice. When researching, it is important to find out what the starting salary base is and the cap salary for that particular career. Be sure you look at the starting salary because that is where you are going to be when you get out of school and starting out. Be realistic about the income level you will be receiving when you get out of school. This will help when you are calculating your ROI and how fast you can repay the loan. Do not just use the national average when assessing your salary, but be specific to the area where you plan to live.

Let's take a look at an income level of a particular career so we can get a clear picture of an ROI on education. Let's again use a dentist as an example of a career. Go online and do some research on what a dentist income level will be throughout the entire country. The national average is $133,680 per year, and that is just starting out. So, if you happen to incur $100,000 worth of student loans or debt, you will want to know your earning potential, and the job availability across the country, in that profession. You also want to look at the possibilities of dentistry careers open in your area, or if the profession of a dentist is in high demand. It is one thing to look at the numbers and another to be sure there is room in the industry for employment or for opening your own business. Therefore, what you want to do is look at the national averages for potential job placement, income levels, and from there you can make your decision. You are going to look at your realistic salary base for when you get out of school, entry-level positions, and your potential for paying back your loan. You want to make sure that you are factoring in your interest and fees. Many student loans, on average, are around 3.4 to 6.8% (the interest rate can change from year to year and state to state), which is a really low percentage rate. So, this can be well worth your investment because, over time, you will have a high return on your investment. When you are employed as a dentist and if you are making $133,680, you can certainly pay back $100,000 loan in a fair amount of time. It's not going to take you that long, especially if you are accustomed to living on, let's say, $30,000 a year. And if you have roommates you can certainly take on the debt, just don't jump into a new high-priced lifestyle as soon as you get out of college. This is the all too common mistake that most people make. They move up their lifestyle too quickly, before it is financially safe to do so. You may want to remember to take baby steps, gradually. Keep your same lifestyle. Maybe you still want to take on that roommate, so you can have a low overhead. Then you can pay back the debt at a faster pace. That is a personal choice and a decision you will have to make. My advice is to not spend too much too fast and you can keep your good debt from turning into bad debt. In the long run, this gives you a much better lifestyle with less stress.

The mistake that people make with good debt turning to bad debt is that they let it get out of hand. They will start to get a salary coming in and the feeling of having the money. After all, it's been a while since they have had money in their pocket. They haven't been able to afford vacations, fancy cars, or clothes, and with this new salary at their leisure, their spending can get out of hand. When they get out of school they think they are making up for lost time or they have an unrealistic outlook on spending the money. They may very well go too far and incur more debt, which is the bad debt. They spend money on things they want but don't necessarily need. That type of spending gets you into bad debt and what happens is you become overwhelmed. You find yourself not paying off the good debt, the student loan, as rapidly as you would like. Now the bills keep piling up. You have to be realistic about your potential income or about the income that you are making. Look at creating a budget and making sure that you can pay your loans and can afford your spending habits.

Continued education is also a wonderful way where debt is a good thing. It doesn't have to be in the form of a large student loan, it can be as simple as one business class. Maybe you are looking to better yourself for your business or get a competitive edge or a higher income. You can take a look at continued education in your local schools or community centers. You may want to consider online courses. There are a multitude of courses online that are convenient and will help to raise your income levels. Local businesses sometimes offer higher education, not necessarily degrees. However, it will still help you to excel in your business. So, this is another good investment. Let's say you take a higher education course that is going to let you have a higher skill in the business you are already performing. You can now take your business to a new level because you now have more education, and again, you are getting a great ROI. Let's say a class costs you $250 and it takes you to a level where you are able to bring in ten new customers, making $500 for each new customer. That is $5,000 extra income. Paying $250 to make $5,000 is a great ROI. You have now paid back the $250 for your education and received a profit of $4,750! Just one new customer will pay back the debt and leave you a nice profit. This example shows how it is definitely worth paying the money for the course, and another example of how debt can be a good thing for education.

Many employers will offer higher or continued education to their employees. This is a great benefit to take advantage of and may possibly give you a higher income in the long run, while making you more valuable to your employer and future employers.

MORTGAGE - GOOD DEBT

When you buy a home or invest in real estate and take out a mortgage for the purchase, most of the time this can be good debt. That is, if you buy right! Yes, again, you must do your research here. The reason why the mortgage you take out is good debt is because it is attached to the real estate, and that is an asset with the hope of gaining an appreciated value. When the real estate market is accelerating or you get a great buy you are gaining equity. Equity on that home is your return on your investment (ROI). Over time, real estate has been a good investment and a very sound investment. The real estate market in recent years has not been as favorable, and trying to predict the exact future of real estate is uncertain. We're not quite sure when it's going to take a turn for the better, however you can take a look at history. Records show everything is cyclical and that things will take a shift and they will come back up in time. If you have the credit or the cash, with this economy, right now is a great time to make real estate investments. Right now there are great buys available to you. If you can purchase now, I would certainly advise doing so. Be sure you can afford to make the purchase and investment. It's only going to go back up in time and if you don't need to cash out the investment any time soon, you could end up with a nice profit and a really good deal.

Again, I am going to advise you to do your due diligence and your research in the area you intend to purchase, making sure that you are looking at the growth history or the potential for growth in the area. Educate yourself so you can determine whether an area is growing, what the growth span is, future projections for that area, and then you can make a sound decision in buying real estate. Usually with real estate the old saying location, location, location is true. When I invest in real estate I do very thorough research of the location beforehand. This really pays off since the areas that I have invested in have not been hit as hard as most of the real estate throughout the country. There are never guarantees on any real estate investment. You will have a much better chance for higher returns when you make a wise investment after doing your research.

There are many, many different ways to buy real estate, which is another book altogether and one of my passions. For now, one of the prime rules that I always implement when buying is location and location strategy. I do love investing in real estate and have had a good share of success. Even though I'm an advocate of only buying real estate as a good investment, sometimes purchasing real estate is not only taking into consideration that it is a great investment. For instance, If you are set on living in a certain area because of your job, your family is there, the kid's schools are good, your husband or wife has a job there, or it's where you have to live, make sure to look at the surrounding areas to ensure the property you choose is the better investment for you. Look at the commute; is it going to be worth it to you? Weigh all your options before purchasing a home. Buying a home is one of the largest purchases that you can make in your entire life, so you want to take it seriously. Do your research and due diligence with a good realtor, helping you in the area you are looking to purchase in. Sometimes it's better to rent in the area you have to live in if it is not the best area to invest in. You can purchase real estate in another area or state and have that purchase be a rental property where it is a better investment. You will have to work out the numbers.

Personally, I always buy real estate as an investment opportunity. I don't buy a home just to live in it. I always look at it as if it's going to be a good sound investment. This is the true key to having real estate be a wise investment and good debt. There is one home that I am thinking about purchasing that is for lifestyle purposes and is the kind of lifestyle I love to live in. But again, it is all about location, location, location, so I know I wouldn't ever have a hard time trying to sell it and get a return on my investment. This type of lifestyle is high in demand, which means this type of property will always be high in demand. Whenever I do buy real estate for investments it is all about the location, the rate of growth and the rental potential. When I buy properties I look at them as possibly being a rental property at some point, or how easy and how fast I can sell it.

Mortgage debt is good type of debt for you to have because it is a secured asset, which means the debt has collateral. The bank is looking at that as a secure investment because they know what the property is worth. This is a debt they can secure if for any reason you default on the loan.

Before making a real estate purchase be sure to read the chapters later in this book, called "A Piece of the American Pie," which teaches you about mortgages. Also, read "The Great Escape" chapter, which teaches you about escaping foreclosure. Make sound decisions about your purchase and make sure that you get a mortgage that is affordable to you. Be realistic with your current earnings and your earning potential. People get in trouble when they tend to go with the pie in the sky and they push and push, and they really want this bigger and better house. Keeping up with Jones's and all of those different things that get us into trouble or turn our good debt into bad debt. This is something you do not want to do. I suggest getting help from professional realtors and/or other real estate investors. Take the time to do your research before buying. It's well worth the time and will help you avoid creating stress and give you a better chance of not falling into foreclosure.

You also want to do your research when you are looking into buying income generating real estate, such as, apartments, condominiums or houses that you want to rent out. You can never do too much research when you are purchasing any kind of real estate. And when you are looking into purchasing an income generating property, look at what that area holds as far as rents. You also want to look at the job opportunities in that area, making sure it will be stable for the rental growth. In other words, it's not just a town that is led by one large company. An example of this is a large printing company in Florida was one of the biggest corporations in that area, however, there were no other large corporations. There is great potential because there are a lot of job opportunities with this company employing thousands of employees in that area. The only problem is, if that one company closes down and moves out, you are now at a risk with your income generating property. The whole town could be looking at devastation and you're stuck with the real estate. So, if you are looking at income generating properties you want to look at places that have more than one high potential for job placement and job opportunities. You need to make sure that the population stays in that area so that you can continue occupancy on your rental, or if you intend to sell it you may ensure to sell it for a higher price. Be sure that the numbers are going to work out for you to gain a profit. Make sure when running the numbers you are including, not only your mortgage, but also include the property taxes, any HOA dues, the garbage, water, insurance, repair, management cost, if any, and upkeep, as well as, vacancy rates (typically 5% could be higher or lower in different areas). Compare the numbers from your bills to the rent that you will be getting. Then measure the return for what the market holds, as far as a rent value. Also, you can factor in some of the possible tax benefits from owning the property.

Another way to have debt be a good thing is commercial real estate. Do your research and run the numbers and make sure it will be profitable and practical to lease out the commercial real estate. Let's say for instance, it's a shopping center or a strip mall or investment of this type. You will want to look at the history of the property. There is a lot that goes into buying commercial real estate, a lot more than can fit into this chapter. One quick piece of advice for this area is to be sure you have a good staple store or restaurant in your center. This will be the draw for traffic and other renters. Remember this as a general rule for buying commercial real estate.

Sometimes people will be upside down when they have a piece of real estate. For one example, they have a piece of real estate they are using for the tax benefit because they need the tax write off. Check with a tax professional to see if the investment has tax advantages for you. Sometimes the property tax may be higher and can put the owner over what they are collecting in rent. This puts the owner in what we call, in the red. The tax benefit may create more income than what they are paying out for the property. This puts them in the black for the investment. If it works out to be a tax benefit because they needed that tax deduction, this is beneficial because property possibly gains income and equity. What's so wonderful about gaining equity is it can be a giant savings account that just sits there. That is, of course, if the market stays good. If the market goes lower than your equity, obviously, your equity is lowered in the property. You need to be able to have the time for it to bounce back or take that risk. Real estate is usually a pretty sound investment, however, in today's market you need to be sure you can afford this investment and the time it will take for the market to bounce back.

If you can, then now is the time to get some great buys!

We are never really sure about the real estate market. Some people's strategy is to watch the market and just when it starts to creep up a little bit they are ready to buy. Keep in mind that that's what most people are doing, so there will be more competition. You may not get in on those deals because most people see that the market is going up. They also see that the interest rates will be going up so they jump quickly. They figure this is their opportunity to get in, knowing that the market is going to get higher. This is a great time to make an investment, and if you can do so I certainly suggest you be ready. Start looking and jump onboard for making some great sound investments in real estate.

Having no mortgage can be a high priority for some people. Ultimately, only you can make the decision on whether or not it is best for you to carry a mortgage debt. I am going to give you some guidelines to help you make your decision:

Benefits from paying off your mortgage:
- Security in owning your property free and clear
- Other investments can give you a higher rate of return
- You have no other consumer debt
- You do not like the stress of a mortgage
- You are planning on downsizing with a new property
- You can afford to pay off your mortgage and still have a good savings and investment plan
- You would rather use your mortgage money to invest elsewhere
- You have a 30-year mortgage and maybe less than 10 years remaining on the loan, so you are not getting a good tax deduction from the mortgage
- You are not getting any tax deduction

Consider keeping a mortgage:
- If your mortgage is affordable with your current income and projections for your future income and growth
- If your mortgage rate is low and you could not get a good investment for that money elsewhere
- If you have the discipline necessary to invest your extra money and create a good plan

- If your primary goal is saving and investing for your future
- If you are in a high tax bracket and you need the tax deductions
- If you have a 30-year loan and you are in the early part of the loan, creating a tax advantage
- If you plan on retiring in 10 years or more
- If your primary goal is paying off your credit cards or other high interest debt

If you are interested in learning more about investing in real estate be sure to check out my website. I have some very helpful information to get you started or take you to the next level with your real estate investing.

STARTING YOUR OWN BUSINESS OR GROWING YOUR BUSINESS

Another area where debt can be a good thing is starting a business or taking your business to the next level. Business debt is a good thing or can be a good thing. Once again, you want to make sure it doesn't turn into a bad thing. Don't let this be an excuse to spend money and think that Michelle said, debt is a good thing, start a business. I am not saying every business that you start is going to be good debt. You have to be willing to do your due diligence. I can never say that enough. You have to do your research when you are looking at investments. If you are starting a business, you absolutely want a business plan. You want to make sure that your numbers are going to work out and that you have a full-fledged plan. A business plan can sometimes allow you to get a business loan. A business loan and a business credit card are good things because you are establishing credit for your business and building it. When you are looking at starting a business, there are so many things to consider in making sure that you make a sound decision. My client, Tammy, is really chomping at the bit to get working on her own business. I have advised her to slow down.

We are working with her assets and her new business aspirations; she moved from another country and doesn't have capital to start her own business. A new business does take capital, so you have to be able to have the resources to pay it back with your business plan. You have to know that you are going to be generating income to pay back that loan or have the capital saved up to be able to start with or possibly take in business partners. Partners can help you with capital, and when you take on partners you will have to know you will be giving up a piece of the pie. This is certainly worth it if they are bringing in the capital necessary to start your business. If you are looking at taking out a personal loan or a business loan for starting a business, you will want to get the best interest rates. They are going to be looking at your credit and your credit score. Now, that doesn't mean you can't qualify for a loan if you have a low credit score. Again, I always talk about the relationships. Relationships are everything, so build a relationship with your bankers. If you walk into your bank and you have a relationship built with them, and they see you on a regular basis depositing checks, they know you don't bounce checks, you pay your bills on time, and anything having to do with the bank, you then become trustworthy to them. What happens then, is they become more willing to lend you money. They now feel more confident that their money will be paid back. When you are inquiring about a business loan, if you go in with a great business plan you can most likely get a business loan. The goal is to get your loan officer to get behind you so they can help get the loan approved. You want to make sure you bring a lot of documentation, a lot of research, and that is what will back up the decision for them to be able to give you the loan.

Another way to have debt as a good thing is by building your business or taking it to the next level. If you want to take your business to the next level and you need more capital, you are going to need a loan and a great plan to expand. Let's say, for instance, you have a wonderful ten-table restaurant. You want to expand it to fifteen tables because you have a line outside the door every Friday and Saturday night. You have the opportunity through your landlord to be able to expand and knock out a wall and gain five more tables, which will instantly increase the value of your business, and also instantly generate income. This is where debt is a good thing. The renovations you will be making will require taking out a loan to do the construction. The construction will include knocking out the wall so you can add more tables. In your business plan you have allotted a certain amount of time and you have worked out the numbers so you know you will be able to pay the loan back within the year, and you are able to grow your business. Over the next few years you are generating a much larger income for yourself and your business, and you have the debt paid off within a year.

Here is an example of thinking the debt was going to be a good debt and having it turn south into a bad debt. Let's say you take that same restaurant and somebody who might have a larger ego, who thinks, "Oh my gosh, I have a line outside the door with ten tables. I am going to make my business huge and take it to a massive amount." This restaurant owner did not do any research and assumed they should just make it a forty-table restaurant. They lease the store next door and incur huge debt, more than doubling their debt from the past. Again, they have not done their research and don't realize there is another restaurant going in around the corner that happens to serve similar food. Now they have expanded, they have incurred all of this debt, more than doubling what they had before. There is no longer a line outside and the restaurant is now filled with the forty tables that are more than half empty. They are losing money because they let their ego get in the way and did not do their research. They expanded much too quickly and are paying the price for their mistakes. Those are two examples where you can see how debt can be a good thing for building your business and taking it to the next level, and you can also see how good intentions for your business can turn into bad debt. We want to avoid bad debt at all costs! Once again, I will keep saying it over and over again, research and due diligence are your best friends. Make sure that you have done the comparisons for the competition and that you have looked at every level for taking your business to the next step. Be sure you are making a wise choice with the expansion and the numbers you are looking at with your business plan.

Another area where debt can be a good thing is business equipment. Again, let's look at a restaurant for our example. You need tables, accessories, kitchenware, and everything that is needed to expand the business. When you are considering purchasing ten more pots so you can serve more dishes of pasta per day, then you are looking at having a great ROI. You are generating more income by having those extra pots in the kitchen; more food going out, more income coming in and you can certainly pay off that debt more rapidly. Again, make sure you have done your due diligence and that the numbers do weigh out. Every business has different equipment that is needed and it is certainly a good way for your debt to be a good thing. One thing I would like to bring to your attention is that many times we look at a car as not being a good debt. The instant we drive it off the lot it loses its value. So, most people look at a car as not being a wise investment. However, if you have one or more cars for a delivery service with your restaurant, and you are getting a tax benefit, then that debt could possibly be a good thing. If you're a salesman and you travel throughout the state in your car, and you take clients in your car, the car can be used for a tax benefit. That is another way that debt can be a good thing. Again, we really want to be careful about not letting our ego get ahead of us. We do not want to do entitlement spending and get in over our heads. You need to be realistic with your income or potential income. Once again, make sure these are things you can afford. There are great tax benefits for your business equipment, and sometimes a car can be considered a part of this, depending on your business. Remember, there are very specific and great tax benefits for each type of business that is out there. This is something you will want to look into because you will want to out weigh the tax benefit to see if it will help you increase your income and build wealth. Whenever you gain from a benefit or anything that is of value then that is helping you build your wealth. That is why I say debt can be a good thing, and there are many ways that debt can be a good thing.

If you are considering your own business here are some things to consider:

Possible Pros:
> You are your own boss
> Greater profit and income potential
> Your money works for you
> Possible tax benefits
> Expanding your business and community connections
> Doing what you love
> Fulfilling your dreams
> Control of your schedule
> Hire employees to give you freedom

Possible Cons:
> Startup for a new business can be very time consuming
> Now consumer or client problems are your problems
> Overhead cost and startup
> Business licenses
> City licenses
> Zoning for the area if you have customers

Parking
Local taxes
Employee wages
Insurance
Equipment cost
Operating expenses

Among the issues you will research are supply and demand, your competition in this field, how much capital you will need to get started, the legal issues affecting it, such as, if a license is required, and whether you can realistically make a profit from your service or product, after your expenses. You will need to analyze what you already know about running a business and what you need to learn. Then find the correct way to fill your information gap. A smart entrepreneur is one who has prepared for the ups and downs of business. Too many people get an idea and rush out to get started without doing the proper research and preparation. That is why more than 90% of all new businesses fail in the first five years. It is not because the new owners are not dedicated or passionate about what they are trying to do. It's because they didn't do their homework before they began. That is why I am asking you to start slowly and take one step at a time. If you take the proper steps, one at a time, those little steps will turn into a wonderful journey and help you become successful.

After you have completed your research and you are certain that the business has a financially successful potential, it is time for you to begin to plan your business venture. There are several ways you can start. You can become an independent owner, you can have partners, you can form an alliance with others whose work supports you, or you can incorporate. Whatever way you decide to go will have a lot to do with how independent you can be and how fast decisions can be made. Each way has many benefits and drawbacks that you need to study before you decide. One way to make such an important decision is to take the time to seek advice from a non-partial party, such as a banker or financial business attorney.

There are other issues that help a business start and stay successful that you will want to consider, such as, correct bookkeeping practices, the best way to market yourself, or even the best place to locate the business you are investigating. If you are considering starting a home based business, you will need to investigate the zoning laws of your neighborhood and the feelings of your neighbors. How many cars can you park on your street and how many people will enter your home each day are important issues if you plan to have a product or service for sale. The impact of parking in the neighborhood is important if you plan to have high traffic. These issues are not important if you plan to have a home office but you travel to the customer or do work outside of the home.

You may also want to consider selling information or ideas based on the work or profession you are now engaged in. This type of entrepreneur is usually called a consultant and they have made great impacts on many types of businesses in the last twenty years. Before you discard or abandon what you are doing now, be certain to analyze all of the information you have learned and decide how it might help you in a future occupation. Nothing learned is ever wasted. Sometimes it takes a while to visualize how it might help you, but don't forget this information as your plan. Nor do you want to forget all the contacts you've made in your social and business life. They very well may be your first clients or customers. Whatever it is that you plan to do, remember, the way to becoming the person in your imagination is to focus on going forward slowly and with responsibility.

None of these cautions are meant to discourage you from being an entrepreneur; rather, they are mentioned here because I want you to become a successful business owner.... if that is what you want to do. If your dream is to become an independent business owner, nothing should be able to hold you back. There is always a way to get started, you just might need to get creative in finding where you can best serve yourself and others. For financial reasons, some people find it necessary to start a business on the side while they "wean" themselves away from their full-time salaried job. This could be a good way to start a new business. It gives you a chance to explore whether you really like selling a service or products on your own before you invest too much capital. It gives you the opportunity to use your special talents and unique gifts to explore the realistic possibility of the dream that you have. And don't forget to examine and think about non-traditional professions and careers. In this day and age, people are involved in more different occupations than ever before. Getting a loan for a non-traditional business may take a little longer, but when you find the right banker, one who understands your keen desire, the money can be found.

As I mentioned at the start of this chapter, the financial advantages of owning your own business are tremendous. However, being an entrepreneur is not for everyone. There are some risks involved and you will need to know your personal risk factor before you make a firm decision about owning your own business. In the meantime, if you've been dreaming of becoming an entrepreneur and of starting your own business, here is a simple method that may help you get started. Approach the idea with a feeling of optimism. Take those areas that you consider problems and then think of each problem as an opportunity to use your inspiration and creativity to create a solution, while offering a service or product.

Write the "problem" out on a piece of paper. Write it out clearly, exactly as you think of it. Then write down all the possible solutions that you can think of to handle this "opportunity." Don't worry if the idea that comes into your mind seems impossible. If your imagination thought of it, there is probably a reason for this idea. Then choose the best solution and decide how to make it come true. Do this for each reason you have, why you can't get started. Soon you will have solutions for the problems, as the creative side of you works toward your desired solution. If you get stuck on a solution, you can partner with someone for some ideas. Sometimes two minds are better than one.

If you are interested in learning more about starting a business, check out my website for all that I offer on helping you to get started. I offer many different types of opportunities and solutions that meet your needs.

Solution Summary

3: DEBT A GOOD THING?: EXAMPLES OF GOOD DEBT

Education
- Education can be good debt, as it can increase earning potential.
- Know what your starting salary is going to be and the cap.
- Research student loans and grants.
- Research the ROI, remember to factor in the time it will take to get your return.
- Consider continuing education for higher earning potential.
- Check with your employer to see if they offer support for higher education.

Mortgage
- Mortgage can be good debt if you make a wise purchase and have the right mortgage.
- Buy when the market is low and sell when the market is high to guarantee success.
- Make a reasonable commitment, considering your income, expenses and earning potential, when getting a mortgage.
- Remember location, location, location - one of the most important rules of real estate.
- Do research and educate yourself, calculating your ROI before investing in real estate.
- Be sure when calculating the numbers to include all expenses, the mortgage, property taxes, HOA dues, utilities, insurance, repairs, and management costs, etc.
- Factor in the tax benefits.

Business
- Business debt can be good if you do your research and know your risk factor.
- Create a business plan.
- Know how much capital you will need to get started.
- If you don't have capital, an option is taking on business partners.
- Before starting a business know all of your operating expenses.
- Research supply and demand, as well as competition in this field.
- Figure out if it is realistic that you will make a profit on your service or product after you factor in start up costs, loans, and your expenses.
- Seek advice from bankers, financial business attorneys, as they can help you avoid costly mistakes.
- Consider selling your expertise as a consultant.

Chapter

Plastic Jungle

CREDIT CARDS

As we move into the chapter dealing with the credit card industry, I affectionately named the "Plastic Jungle," I want you to know credit and credit cards are not necessarily a bad thing. In fact, I am an advocate of having credit, credit cards, and good credit. What I want is for you stop throwing away your hard earned money on unnecessary fees and high interest rates. Instead, I would like you to use the credit industry to your benefit. This one chapter can teach many of you how to go from debt elimination to wealth creation. Becoming financially savvy with your credit cards will give you freedom, and for many of you, alleviate your debt completely!

Too much credit card debt is a big problem! However, you really do need credit cards to do certain things. They are very convenient. Credit cards, when used correctly can be a convenient tool that serves you. They are great for tracking expenses for your taxes, making online purchases or phone purchases, for gaining airline miles, and many other bonuses. The key is to pay them off every month and to not fall behind. The credit card companies offer you all of these bonuses to entice you to use the cards. Their hopes are that you will fall behind, therefore, owing fees and interest. Don't get taken advantage of with overwhelming interest payments and frustrating fees, where you end up serving your credit card companies!

Here are some remarkable statistics on credit card debt:

- 20% of Americans have maxed out their credits cards
- Roughly 24% of people making purchases in the United States are using retail store cards, debit cards and bank credit cards
- For 2006 total credit card debt in the United States totaled about six hundred and sixty five BILLION dollars on bank credit cards and about one hundred and five BILLION dollars on store or gas credit cards, according to the Federal Reserve. According to the Fed's G19 (Federal Reserve Statistical Release), the total is roughly eight hundred billion dollars for 2006
- Approximately 185 million people have at least one credit card
- The reliance on plastic, most of which are credit cards, rose 7.8% of its adjusted annual rate to a record 943.5 BILLION in 2007, according to the Federal Reserve

If you have credit card debt, as you can see from the numbers above, you are not alone!

A GUIDE TO COMPARING CREDIT CARD OFFERS

I'm sure if you are like millions of others in the country you get credit offers in the mail by the handfuls. You may throw them away or you may save them up. How do you decide which ones to go with?

Compare the disclosure chart that is on every credit card offer or solicitation. It is now mandatory to have this disclosure chart. It is called the Schumer Box, named after Senator Charles Schumer from New York, who spearheaded the legislation. The problem is that the credit card companies still make it very confusing for you. So you want to read carefully.

Remember, you are the customer. If you have a good credit score, you are an even better customer. However, even if you do not have a good credit score, they still want you as a customer. Reason being, the credit card company is betting they will be making money from you. But you do have the power of choice and I suggest shopping around for the best companies and offers.

What you will want to consider:

- The introductory or teaser rate and the actual APR – looking for the lowest rates
- The annual fee (or if there isn't one, this is most preferable)
- Any transaction fees
- The minimum finance charge
- How they calculate the variable APR...the longer grace period the better
- Over limit/late payment fees
- How they compute your balance... the best is the "adjusted balance"... second best is "average daily balance"... the worst for the consumer is the two cycle balance

In addition to the above list, consider if the card is offering you airline miles, bonus points for hotels or rental cars. They may even offer you cash back and other offers. These can help you to decide whom to go with. Make sure to read the fine print or make a phone call to clear up any questions you have. The offers are set up to entice you into using their card. Sometimes they are a good deal and sometimes they are not! I have clients that have a credit card that is an airline miles card. They charge everything on their credit card, paying it off each month, and never carry a balance on their card. And the best part about it, aside from not being in debt, is they haven't paid for an airline ticket in years. They always use their free miles from their credit card company. They are using the credit card companies to their advantage, as opposed to the opposite.

If you need to get a credit card, even if you have the worst credit imaginable or have no credit and are just starting out, you can get a credit card. But I am not talking about a secured credit card. Here is one of my credit building and credit repair techniques that is easy to do. I suggest going to a family member, loved one or a good friend and become an authorized user on their account. You are building your credit, and you need to use it wisely. The person adding you to their card is trusting you, and in the meantime, helping you build your credit. After a period of time, 6 months to a year of making your scheduled payments, you can now leverage that card to open one under your own name with the same company or another company. Now you are building or rebuilding your credit.

At the top of the list, concerning your credit cards, is to be extremely aware of late payments. Don't be fooled, they are out to get your money with late payments. If you are late on a payment they can completely change the terms of your credit card agreement and set you up to spiral into huge debt. In some cases it can be considered late if it comes in past a certain time, on the exact same day the payment is due. And if you have late payment fees, it can really catch up with you. On average, they will charge you $35 per late payment. Just one late payment can cause your interest rate to skyrocket upwards to 29% or higher.

Let me ask you this, do you know what interest rate you are paying on every credit card you have? If you answered, no, you really need to find out. The sooner the better! And don't think that you are paying what you did when you first signed up. Credit Card companies change the interest rates all the time. You may think you signed up at a teaser rate of 0 - 8% and now you are paying 25% - 30% or more and you don't even know it! Your credit card rates can also change because they are legally adjustable. It doesn't matter if you have good credit; they can make it higher legally, so they do.

The single most beneficial tool that can help you get out of debt is to **call your credit card company and ask them to lower your interest rate ASAP!** Did you know that there is a very high percentage of consumers that get their interest rate lowered? Over half! This can be done in as little as five minutes of your precious time, and with the results ending in your favor.

The credit card companies operate with the motivation of selling you the highest rate that they think they can get away with. There are usually, if not always, other offers they can give you if you ask. You just have to ask and get to the right person. This technique is the most successful for all of my clients to lower debt immediately. I suggest everyone to do this, even if you presently have a good rate. Even if you don't use the card still call and try to get the percentage rate lowered. You never know when you might need to use the card.

You must remember the credit industry is in a business, first and foremost – they're in the business of taking your money. That's all they care about. Also note, just as any other business is competitive, so is the credit industry. So you can use the competitive edge to your advantage, remembering you are the consumer. You can take your business elsewhere. This is the position you always want to be in with the credit industry. Even if you have no other offers, even if you have no other credit cards, you should always let them feel that they could lose your business at any time to another competitor.

Gather your credit card statements and call the customer service number. Direct yourself to the credit analyst or the credit specialist. Every company has their own titles for the person who handles rates and new business. You just need to get to the right person. If for any reason they deny your request you can try again and again. I have a client named Dawn who had to get through five different people to get her rate lowered. She did not give up, and as a result, she got her interest rate lowered by 9.95%, instantly saving her thousands. The original rate was 17.95% and now she is only paying 8 %. In a short period of time, Dawn had her interest rate lowered on nine credit cards. She did it all with my technique of calling the credit card company and telling them her entire story. She told them how she is a manicurist and that she had an injury on her thumb last year that put her into debt. She had to have surgery and her medical expenses were adding up with her loss of income, due to down time. She would go into detail and befriend the person on the phone. When you are befriending someone, using a touching story or humor will usually work. Since she was unable to work for a period of time and she is doing her best to catch up, it has been difficult for her but she always stays in communication with her creditors. She even had one creditor remove a large fee, simply because she befriended the woman on the phone. Dawn made a balance transfer to move one of her credit card balances to another card that had a 0% interest rate. After talking to the representative on the phone, and again, befriending her with her story, the representative decided to waive the transfer fee, saving Dawn over $ 300, instantly.

Call the credit company and you can have the same results. After getting to the right person you can begin by telling them how wonderful their company is and that you would like to keep your business with them. However, you have offers from several credit card companies and even though you don't want to take the business away from them, you have to go where they are giving the best offer. Please note, that even when using these tactics, I don't suggest for you to close your account. Think carefully about that.

As your length of credit history is a factor contributing to a higher credit score. Certainly consider transferring balances if they are not willing to work with you. Then you begin to negotiate the best offer they have available, or have them lower the interest rate that you are currently paying. If you have a high credit score tell them what it is. For example, if you have a 780 credit score, tell them you are never late and everyone's offering you credit. Your hope is that they can be competitive with what others are offering you so that you may keep using their card. If you have had the card for a long time you will want to use that towards your benefit. The longer your history is with that bank, loan or card, I suggest using that for leverage. You'll have more bargaining power. Remember again, you are a valuable consumer considering your credit history. However, don't be concerned if you don't have a long history with them. They will still work with you to build a relationship. They want to get all of your hard earned money in interest and fees. Let them know you have been a loyal and good customer. Be sure to keep records of dates and times of everyone that you talked to. The other thing I want you to remember is to not give up, even if they say no, ask for someone in a higher position. Who do they report to, who makes the final decision? And be sure to come across in a polite manner. Remember, there are always ways to convey your value as a consumer and acquiring your desired results which is getting the best rates.

Several of my clients have been able to save thousands to even tens of thousands of dollars in just a five minute phone call with the end result in mind of lowering interest rates and eliminating unwanted fees. Over a lengthy period of time this can really add up.

Think about this, if you buy a $20 lunch and it puts you $1 over your credit card limit, you end up paying another $30 in an over-the-limit fee. That $20 lunch has now cost you $50. My suggestion is for you to really be aware of your limits at all times on all of your cards. This will alleviate so many fees. Additionally, I suggest you call and have the credit limits raised on all of your cards, if you carry high balances. Often times, the credit card companies will raise your limit if you are in good standing with them, all you have to do is ask. They also may make you another offer, eliminating fees if you ask. Ultimately the end goal is to stay in the habit of keeping your credit cards under the limit and paying in full each month, without overspending. If you are making payments and are near your limit, try not to carry this card with you so you will not be tempted to overuse it.

You can save hundreds to thousands of dollars by calling your credit card companies and asking to have your late or over-the-limit fees removed! They have the power and they do remove the fees. They won't always do this, but what do you have to lose by trying? Call and use the same techniques that I mentioned Dawn using and leverage them to remove your fees! You will need to watch yourself in the future, as often, they will say they are doing this as a one-time courtesy. If you become good enough with the calls you can do this more than once.

My client Victoria is 25 years old, does not have children, and has been engaged for about two years. Her fiancé's financial situation is stable, while hers involved frequently charging on her cards. She used her debit card to make most purchases, but with large purchases she had gotten into the habit of using her credit card. She lives in Boston, Massachusetts and works as a Job Coach. She loves her job and is happy with her current salary. What she needs to do is work within her current income, considering that is what she will be receiving for a while. She has been following my techniques and now finds herself paying off her credit card balance in full, every month. Though, lately she has gotten into the bad habit of charging more and just ends up adding to the balance. She now knows that after paying off her complete balance every month, it is not in her best interest to charge up her credit card again with hundreds of dollars. She is working on changing this habit. Currently, she has some credit card debt on one of her cards that amounts to $3,240. That credit card has several fees that are applied to her account every month. The fees are starting to add up quickly. Each month she was finding herself losing money rather than having it go towards her debt. I'm sure you can imagine how frustrating this is for Victoria.

I suggested that she transfer the remaining balance to a card that does not have an annual fee and has a lower interest rate. Victoria also called her credit card company and instantly lowered her interest rate for future purchases. This was simple for her to do and saves her hundreds of dollars per month and thousands per year.

Marriages are hard enough, but consider that the divorce rate is an extraordinary 50-70%, and that the number one reason they fail is due to financial difficulties. Maggie and Jay are one of the couples I consulted that started their marriage $70,000 in debt. That was mostly, if not all, in credit card debt. You can imagine the stress and strain that caused their marriage! They applied my technique of borrowing money at a lower interest rate from a family member. They even managed to get another loan from a family member at no interest. You can imagine their relief when they were able to get rid of all their credit card debt and interest within one week! They now were on a mission to stay out of credit card debt! They took this mission seriously and were bound and determined to be successful, and to not default on their family loans. They had a legal agreement drawn up that was simple and basic, and stated all the terms of their agreement.

As they started their plan of attack on the debt, they started paying cash for all of their purchases. They cut back on excessive purchases, like, eating out on a regular basis, ordering alcohol out, excessive clothing, and cutting back on entertainment expenses. They did not completely stop all things pleasurable, but they did cut back in large quantity. As I'm sure you can see, there is nothing from the above list that is absolutely needed to survive! At the time, it was not the most convenient thing for them to make this change, but it turned out to be much easier to do than they had thought. Now, think about this, if they were never overspending in the first place, they wouldn't have had to go through the temporary discomfort. They also used the techniques of calling the credit card companies and lowering their interest rates and getting no annual fee cards. Now, with their new knowledge, they watch their credit card statements like hawks, never allowing for hidden fees or other charges. And believe me, they have had their share of fees trying to sneak in. Maggie always catches them now and handles the situation immediately. She will call the companies, get to the right person, and have the fee removed or waived. Now, Jay and Maggie always pay their credit cards in full every month and never pay any interest! This is a good habit to get into and all you have to do is follow your **Debt Eliminator** and **Wealth Creator** chart. You too can get on the pay no interest plan. One month, Maggie noticed that her purchases started creeping up, and she had found herself with a higher balance than she was used to. She was surprised to see that the balance had reached a total of $5,042. She knew she had $5,000 in her bank account in reserve, so she diligently paid the $5,000, leaving herself with a balance of $42. On her next statement, much to her surprise, she found her balance of $42 now had a $97 interest payment that was also due. In shock and wanting an explanation, she immediately contacted the credit card company. They explained to her that even though she had paid such a large amount, since she didn't pay it in full, the interest was still charged to her for the full amount. She would have been better served keeping her money in her bank account where it would have been collecting interest. Instead, she paid them a large amount thinking she would only be paying interest on $42. When she called she was kind and professional and explained her disbelief over the interest charge. At the same time she was firm with the person over the phone, saying she knew it wasn't their fault and could they do anything about this? They did end up giving her a one-time grace period, removing the interest. Maggie was happy and learned a good lesson with this story.

With their new plan, Jay and Maggie were able to pay off all of the $70,000 debt in just over 1 year. Through this principle and applying the techniques in this book they now have NO credit card debt! Absolutely no credit card debt. Jay and Maggie now have a beautiful home in the Hollywood Hills, rental properties, horses, and they live credit card debt free. They now have a sound relationship, and Jay is thrilled that Maggie has been proactive in learning about handling their finances. At the beginning of the marriage it was Maggie that was mostly responsible for their credit card debt, so it was a huge relief to get it under control and paid off. Because of their new way of living they are now able to enjoy a much better relationship with each other.

A beneficial tool to help you get out of debt is to immediately transfer your outstanding balances on higher rate credit cards to ones with 0% interest. This can save you thousands in interest! WARNING! WATCH THE FINE PRINT, THE TRANSFER FEES, AND EXAMINE ALL THE TERMS. DO NOT PAY LATE OR GO OVER THE LIMIT, OR YOU MAY INSTANTLY LOSE YOUR 0% RATE!

This is a great way to immediately reduce interest fees and debt, but you must be sure to read and know what you are getting into. Even with the transfer fee, you will, in all likelihood, save money. A transfer fee could be far less, in the long run, than the interest you could be paying on the higher rate card. You can call your existing credit card companies and ask what the best balance transfer offer is that they currently have available. Let them know that you have an offer for a card with 0% interest for a year. Ask if they can match that or what their best offer is.

If you have any questions, call the customer service number on the offer and ask for the credit analyst or credit specialist. Remember, every company has their own titles for the person who handles rates and new business.

Ask them these following questions:
How long does the 0% last?
Are there any balance transfer fees?
How much credit is available to me? (Only transfer an amount that will not put you over the limit, including the transfer fee)

Another great way to get rid of your credit card debt, if you own a home, is to transfer it to a HELOC (home equity line of credit). You can get fabulous rates if you transfer to a HELOC, and in most cases, the interest you are paying on your HELOC, can be written off on your taxes. Then, if you have more than one card, you will now only have one monthly payment, which can alleviate a lot of stress. And you can have the balances transferred in as little as one week!

Your monthly payments will usually go down, which will be another nice form of stress relief. The key is not to slip up and feel as though you can go back to charging on your credit cards again. A good technique to make sure you're not tempted to frivolously use your credit cards is to not carry them with you. Keep them in a safe place at home and use them only when needed, for building wealth or in emergencies. For example, you can build wealth with credit cards when you are growing a business or investing in your higher education.

The average American household has at least one credit card with $9,200 in debt. The average interest rate they pay runs between 15-25%. The sad part is that most people can only afford to make the minimum payment, which will never get them anywhere. Here is what happens if you only make a minimum payment...you will be paying on that credit card for the better part of your life.

Let me show you an example. Let's say you have a credit card with an average debt of $9,200 dollars and a 25% interest rate. If you only make a minimum monthly payment of $172 a month, 30 years later you will still owe all of the $9,200. Yes, you heard me correctly. When you make a minimum payment you're barely covering the interest owed each month. In fact, to pay off the original debt of $9,200, you will end up paying an additional $53,040 in interest. So you will end up paying the credit card company a grand total of over $62,000. Look at it another way. Say you were looking for a high-definition flat screen TV and found a nice one on sale for only $999. Initially, that might sound like a good deal. You don't have the cash so you put it on your credit card, thinking you will gradually pay it off, but meanwhile, you have the satisfaction of having the TV now. If you only made minimum monthly payments on the TV, after interest accrued, you would end up paying the credit card company over $6,700 for that TV. If that TV were priced in the store at over $6,700 you'd never buy it. But when you use a credit card and only make the minimum monthly payment, that's exactly how much you would pay for it.

The numbers are staggering when you are only making minimum payments. For $9,200 in debt you would be paying over $53,000 in interest. That's like having the credit card companies running your entire life! It's like you're working for them.

I have a client, Lori, who is the perfect example of what happens when you make minimum monthly payments. She had a debt of $8,530 and had been making minimum payments for 7 years. She had not really been paying attention to the balance until she started working with me. As with all my clients, we started with the **Debt Eliminator Chart** and that is when she realized she now owed more than when she started!!! Obviously, this was not good news to Lori. As I gave her an assignment to get the interest rate lowered, she diligently made the phone call to her credit card company. Initially, they told her they could not lower her rate. She explained that she was going through a divorce and had noticed that her ex-husband had only been making minimum payments. She also told them she was trying to keep her son in the school he had attended for years. She told them it was tough for her to make ends meet and was there anything they could do for her. I suggested she ask the credit card company if they could give some type of consideration for hardship.

Many companies will offer some sort of a hardship concession for loss of job, divorce, death of a family member, medical issues, etc. The credit specialist she was talking to said that in consideration of her divorce they could freeze her interest for 4 months. Lori was able to get money out of a home she had in Florida with a HELOC and move some other money around so she could work on eliminating the debt in 4 months and not have any extra interest! This saved thousands of dollars instantly, and once again, the phone call only took 5 minutes. You can imagine how much stress this has alleviated for Lori.

Lori had another card that was causing her stress. She had a teaser rate credit card that had a 0% interest on it for one year. Before Lori came to me and used her **Debt Eliminator Chart** she had missed a payment, which made her 0% rate skyrocket to 26%. She had a long history with the company of making her payments on time, so I suggested she call and talk to the credit specialist or supervisor. She made the call. Remember, as I always suggest when making that call, be considerate and kind, however, still be firm about having options with other credit card companies. She explained to the credit specialist that she had this card for 11 years and had never made a late payment. She apologized for the payment being late and explained that she was traveling back from her son's school function, and that the envelope got mailed later than anticipated. She said that this was very out of character for her, and that because of her divorce she had been under a lot of stress. She continued to say that she liked their company and would like to continue doing business with them, and asked if they would consider giving her a grace on this one late payment and reinstate her teaser rate? She again, very kindly said that if they did not she would have to transfer the balance to another card that has a 0% offer. She would also never use their card again. She said that she did not want to have to resort to this, however, she would have no choice. The specialist put her on hold for a brief time. When the specialist returned she said that she could see from her history, she had never been late. She said that she would give her this one grace and reinstate her teaser rate. However, this was a one-time only deal and that she would not receive it again. Lori thanked her and now that she is working with the **Debt Eliminator Chart** she will not be late on her payments again. She now closely watches her due dates so they do not slip and cause her unnecessary stress. Consider using these same techniques for yourself and you could eliminate your debt or save thousands!

Most people don't realize that a large part of their debt on credit cards is made up of interest and fees. For example, if you buy a leather coat for $100, over time, with interest and fees paid you could end up paying $210 for that $100 coat! I am sure you did not sign up to pay nearly double for that purchase. The biggest part of your debt is not what you actually buy; it's the interest and fees you pay when not paying off the balance each month.

When you are negotiating with your credit card companies, it is important for you to know, if you claim bankruptcy there is a good chance they will never get paid for your debt. So, if you are considering claiming bankruptcy, it is in their best interest to give you some kind of a payment plan. It is better for them to get some payment for the debt than nothing at all. You just have to know it will be a win/win for everyone. Everyone wins when you get them off your back and they get some kind of a payment plan. Also, look closely at the next chapter, "Taming the Beast", as some collection companies break the law on a daily basis. Know the law and your rights.

When using credit cards always be aware of the fine print. There is always a hidden agenda in the fine print, from balance transfer offers to huge fees. There can be different rates for new purchases and cash advances. Sometimes the checks they mail you can be a separate fee all together. Read the fine print carefully. The credit card companies are in the business to confuse you; it means billions of dollars to them. They set up confusing offers all the time, and just when you think you have the offer down they will change it, hoping to trick you into accepting it without looking at the changes. The reason why they continue to do this is because it works on millions of people across America, who keep falling for their tricks. It's a lucrative business for them, so the companies keep doing it, and siphoning away your hard earned money. Be aware that you may not be getting as good of a deal as you think you are.

Now lets take a look at some typical offers that are mailed to millions across the country. Let these examples spark your discerning eye on all the offers that come to you. READ CAREFULLY before accepting any offer!

One of my clients received an offer in the mail that stated in large bold letters, "ZERO BALANCE OFFER." He had some debt, so he was interested in this seemingly good offer. He was about to take this offer until I took a good look at the fine print and found the hidden "bait and switch" clause. What they were really saying is that once you transfer your balance to them, you will have a zero balance on the card you are transferring from! What they failed to mention in the teaser, which was written in the small print, was there was a 9.75% APR plus prime that went up to a whopping 17.75%. My client has an 800 credit score and it is absurd for him to be paying 17+% interest on anything. The point is, he almost took advantage of this offer and he would have been charged fees and paid high interest.

Hidden fees change on balance transfer offers all the time. You have to be on your toes, because the credit card industry changes so they can take advantage of you when you're not expecting it. For instance, a card may have previously made an offer of a balance transfer with a 3% service charge and maximum fee of $75. People became accustomed to the max fees and think it is a trade off to get the zero interest balance transfer. What they are really doing is changing the terms the next time they send you the offer, in the teeny tiny print you can't see without a magnifying glass, now states that there is a 3% fee and there is **no maximum**. If you're transferring large amounts you could end up paying hundreds, to possibly thousands of dollars in just one fee.

If you are like most people, and you have any type of debt, you are probably paying interest. So, you can imagine that getting an envelope in the mail with the large 0% fixed APR for one year would be pretty exciting. It could seem like a huge relief and a very tempting offer! Now, when you look inside you see in large type, $100,000! Wow, the things you could do with $100,000. You could maybe even get into an investment and cash out the profit before the year's up. Very tempting, right!

If you look at the fine print, and again believe me, you will need a magnifying glass for this, it says, "balance transfers and cash advance checks are subject to a 3% transaction fee, no less than $10." What that means is, if you take advantage of this offer and go for the $100,000, your transaction fee is a whopping $3,000!!! Now take a look at the other document enclosed in the envelope, that most people never read. It is the Disclosure Summary. Wow, the fine print is even smaller in this one. If you look at the Default APR it says, "Up to 29.99% for all Purchase, Balance Transfer, and Cash Advance balances if late or over the limit for both Platinum Plus and Preferred accounts." It says, "See Explanation 1 on Page 2." You now have to flip the page to even smaller writing on the back. On page 2 it explains that if your minimum payment is late (i.e., not received by 5 p.m., ET on its Payment Due Date), or the account balance is over the credit limit, they may increase your account's Standard APR's up to the Default APR. The Default APR will be applied to all new and outstanding balances.

Are you confused yet??? Of course you are, and that is how they want it! Let's look at this again. The Default APR is up to 29.99% for all Purchase, Balance Transfer, and Cash Advance balances if late or over limit.

If you use the $100,000 available to you and you now have the 3% fee, adding $3,000, YOU HAVE INSTANTLY GONE OVER YOUR CREDIT LIMIT!!! The $3,000 fee just put you over the limit! This has happened to my clients and they are devastated. THEY THOUGHT THEY HAD 0% AND NOW THEY ARE CONTRACTUALLY OBLIGATED TO A WHOPPING 29.99% IN INTEREST. Even if you realized this and instantly paid back the $100,000, you are still obligated to pay them the $3,000 with 29.99%. You also might be obligated to pay 29.99% in interest on the $100,000, even for only having it for a short time. 29.99% is basically a 30% interest rate, a far cry from the 0% advertised. So that 0% is not so ZERO anymore.

I know it's hard to believe that they can get away with that! The biggest part of your debt is not what you actually buy; it's the interest and fees you pay.

Here's another one...

They send a check made out to "you," the credit card customer, for a little over $9. You normally would think it's a refund for overpayment or a thank you gift. In reality, the fine print says, "Upon cashing this check you agree to a pre-paid one-year membership" with an auto club or some other form of membership. You cashed their check for a little over $9 and now you legally owe them a $100 membership fee that you aren't allowed to cancel, according to the fine print. This is a perfect example of what giant companies are doing. It's legal, but it's not right. Remember, the credit industry is a business, and they are in the business of taking your money. People just don't know what's going on, and that's why I say it's not your fault you have debt problems. YOU REALLY NEED TO READ THE FINE PRINT, that is, if you can even find it. The excessive interest rates and fees are taking a staggering toll on all of us, and most people don't even realize it's happening! I think it is important to expose these scams.

Unless you are completely out of control with spending, I highly recommend you have at least one credit card! The **Debt Eliminator Chart** will help you to pay on time and keep track of your statements. I actually suggest having at least 3 revolving cards (general credit cards, department store, gas, etc...) at any given time. If you at least start with one and eventually move on up to 3, that would be good for now. The reason you should always have credit cards is because it gives you power with your credit score and the lending institutions. They want to be able to see that you are responsible with your payments. They also like it if you have length of credit history. The longer you have a card the better it is for your credit score. If you find it highly irresistible to use the cards, and often spend excessively, let me give you some tips that may help. You can have the credit cards, just don't carry them in your wallet! Keep them in a safe secure place at home as you will not be tempted to spend randomly. If you feel this would still not work for you and you would be tempted to go and dig out the credit cards then I suggest keeping the account open however cut up the cards. Make note of the account number and expiration date. Keeping the accounts open will add to your length of credit history. Another solution is to carry one card and use it in emergencies only. Use each card periodically. When cards are not used at all, the account might go dormant. And since length of history is a portion of your credit score, you want to be mindful and keep all cards active. You can do this WITHOUT going into debt. You can simply charge a $10 lunch, gas, or another small purchase, paying in full by month's end. Do this every once in a while or months before you plan on making a large purchase, like a home or a car. This can be beneficial to your credit score, giving you buying power. Charging these small amounts will reactivate the card and add to your length of history.

A good money saving tip is this: STOP UNNECESSARY DEFICIT SPENDING. Spending into debt can be so easy with a credit card.

The reason is purely psychological. When you give a clerk a credit card, it's not the same as handing over a stack of green dollar bills. Could you hand the clerk a fist of ten or twenty dollar bills as easily as you could hand her your credit card? I venture to say, probably not.

Credit cards can easily put you into debt. Even people with very good incomes can get into a hole. This is where the credit card companies want to keep you. Paying down the credit card to zero is difficult and can become more difficult with each month that goes by. Using the credit card by choice, too quickly turns into using it for need. When you get to the point where you are using your card out of NEED because you don't have enough cash, this is a sign you are in trouble. The truth is, credit card debt can zap your financial strength and deplete your physical body, as you get stressed.

The secret to freeing yourself from the credit card game is not to overspend, and choose the best cards with the lowest interest rates and no fees, or the lowest fees. Begin by using an aggressive plan to pay them down as soon as possible. Pay more than the minimum amount, even if it's only $10 extra. Once you stop adding to the debt, you will eventually get them paid off. That is only, IF you always pay more than the minimum amount. Everyone can get out of debt if they are patient and disciplined and follow the techniques I teach. Once you are out of debt, YOU MUST work with your **Debt Elimination** and **Wealth Creation Charts**. Adopt a strict policy of paying your credit cards off each month or paying cash. I suggest changing the habit of buying now and paying later. Save your credit for when you really need it, like emergencies, or starting a business, investments, things that will bring you an ROI. It may surprise you, but sometimes clothing can be a great investment if it is going to help you in your job. You just have to be wise with your spending.

You are not on this earth to constantly worry about money, how your bills will be paid, or what your financial future will be. That is wasted energy that could prevent you from getting where you want to go, and achieving all you desire.

It's too easy to be lured in by all the credit card offers and the American philosophy of instant gratification. Stopping credit over-consumption is one of the most powerful financial tools available to us all.

Solution Summary

4: PLASTIC JUNGLE: CREDIT CARDS

- Credit and credit cards can be good when you use discernment.

- Become savvy with credit cards and you can have financial freedom.

- Pay your balances off each month - don't fall behind.

- Sort card offers by disclosure details: APR - look for the lowest rates, the annual fee - if none even better, transaction fees, the minimum finance charge, over limit, late payment fees, etc.

- Read the fine print for hidden fees - if needed, call to answer any questions about new credit card offers.

- Know the interest rates for each of your credit cards.

- Call your credit card companies and ask them to lower your interest rates. Be persistent and polite and get to the right person - ask for someone in higher position if the current person denies your request. Call back again if they still deny you.

- Call and request they remove fees and penalties if you have any.

- Transfer balances to cards with better interest rates and lower fees.

- Be sure to know how long promotional rates last with new cards or existing cards and if there is balance transfer fees.

- Pay higher interest cards first.

- Leave your cards at home in a safe place - do not be tempted to use them!

- Stop unnecessary deficit spending.

Chapter V

Taming the Beast

COLLECTION AGENCIES

This chapter will teach you how to deal with the collection agencies. With the recent tightening of the lending practices, and the general population being in over their heads with debt, collection agencies are in demand, more than ever. The lenders, health care professionals, hospitals, cities, taxes, landlords, etc, are turning to collections in an effort to get back some of their losses or recoup losses. As a result, there have been unfair practices at the hands of the collection agencies, and there are laws that are out there to protect you. In many cases, when the collection agencies are trying to collect they will use tactics that break the law. Considering the fact that more and more Americans are having an issue with collections, I want you to be aware of your rights and how to protect yourself.

Many studies within the last twelve months have shown that there are drastic changes and huge complaints with the collection agencies, in regards to unfair tactics being used to collect. I will teach you techniques on how to possibly avoid collections all together, and how to protect yourself if you find yourself in a collection situation. Many times it may not even be your fault or may not be your debt that they are trying to collect on. With the surge of the recession and economics on a downswing, collections are on a high, and therefore, more likely for there to be errors. My goal is for you to be aware and be able to protect yourself. With four out of five Americans having an error on their credit reports you can imagine how many errors there are in collections.

The first line of action, if possible, is for you to avoid collections all together. The reason why is that a collection has a judgmental affect on your credit report and your credit scores. Collections are never a good thing so you want to make sure you avoid them, if at all possible. Collections can also be very difficult to remove.

First and foremost, I want you to understand what a collection means. When a debt on your record has gone into collection, that means that the creditor is going to handle the outstanding collection in house or by an outside source, which is a collection agency. When they give it to an outside source, sometimes that collection agency is buying that debt outright so that they can collect on it. This is actually a business. This type of collection agency is a business, in the business of buying old debt from people. Whether it's a doctor's office, a mortgage, an auto payment, whatever that debt is, they purchase it for pennies of what is owed. The lender or the service provider is recouping some of their losses and turning it over to the collection agency for an agreed price. The collection agency now owns the debt. The collection agency is in the business of collecting money and that is all they do all day long. If they do not collect they make no money. Their objective is to be able to collect as much as they can for the debt, and they will often resort to intimidating you. They will try collecting old debts, new debts, debts that are not yours due to errors, or even if you have a relative with the same name. They will try to use any kind of tactic and get as much money as possible. Another way collection agencies operate is on a percentage basis. The lender or creditor will hire an outside collection agency that gets a percentage of the debt collected. In some cases it can be up to fifty percent. As you can imagine, this gives them a huge incentive to be able to make higher dollar amounts and to gather as much money as possible. In many cases, unfortunately, they are not concerned about how they collect.

There are laws in place to protect you. In some cases collection agencies do follow the laws. However, in many cases, they are breaking the laws. Often, collection agencies will get reported to the FTC or BBB, and can get large fines if they are breaking the law. There are many cases where the agency will close down, claim bankruptcy and re-open under another collection agency name to avoid fees and fines. In a case such as that, they would not be going after the same debt since it may be the reason they closed down to begin with. Know that you do have options, you are protected, and you must know your rights. The goal is to have you stay out of collections or to make sure the collection agencies are complying with the laws. Knowing your rights is important so they can't intimidate you into wrongful actions or payments.

Collection agencies may also offer incentives to their employees, such as, bonuses for collecting the most amount of debt. That again, creates a very high incentive. Unfortunately, you have predatory people who are working for these agencies. At times, they are not following guidelines and can be extremely unethical in their practices and breaking the law.

I have heard this over and over again from my clients who will hold out on paying a bill because they feel the bill is unfair, they don't agree with the charge, or in some cases it's a couple dollars more than what they thought they owed. It all depends on how far you want to take it and get involved with the fight to make sure you're getting the right service or bill. Say for example, someone will have a situation where there is a forty-dollar charge that they don't want to pay. There is a lot of going back and forth and arguing over the amount, and there is the possibility of the person's credit score being adversely affected. And this can be over something as simple as a $40 telephone charge. If you were in the market to buy a house you would not want a negative mark on your credit score over a $40 dispute. In a situation like that you need to weigh your options. If you feel it's right to go against them, then by all means, you should pursue it. Many times you can win, and in this book I will show you different ways to do just that. However, if you are making any major purchase, like a home or a car where your credit score is going to be looked at, this may not be worth it. Paying the small amount of $40 to avoid paying a much higher dollar amount in the long run would make more sense. Because, if you are looking to get a loan qualified, you will have that collection on your credit score when the loan is being evaluated. Your interest rate could cost you much more than the $40 over the time of your loan. It could even cost you thousands more, so it may not be worth the fight over $40, and the principle of the matter. You have to make the best decision for yourself and determine what will save you the most money in the long run. It might be best to give in on your fight for what is right in some cases. The collection agencies are banking on your desperation or lack of knowledge to make more money on you. That is why it is so important to keep a close watch over your credit score and history so these predators are not able to take advantage of innocent people.

I would like you to be armed with the knowledge necessary when you're dealing with collections. By paying your bills on time you can avoid this all together. Also, make sure that you keep up with your credit report, your credit history, and keep organized, so that you can avoid finding yourself in a bad situation. I am not saying there won't be errors, because remember, four out of five of you have errors on your credit report. That does not mean you have to give into them, it just means to watch it carefully, fixing errors as they arise. This way you have a better chance of avoiding the stress at the time of a big purchase and qualifying for a loan.

I know that collections sometimes are unavoidable. There are situations in life that are unavoidable, such as, divorce, a spouse's death, an illness, unforeseen job loss, etc. There are many things that can happen in life that can be detrimental to your financial history. In many of these cases collection is unavoidable. In those cases, what you need to do is know your rights. I will give you some guidelines and some rules that the collection agencies have to follow, and just knowing your rights will help you. I know it can be a very stressful time when you're going through any one of the above situations. Let's take a look at what your options are and what you can do. The first one is, know the law, which I will explain for you in simple terms. The Fair Debt Collections Practices Act (FDCPA) is there for you and your rights are completely outlined. If you have been contacted by a collection agency you have 30 days to dispute that debt, or you can also ask for a request for the lender or creditor to validate the debt.

Taming the beast is really not as difficult as it may seem. There are a multitude of illegal predatory debt collectors out there. You do have rights and there are laws in place to protect you.

I advise you to keep very accurate records of all correspondence with creditors and debt collectors, including, contact letters, and phone calls. Whenever you send letters of dispute or any types of correspondence letters, send them by official mail with a return receipt requested. Make sure that you always keep a copy for your own records. If need be, if you are trying to prove a case at a later date this will aid in your proof of verification.

It is within your rights to report any violations of the law to your State Attorney General, the Federal Trade Commission, and the Better Business Bureau.

The Federal Reserve has reported that with our economy the way it is, Americans are using their credit cards more than ever before. Debt collectors are now reaching new lows to make you pay outstanding debts, while consumer debt is reaching new heights. I watched an investigation the other day with unethical tactics caught on tape. I was shocked to hear how these collectors were treating people and breaking the law. If you are experiencing bad behavior from any credit collectors, please know that the law does protect you.

I witnessed a credit collector calling somebody using foul language saying, "I guarantee you everyone you know is going to hear this in your @#$@# neighborhood, you're a piece of @#$#@ and you don't pay your bills." Now, imagine phone calls like this just over unpaid bills. No wonder why some people complain about debt collectors and are reporting abuse. Clients have even stated that people were getting fired from their jobs from these dirty debt collectors illegal tactics. Consumers have even reported getting threatened that they will go to jail, which is not true. The collectors terrorize the consumers making them feel like a criminal who will be locked up behind bars. Lawyers are saying that many debt collectors are out of control and terrorizing people. As a result, the consumers have been filing numerous complaints for damages and injunctive relief. Collectors have called and said things like "I'm going to call you until you die and I get my money." Or other horrible things, such as, "You are a @$@@$%$ piece of @#$# and you will always be, because you do not pay your bills."

Debt collector calls like this are at the top of the complaint list at the Federal Trade Commission. **However, the Federal Trade**

Commission says that the federal law protects the consumer, setting down clear rules that debt collectors must obey.

No deception – debt collectors cannot imply or state that they are someone they are not. One client of mine reported a debt collector that said he was a detective. If they are implying or stating that they are a police officer that is a clear violation of the law. I have a client that says they got a call stating, "If I don't hear from you I will have the Sheriff's department at your doorstep." This could be a violation and should be reported to the FTC.

I have a client who was in a dispute over a TV purchase – she got a call from a so-called "detective" who implied that she might be charged with a crime. He stated on the phone that the crime was in regards to the consumer charges and claimed this was a felony. She thought he was the police. She was frightened, but when she realized the supposed detective was really a debt collector, she told him to back off. He threatened to call her employer, and she was firm about telling him not to. He then said he was going to come to her place of employment, and she informed him that this was not acceptable. He continued to threaten her. The FTC says that there is a good chance that this might be a violation.

No Job Harassment
If the consumer says not to call them at work, then the debt collector must stop calling them at work. One of my clients worked two jobs to afford the new TV she bought on credit. But when she was late on just one payment, they were calling her five times a day. They even called her boss and complained to her bosses, and she was fired from both jobs. They are not allowed to do things that they know will cost you your job!

No Profanity
Debt collectors can also not use profanity or other harassing language with the consumer. If they do so, the debt collector can be sued for harassment. Debt collectors must treat consumers with truth, fairness, dignity and respect. If you want to get through this difficult time without getting sick to your stomach and not being able to sleep at night, you need to know your rights. If the two examples I used above had known their rights they would have been able to stop debt collectors in their tracks.

Reputable collection agencies will work with you if you contact them to set up payments. If you are being harassed, the FTC encourages you to file a complaint, and I will show you exactly how to do this.

Fair Debt Collection Practices Act (FDCPA)

The Fair Debt Collection Practices Act was set in place to protect you from the predatory misuse of debt collectors.

One of your rights that you should know about is in accordance with the Fair Debt Collection Practices Act, Section 809(b): Validating Debts:

(b) If the consumer notifies the debt collector in writing within the thirty-day period described in subsection (a) that the debt, or any portion thereof, is disputed, or that the consumer requests the name and address of the original creditor, the debt collector shall cease collection of the debt, or any disputed portion thereof, until the debt collector obtains verification of the debt or any copy of a judgment, or the name and address of the original creditor, and a copy of such verification or judgment, or name and address of the original creditor, is mailed to the consumer by the debt collector.

If you dispute a debt, until the debt collector or creditor validates the information, the information concerning that particular debt is considered inaccurate. If a creditor or debt collector reports information that they know is invalid or inaccurate it violates the Fair Credit Reporting Act § 1681s-2. Even if the creditor or debt collector chooses to pursue a judgment without verifying or validating the debt, you can request to the judge that the case be dismissed due to the failure of compliance with the FDCPA.

It is your right to request the following information from a debt collector:

- The amount of the debt
- The name of the creditor to whom the debt is owed - not just the name of the credit collector but the actual creditor
- If there is any judgment it is your right to have them provide verification or copy of any judgment (if applicable)
- It's also your right to request proof that they are licensed to collect debts in your state

Also, it is within your rights to dispute the debt in writing within 30 days of the notice. You have the right to obtain verification of the debt or of the judgment and they have to mail it to you at the collector's expense. No fees or interest can be legally added, except if allowed by state law or the original contract.

Any attempt to collect the debt without validating it violates the FDCPA.

Your letter is considered an official notification and if they don't respond to your letter of dispute, it is within your rights to let them know you're considering the matter closed. That you do not intend to correspond with them any further unless they comply with your request of proof, or that they comply with the FDCPA and the FCRA (FAIR CREDIT REPORTING ACT).

Please note, if they do not provide you with your request of proof, any attempt to collect the debt without validation will put them in violation of the FDCPA, and you can report all violations.

Anything that is not validated is an alleged debt at that point. You have the right to protect yourself from anyone harassing or being predatory towards you. There is a lot you can do, so I want you to make sure you know your rights. One of the things you need to make sure of is to periodically check for updates, as the laws continuously change. My website often has updates available to you, so keep checking in. One resource that I suggest you check out is the Fair Debt Collection Practices Act at www.ftc.gov.

The following information is about your rights as a consumer, and is quoted from the Federal Trade Commission Website:

CREDIT AND YOUR CONSUMER RIGHTS

A good credit rating is very important. Businesses inspect your credit history when they evaluate your applications for credit, insurance, employment, and even leases. They can use it when they choose to give or deny you credit or insurance, provided that you receive fair and equal treatment. Sometimes, things happen that can cause credit problems: a temporary loss of income, an illness, or even a computer error. Solving credit problems may take time and patience, but it doesn't have to be an ordeal.

The Federal Trade Commission (FTC) enforces the credit laws that protect your right to get, use, and maintain credit. These laws do not guarantee that everyone will receive credit. Instead, the credit laws protect your rights by requiring businesses to give all consumers a fair and equal opportunity to get credit and to resolve disputes over credit errors. This brochure explains your rights under these laws and offers practical tips to help you solve credit problems.

YOUR CREDIT REPORT

Your credit report contains information about where you live, how you pay your bills, and whether you've been sued, arrested, or filed for bankruptcy. Consumer reporting companies sell the information in your report to businesses that use it to evaluate your applications for credit, insurance, employment, or renting a home.

The Federal Fair Credit Reporting Act (FCRA) promotes the accuracy and privacy of information in the files of the nation's consumer reporting companies. Under the Fair Credit Reporting Act:

1. *You have the right to receive a copy of your credit report. The copy of your report must contain all the information in your file at the time of your request.*

2. *Each of the nationwide consumer reporting companies – Equifax, Experian, and TransUnion – is required to provide, at your request, a free copy of your credit report, once every 12 months. For details, see Your Access to Free Credit Reports at ftc.gov/credit.*

3. *Under federal law, you're also entitled to a free report if a company takes adverse action against you, like denying your application for credit, insurance, or employment, and you ask for your report within 60 days of receiving notice of the action. The notice will give you the name, address, and phone number of the consumer reporting company. You're also entitled to one free report a year if you're unemployed and plan to look for a job within 60 days; if you're on welfare; or if your report is inaccurate because of fraud, including identity theft.*

4. *Otherwise, a consumer reporting company may charge $9.50 or more for another copy of your report within a 12-month period.*

5. *You have the right to know who asked for your report within the past year – two years for employment related requests.*

6. *If a company denies your application, you have the right to the name and address of the consumer reporting company they contacted, provided the denial was based on information given by the consumer reporting company.*

7. *If you question the accuracy or completeness of information in your report, you have the right to file a dispute with the consumer reporting company and the information provider (that is, the person, company, or organization that provided information about you to the consumer reporting company). Both the consumer reporting company and the information provider are obligated to investigate your claim, and responsible for correcting inaccurate or incomplete information in your report. For details, see How to Dispute Credit Report Errors at ftc.gov/credit.*

8. *You have a right to add a summary explanation to your credit report if your dispute is not resolved to your satisfaction. You also can ask the consumer reporting company to provide your statement to anyone who received a copy of your report in the recent past. You can expect to pay a fee for this service.*

YOUR CREDIT APPLICATION

When creditors evaluate a credit application, they cannot engage in discriminatory practices.

*The **Equal Credit Opportunity Act (ECOA)** prohibits credit discrimination on the basis of sex, race, marital status, religion, national origin, age, or receipt of public assistance. Creditors may ask for this information (except religion) in certain situations, but they may not use it to discriminate against you when deciding whether to grant you credit.*

The ECOA protects consumers who deal with companies that regularly extend credit, including banks, small loan and finance companies, retail and department stores, credit card companies, and credit unions. Everyone who participates in the decision to grant credit, including real estate brokers who arrange financing, must follow this law. This law also protects businesses applying for credit. Under the Equal Credit Opportunity Act:

1. *You cannot be denied credit based on your race, sex, marital status, religion, age, national origin, or receipt of public assistance.*

2. *You have the right to have reliable public assistance considered in the same manner as other income.*

3. *If you are denied credit, you have a legal right to know why. For details, see Equal Credit Opportunity at ftc.gov/credit.*

YOUR CREDIT BILLING AND ELECTRONIC FUND TRANSFER STATEMENTS

*It is important to check credit billing and electronic fund transfer account statements regularly because these documents may contain mistakes that could damage your credit status or reflect improper charges or transfers. If you find an error or discrepancy, notify the company and dispute the error immediately. **The Fair Credit Billing Act (FCBA)** and **Electronic Fund Transfer Act (EFTA)** establish procedures for resolving mistakes on credit billing and electronic fund transfer account statements, including:*

1. *Charges or electronic fund transfers that you – or anyone you have authorized to use your account – have not made*

2. *Charges or electronic fund transfers that are incorrectly identified or show the wrong date or amount*

3. *Math errors*

4. *Failure to post payments, credits, or electronic fund transfers properly*

5. *Failure to send bills to your current address – provided the creditor receives your change of address, in writing, at least 20 days before the billing period ends*

6. *Charges or electronic fund transfers for which you ask for an explanation or written proof of purchase along with a claimed error or request for clarification.*

The FCBA generally applies only to "open end" credit accounts – credit cards and revolving charge accounts, like department store accounts. It does not apply to loans or credit sales that are paid according to a fixed schedule until the entire amount is paid back, like an automobile loan. The EFTA applies to electronic fund transfers, like those involving automatic teller machines (ATMs), point-of-sale debit transactions, and other electronic banking transactions.

For details, see Fair Credit Billing and A Consumer's Guide to E-Payments at ftc.gov/credit.

YOUR DEBTS AND DEBT COLLECTORS

You are responsible for your debts. If you fall behind in paying your creditors, or if an error is made on your account, you may be contacted by a debt collector. A debt collector is any person, other than the creditor, who regularly collects debts owed to others, including lawyers who collect debts on a regular basis. You have the right to be treated fairly by debt collectors.

The Fair Debt Collection Practices Act (FDCPA) *applies to personal, family, and household debts. This includes money you owe for the purchase of a car, for medical care, or for charge accounts. The FDCPA prohibits debt collectors from engaging in unfair, deceptive, or abusive practices while collecting these debts. Under the Fair Debt Collection Practices Act:*

1. *Debt collectors may contact you only between 8 a.m. and 9 p.m.*

2. *Debt collectors may not contact you at work if they know your employer disapproves*

3. *Debt collectors may not harass, oppress, or abuse you*

4. *Debt collectors may not lie when collecting debts, such as falsely implying that you have committed a crime*

5. *Debt collectors must identify themselves to you on the phone*

6. *Debt collectors must stop contacting you if you ask them to do so in writing*

For details, see Fair Debt Collection at: ftc.gov/credit.

SOLVING YOUR CREDIT PROBLEMS

If you are having problems paying your bills, contact your creditors immediately. Try to work out a modified payment plan with them that reduces your payments to a more manageable level. Don't wait until your account has been turned over to a debt collector.

Here are some additional tips for solving credit problems:

1. *If you want to dispute a credit report, bill or credit denial, write to the appropriate company and send your letter "return receipt requested"*

2. *When you dispute a billing error, include your name, account number, the dollar amount in question, and the reason you believe the bill is wrong*

3. *If in doubt, request written verification of a debt*

4. *Keep all your original documents, especially receipts, sales slips, and billing statements. You will need them if you dispute a credit bill or report. Send copies only. It may take more than one letter to correct a problem.*

5. *Be skeptical of businesses that offer instant solutions to credit problems.*

6. *Be persistent. Resolving credit problems can take time and patience*

7. *Only in rare situations can a credit repair company charge you for things you cannot do for yourself for little or no cost*

STATUTE OF LIMITATIONS

The statute of limitations is the next thing that I want to cover. The statute of limitations, or the actual length of time they can sue for the contract can be confusing, due to different time frames. The creditors are able to sue you for the contract debt over a span of time that may be longer than what the requirement is to legally report a debt to the credit reporting bureaus. People get confused on the statute of limitations of a debt and the credit-reporting bureau listing duration of a debt. The difference with the credit reporting duration is it harms your credit score and the statute of limitations is how long they can legally collect a debt from you. Collectors are suing more frequently because businesses are hurting, due to people having financial difficulties. Unpaid debts are going into collections and companies are going into courts, trying to sue for whatever money they can collect. If you have a judgment against you or a lawsuit, that will have an adverse affect on you and your credit score. What I advise you to do is even if you're close to approaching the statute of limitations on a debt, and they are coming after you, if you are able to pay or settle it, do so. If they come to you after the statute of limitations has expired, then they have no legal recourse. Laws are always updating and changing, so I suggest checking the Internet for the latest updates on the statute of limitations.

The following is an explanation for the different types of debt:

Oral Contract: You agree to pay money loaned to you by someone, but this contract or agreement is verbal (i.e., no written contract, "handshake agreement"). Remember, a verbal contract is legal, but tougher to prove in court. Written Contract: You agree to pay on a loan under the terms written in a document, which you and your debtor have signed.

Promissory Note: You agree to pay on a loan via a written contract, just like the written contract. The big difference between a promissory note and a regular written contract is that the scheduled payments and interest on the loan are also spelled out in the promissory note. A mortgage is an example of a promissory note.

Open-Ended Accounts: These are revolving lines of credit with varying balances. The best example is a credit card account. Please note: a credit card is ALWAYS an open account.

STATUTE OF LIMITATIONS

State	Oral (Years)	Written (Years)	Promissory (Years)	Open-Ended Accounts (Years)
AL	6	6	6	3
AR	5	5	5	3
AK	6	6	3	3
AZ	3	6	6	3
CA	2	4	4	4
CO	6	6	6	3
CT	3	6	6	3
DE	3	3	3	4
DC	3	3	3	3
FL	4	5	5	4
GA	4	6	6	6
HI	6	6	6	6
IA	5	10	5	5
ID	4	5	5	4
IL	5	10	10	5
IN	6	10	10	6
KS	3	6	5	3
KY	5	15	15	5
LA	10	10	10	3
ME	6	6	6	6
MD	3	3	6	3
MA	6	6	6	6
MI	6	6	6	6
MN	6	6	6	6
MS	3	3	3	3
MO	5	10	10	5
MT	3	8	8	5
NC	3	3	5	3
ND	6	6	6	6
NE	4	5	5	4
NH	3	3	6	3
NJ	6	6	6	3
NM	4	6	6	4
NV	4	6	3	4
NY	6	6	6	6
OH	6	15	15	6
OK	3	5	5	3

STATUTE OF LIMITATIONS

State	Oral (Years)	Written (Years)	Promissory (Years)	Open-Ended Accounts (Years)
OR	6	6	6	6
PA	4	4	4	4
RI	10	5	6	4
SC	3	3	3	3
SD	6	6	6	6
TN	6	6	6	3
TX	4	4	4	4
UT	4	6	6	4
VA	3	5	6	3
VT	6	6	5	3
WA	3	6	6	3
WI	6	6	10	6
WV	8	10	10	8

Imagine if you have high debts that are very old, such as, 20k, 30k, 40k, 50k and even $100,000; by checking the most current listing of the statute of limitations, and also consider consulting with an attorney, this debt could possibly be eliminated all together. You no longer owe it. It is now reduced down to zero.

Do not ignore the collections! I have heard so many stories with different financial advice saying that if you don't have the money to pay for collections, to ignore them and not talk to them. It's always an alleged debt until it's proven to be your debt. However, I would never recommend to you to ignore any collections or anything that has to do with your finances. It can dramatically affect your FICO score. This could harm your financial future and I would never advise that. What I do advise to you is to communicate. Communication is so important. By making phone calls, you could have so much resolved. It is vital and so very important for you to communicate with the collection agencies or the creditors. You just have to know when to communicate and when not to communicate. If you contact a collection agency about a collection that happens to be past the statute of limitations or at the edge of the statute of limitations, and they have not contacted you, **you could reinstate the case** when they were about to drop it. This is one case when you may want to think twice about contacting collections unless they are contacting you, if that debt is outstanding. Also, keep in mind that if you do not address collections it could cost you so much more money than it would cost you in the beginning. If a creditor or collector ends up suing you, you could owe them over thousands of dollars for something that was originally $70. They can possibly even garnish your wages. It is not worth ignoring the debt, and it does not make it go away when you ignore the collection. It can be much more stressful, more time consuming, and much more costly in the long run, if you choose to ignore a collection.

Another option for you is when you're looking at paying a collection you could possibly try to negotiate a settlement. This is very rare because once it goes into collection there is probably a third party involved at that point, unless the creditor or lender has an in-house collection department. The collections agencies are the ones contacting you, so if they are an outside company, remember, mostly likely they are making pennies on the dollar. What they want is to get as much money as possible. They are thinking that you didn't pay the debt to begin with so why should they believe you're going to make any payments in the long run? They just want to get their money and to get it off their books. It doesn't hurt to try and negotiate, so if it's in collections ask them if you can make payments. I have had many clients have success in making payments. It doesn't matter if it's a doctor's office or a lender, they may not have hard set rules and they can possibly go around them. And you can talk to one person and then to another person, and you may get a whole new set of circumstances. So, don't give up. Keep trying. The key is to never ever be rude to these people. Do not use any of the tactics that they are possibly using with you. However, be firm, what you want to do is to be as civil and kind as possible, yet assertive, and let them know you want to do your best to try and make payments. If you can't pay it all, simply try to ask them to settle for possibly 20% of the debt. What you want to do is get a **letter of deletion**, saying that it's paid in full. The reason why it is so important to get the letter is because it will remove the collection from your credit report, and that will have a direct affect on your FICO or credit score.

Please realize that there are predatory collection agencies. Even collections within a company, a lending institution or a creditor that you may think is very reputable, can reduce themselves to unfair tactics. There are also collections agencies that are scamming and doing shady things where they will offer you a payment plan for removal. Always be sure you get this in writing. Do not believe that they are going to remove this from your credit report unless it is in writing. It has to be a letter of deletion. There are very strict rules in place by the credit bureaus to remove past due or collection notices. What you have to do is make sure that you get this in writing. It also has to be wrongful, an error or meet with the statute of limitations. That is the general rule. They must state this in the letter to rectify it. You do need a letter from them first, and before you pay it in full. Otherwise, there is the possibility that it will not be removed, and in some cases your credit score is going to be harmed. Seek professional advice to decide whether or not it is worth it to pay the collection when it's not going to be removed from your credit report, anyway. There are predatory services out there that will offer you a service or offer you an option to pay for the removal, and in some cases that is not anything they plan on doing, so buyers beware.

Some parting advice I would like to leave you with is, anytime you're dealing with someone over the phone or even in person, the best thing to do is take names. Put everything in writing, including the date and time. Receipts would be optimal if you can obtain them from the collection agencies. Be sure that they give you something in writing or a receipt so that you can update the account as paid in your credit reports. Sometimes this can take up to 30 days to update with the credit bureaus. If for some reason it doesn't show up, know that you do have the FTC (Federal Trade Commission) and the BBB (Better Business Bureau) to be able to report these agencies. Also, in summary, please know that it's going to get tougher than ever. So, your first line of action is to try and stay out of collections to begin with so that you don't have any problems. If it's completely unavoidable you will at least have some ammunition to fight back and protect your rights.

For sample letters to send to: creditors, collection agencies and credit bureaus visit my website.

Solution Summary

5: TAMING THE BEAST: COLLECTION AGENCIES

- Avoid collections if possible and pay all your bills on time.
- Do not ignore collections.
- Know the law; it can protect you from the unfair practices of collection agencies.
- The Federal Trade Commission sets clear rules that debt collectors must obey.
- Report any violations to your State Attorney General, the Federal Trade Commission and the Better Business Bureau.
- Equifax, Transunion and Experian are required to provide a free copy of your credit report once every 12 months.
- Watch your credit reports closely and fix errors as they arise - 4 out of 5 people have errors on their credit reports.
- You have the right to dispute information on your credit report.
- Keep accurate, detailed documentation of all communication with creditors and debt collectors.
- Keep original documents, receipts, sales slips and billing statements. When disputing, send copies only.
- Send correspondence and disputes via certified official mail with a return receipt requested. Be sure you keep a copy for your records.
- Work out a modified payment plan that reduces your payments.
- Try and negotiate a settlement.
- The Statute of Limitations sets a time limit on how long a debt can be legally pursued.
- You can reinstate the Statute of Limitations if you make contact on an old debt.
- Negotiate a letter of deletion with any settlement to have the negative item removed from your credit report.
- Don't give up! Be polite and tactful.

Alter Ego

YOUR CREDIT IDENTITY

Establishing your credit could be one of the most important things you will do in your life. Your credit history follows you for life, and this is why I have named this chapter, "Alter Ego." There is no getting away from your credit identity. The good news is your credit identity can help you build wealth and is a great asset to you. You need to understand how it works and what it means. If you have harmed your credit, there are actions steps you can take to rectify the situation. To do this can take time, money, and be painful. It is best you understand how your credit history works and to keep it in good standing. If you don't have credit history, it can seem difficult to get started. If you don't already have established credit, creditors aren't as likely to want to give you credit. Therefore, how do you establish your credit? If no one seems willing to give you credit, this can be frustrating. How do you get started?

Successful people understand that the journey to financial freedom starts with a single step. They add a few more steps and soon those steps turn into miles. Most things in life follow a manner of steps, and I have designed this book in that same way. Learn each step or task as it is presented. Soon you will be along your path to financial security, full of confidence and without fear.

First, you need to take responsibility for where you are and where you are going. In any endeavor, responsibility is the fundamental ingredient to achievement and success. Unless you take responsibility for realizing your own goals and desires, you will not get the necessary results. Ultimately, this will lead to frustration and disappointment. Accepting responsibility for one's self is the first step on the pathway to happiness and peace of mind. An important facet for you to understand is your financial identity and security. By taking responsibility for your financial security, you will be in control of your destiny. If you do this you will have less chance of falling victim of unwanted or unwarranted debt.

Through my research and study of finance, I have discovered that a key factor to financial security is having your own credit identity and understanding how it works. This important piece of information could make a substantial difference in your financial life, and can lead to you building wealth. Unfortunately, it is not one of the life essentials that most people are taught in school. Having a good credit history, FICO, or credit identity, is a very important component. It is necessary to move you more quickly, and with less difficulty, towards a life of financial security and wealth. Everyone who has credit has a credit history. It is important to know how your score is factored in by the credit agencies and how critically it affects all parts of your financial and personal life. You may want to refer to the complimentary, "Guide To Great Credit in a Snap," which will help you better understand your FICO score. The guide also has some helpful hints about building and maintaining your score. In basic terms, your FICO score is what lenders use to determine whether or not they are willing to lend you money. If a lender is considering loaning you money they want to know if you are a credit risk. Bill Fair and Earl Isaac founded Fair Isaac Corporation in 1956, which created the FICO score. The score measures credit risk and is the most widely used credit score system worldwide. Here are a few tips to help you get started in learning to maintain your credit identity.

Start by opening a bank account. This is important for establishing credit and then you will have a payment history. You don't need to have established credit to open a checking account. If you have your own personal checking account and you are starting a small business, you can open a business checking account to establish credit.

To help establish credit, you will want to have credit cards. When using this plastic money, remember to practice discipline using them and NOT to over-extend yourself. When you get your first credit cards, use them sparingly. Make sure you can manage the card payment with your monthly budget. Try to get your first credit cards at a bank, department stores and credit companies. Only if these fail should you consider a secured credit card. A secured credit card means that a bank or credit card company is willing to give you a credit card where there is no risk to carry a balance. Let's say, you have $500 in your bank account and they start you off with a $500 limit on the secured card. This is no risk to them. If you default on the payment they would be able to take the money from your account to secure the debt. If this is your only option, it will get you started. Please always make your payments on time, keep a good track record, and never go over your limit. The goal is that in a short amount of time you will have established some good credit. Then you can get an unsecured card from a bank, credit card companies or a department store, where you don't need a deposit to secure the amount of credit available to you.

When lenders are looking to loan you money they do not value a secured card as highly as an unsecured card. It doesn't rank as high on your credit history. However, it is still letting you have leeway towards building your credit. Ask the company that you have the secured card with about their policy for issuing an unsecured card. These companies will sometimes offer an unsecured card after you have established a payment history. This will be anywhere from six months to a year of paying on time and not going over your limit. Again, a secured credit card should be your last choice in trying to establish credit.

Your history of residence is another factor that lenders will look at to determine whether they will lend you money or credit. They want to see how often you move, how long you stay in one place and whether you rent or own. They are looking for a stable resident history. Owning real estate ranks higher than renting. Even if you're on a home loan as a co-signer, this will still help you.

A good rule in establishing credit is to put utilities in your name. If you have a roommate situation or a spouse, be sure to put the utilities in your name, as often as possible. For example, Mary and Tom, who are married, put all the utilities in Tom's name. Unfortunately, six years later, faced with divorce, Mary was trying to establish credit. She didn't have any credit established in her own name and her name wasn't on any of the utility bills. Cell phone, telephone, cable, water, gas and electric (DWP), were all in her husband's name. If you are married it is a good idea to divide the utilities so you both have your names on them.

Something that may surprise you is that your lenders may also look at your history of employment. They're looking to see your track record for the stability of holding a steady job, and if there is any lengthy period of unemployment.

I am going to give you a rule of thumb that holds true for most anything in life; relationships make everything. I suggest you start or continue building relationships. The first place you can start is with your bank. When you set-up your bank accounts, checking accounts, etc., get to know the people in your bank. Get to know the tellers, the loan specialists, or anyone you come in contact with. The more you get to know them the more they will feel they have a personal relationship with you. When they see your bank accounts are in good standing, you making payments on time, never bouncing checks, and making regular deposits, they will feel comfortable, and trust loaning you money or helping you establish credit. Having bank accounts with good standing records proves that you are a good money manager, and this is what good lenders are looking for. Many banks will offer credit cards, mortgages and auto loans. When you have a good relationship with a bank, this is your first place to start.

Creating a good credit history may take some time, however, it's well worth all the efforts. It may just be a matter of a month or two or a year or two and then you can move into maintaining good credit. The factors to establishing good credit are making payments on time, not over-extending your debt to credit ratio and maintaining relationships with your creditors.

For those of you who are just getting out of school, you may have thought that having good SAT scores were stressful. Your step into adulthood will be no easier a task. In the world of adults, your credit history is what matters. So, when you are thinking about instant gratification purchases that will give you that short-term benefit, you might want to think twice. Too often, we hear horror stories about college students getting way over their heads in debt, thousands to hundred of thousands of dollars, which sometimes leads to depression and suicide. This is sad and unnecessary, and usually originates from a lack of financial knowledge. With the guidance of this book and other resources available, this type of overwhelming debt can be avoided or rectified. There is always help and a way out of any situation, no matter how bad it may seem at the time. If you are in this kind of trouble, get the necessary help onto the right path to building a better financial life.

If you are just now starting off on your financial path, at some point you are going to want to buy a car, house, or maybe a recreation vehicle. To qualify for these big-ticket items lenders are going to be looking at your numbers – meaning, your credit history, FICO or credit identity. When you're looking for a job or going back to school, it is possible your credit history will play a role in whether you are hired or get into school. Don't get caught off guard. Be ready with all of the knowledge you can obtain to keep yourself at the top of the game.

For example, my client Vicky is a 20-year-old college student, who did not have any credit in her name. She came to me to help her with establishing her credit history, and was looking to start by applying for a credit card. She wanted to purchase an item that would require her to pay the item off in installments, so she could build good credit. This was a good way to start. I advised her to research the fees on all credit cards that she was considering, including cards with no fees. Take the time to go through everything, especially the fine print. Find out about hidden fees associated with each card and make sure there aren't any hidden costs that will appear on a later statement. When you are shopping for your first credit card, take your time and be sure to choose one that is offering the best deal available. I explained to Vicky, when you apply for your first credit card you may experience a Catch-22. In order to get a credit card, you need to have good credit. In order to establish good credit, you need a credit card. Lenders won't be able to assess your FICO score from the three credit reporting bureaus because you don't have any established credit yet. This means they will need to review other information to decide your credit worthiness. This includes your bank accounts, employment history, residence history, utilities in your name, and so on. In Vicky's case, she was able to get a credit card as an authorized user on one of her parent's credit cards. This helped her establish a history with that credit card company. I advised her to contact that same credit card company to apply for a new account with a credit card in her own name. Based on the past history with her parents, they approved her.

A suggestion for college students is to use discipline when establishing your credit. You're setting the tone for your financial history. Mistakes can be rectified, however, they can be painful along the way. It's best not to put yourself in that position, in the first place. As with anyone, you want to make sure that you pay all your bills on time. Be sure you keep a close eye on all of your statements so you can correct any mistakes, as soon as possible. Use a discerning eye when getting credit cards, to ensure you get the best rates available. If you have already run up credit card balances, pay as much as you can, as quickly as you can, to reduce the balances. Often times, many people close credit cards, thinking, "I got into trouble and I don't want to use this anymore." You don't want to do that. You want to establish a credit history, and length of history is good. I made the mistake years ago of closing down an account I had since I was 18. I had a long credit history with that card and I really took a hit on my FICO for that mistake. It would have better served me to leave the card at home, not use it, and to just charge a lunch or gas on it once every 6 months. This would have kept the card active on my credit report instead of closing it all together. As a note, if you do not use a credit card for a length of time it can go inactive and that can sometimes harm your credit history. If you do not use a particular card, leave it at home, or if you feel the need, cut it up, just don't close it. You can still charge something very small that you can pay off in full on your next statement, keeping your card active. Even if you cut up your card if you have the card number, expiration date, VIN or security number, you can still use it to charge over the phone. If this is the route you choose to take, keep that information in a safe secured place. The VIN or security number is usually a three-digit number found on the back of your card. Look on the signature strip on a Master Card or Visa. For American Express, look above your account number on the front of the card and you'll find a four-digit number above that.

The first rule of thumb for anyone establishing credit is to try and pay off your debt sooner than later. If you are in a pinch, transferring money to a card with a lower rate can be a good thing, just be sure you read the fine print. If at all possible, I would prefer you to work on better spending habits, and paying as much of your balance off as possible.

I've heard stories of people running into financial ruin. Unfortunately, this is not an uncommon occurrence. In most of the cases, the reason for their financial decline was from lack of knowledge. It wasn't from lack of intelligence but more that they had not been taught the importance of maintaining their financial information. Luckily for you, with your knowledge of the importance of a good credit history and your credit identity, you are well on your way to keeping your financial status in tact.

HANDLING DIVORCE

I will illustrate for you an example of how finances can affect your life. Couples that have been married for 17 years, or even longer, can find themselves suddenly faced with divorce. Devastated from emotional stress, neglecting their daily affairs, sometimes a partner becomes so distracted by the divorce they end up struggling financially. When they finally take a look at their finances they are shocked at how much debt they are in. How did this happen? When they first married they were so in love, neither thinking they would ever part. They both made the flawed decision to let one spouse handle all the finances for their family. One partner may never ask questions about the finances, and they never took the time to learn. They never learned what to do to protect or build their credit identity, or their own finances. In any marriage, I highly advise each partner to keep his or her own credit identity.

Many of my clients, at all ages, are faced with being a single mom or a single dad. One, in particular is Jennifer, age 42. She took on the responsibility of homemaker and raising the kids as her full-time job of the household. Her husband's chosen responsibility was to make sure he kept their lives financially secure. Jennifer never had a full-time career or a financial credit identity of her own. She also had no financial knowledge of how the home finances were handled. However, more than 10 years ago, Jennifer had been a critical part of helping her husband start his business. She worked 12 to 14 hour days during the first months of the business to help him become successful. As soon as the business was off the ground she stopped working in the business and started their family. Her husband felt she could best help the business by staying home and raising their family. She did her job very well, but without any formal compensation or recognition. They collectively agreed on their responsibilities and were both comfortable with how they had chosen to orchestrate their relationship.

Life was good, so Jennifer never asked her husband how he kept the books or where the money went. She was not involved in the planning of the finances, or what their assets were compared to their liabilities. They had both agreed that this was his job. He provided well for the family and she accepted that he was in charge.

Now, years later, faced with divorce, Jennifer's attorney discovered that her husband had hidden money within the company, and in other financial investments. As she looked through the books she found he had made it difficult for her to prove this, and often times he was paid in cash, leaving no records. She was then faced with the devastating news that everything was in his name, and there was no record that she had ever been a vital part of bringing success to the company. She had nothing on paper to show for her hard work and all those years of doing her "job." When I listen to the sounds of fear and disbelief in her voice, it can be devastating. It is heart wrenching to hear from the many who have a similar story to tell. What is most important for you to understand is this was an unnecessary occurrence. It was not a matter of not trusting your spouse; it was a matter of being financially savvy. It is imperative to accept the responsibility of learning about the financial aspects of the family business or the family personal finances. Couples can do this together and make unanimous decisions. Even if the business is too large or difficult to understand, I suggest at least having your own credit identity. It is so important for each partner to establish his or her separate credit identities. In this case, Jennifer must start all over to build her financial future from the bottom up. Fortunately, it is not too late; it just may be painful or uncomfortable for the time being. My goal is to have you avoid this situation altogether. If Jennifer had her own credit identity and her name on investments, she would have been more established to start her new life.

If you are still wondering why it is important to keep your credit history separate from your husband or wife, here's some advice from an attorney. A divorce order does not remove the joint obligation owed to the credit card company. A judge cannot prevent the credit of a spouse from getting damaged if the other spouse does not pay, as ordered by the judge. All the judge can do is sanction the non-complying spouse, but this does not help the innocent spouse who will have their credit hurt as a result. I have heard countless stories where one spouse, in anger, will deliberately charge up a credit card so the other spouse will have to pay it. If the other spouse defaults on payment, it is harming them both. That is why it is extremely important to build separate credit from your spouse or partner. It not only makes a divorce much smoother, should that happen to you, but it also lets you keep your good credit, regardless of what the other person does.

I am not telling you these things to scare you or make you worry about divorce, just be aware of your options. Even if you never go through divorce, there are many reasons why you will want to establish and maintain your own credit identity when you are married. If you and your spouse keep them separate, you can both leverage your position to gain more financial power. If one person's FICO is below good lending standards, you can use the FICO of the other spouse to help you get better loans and better rates. I know a couple that were being faced with foreclosure. Unfortunately, they did not have separate credit identities. If they had separate credit identities and separate FICO scores, they could have possibly qualified for a new loan, and got their house out of foreclosure. Many of my clients will transfer all debt to one spouse and purchase a house with the other spouse's good credit history and FICO score. After the house deal closes, they put both spouse's names on the deed to the house. The loan originally was only in the spouse's name that had the higher FICO to start. When you are married you will be qualified together. One spouse may have a poor work history, low salary, or low FICO, and the other may have a great work history, high salary, and great FICO. If you do not keep your credit identities separate, the lenders will average out the scores and it could lower your overall credit rating. Meanwhile, you could be leveraging the person who has the higher score to get better loans. When you keep them separate, in some cases, it could get you out of trouble.

BEGINNING FROM WHERE YOU ARE

For you, it doesn't matter whether you are 22 or 62, you need to begin where you are and move forward in becoming financially astute. You do this by learning all that you can about money management, credit, credit identity and investments. You don't necessarily have to do it all at once. In the same way you learn other new skills, you gradually change the way you perceive money, savings, and financial success. You do it one step at a time. This book will give you the guidelines you need to become financially savvy and independent.

Your goal is to be financially secure and prepared to make astute financial decisions. As we have talked about, a credit history is used to secure approval for credit, but it is also one of the key ingredients used to approve or disapprove your applications for insurance, employment, and renting. Furthermore, your credit rating is THE factor that determines if you will not get approved at all...or if you will be approved at a high interest rate when you apply to buy a car, real estate, lines of credit, student loans, credit cards, or virtually any type of credit.

When buying property, a low credit rating can possibly cost you more than six figures in added interest over the life of your mortgage. Here is the explanation of how a low FICO works against you.

For example, let's say you have a FICO that is less than 700-720. You are trying to get a mortgage for a $250,000 house on a 30-year-fixed loan. For every 10 point increase in your score you could possibly save an average of more than $100,000 in interest over the life of your loan. As the median house price in the United States in 2007 was at least $213,500, keeping good credit will result in a considerable savings on the purchase of a home.

At first, the system used to determine credit history could seem complex and confusing. If you understand that your credit history is essentially based on five key factors, this will all seem much easier. Your payment history is the first and most important factor when considering your FICO. If your credit identity is kept separate, if you pay your bills on time and your partner does not, you will still keep your score higher. No matter what your marital status, that's always important. If one member of a couple has a higher score, it will help, even if the partner/spouse has a lower score. If both partners have high scores, that's even better.

Thirty five percent of the score is based on how an individual handles his or her debt obligation. This means, pay all of your bills on time and avoid getting a tax lien or judgment entered against you. Either of those will affect your payment history in a highly negative way. If you have a tax lien or a judgment on your credit rating, you will need to consult a credit expert for advice on how to fix this. If you are one of those that are consistently late in your payments, you will want to make a change in your habits. Making your bill payments on time is a critical issue and time well spent. Set aside a specific time you will attend to this each month. Keep your bills in a special place where you won't accidentally forget one. Make every single payment, on time, every month. If you need help to keep organized with timely payments, visit my website, there are tools that can assist you.

Thirty percent is based on amounts owed which has an effect on your debt utilization ratio. Since revolving credit cards make up a significant portion of what ultimately determines your score, it is important to keep this in mind. The credit bureaus determine your Credit Card Utilization Ratio (debt ratio) in the following way: Look at the available credit card limit on each of your cards. Divide how much you owe on each credit card into the card limit amount. That gives you your credit card ratio. Keeping all cards at less than 1/3 of the credit limit is an excellent rule to follow. The closer you are to zero, the better for your score. It just makes sense to keep your card balances as low as possible when it has such a detrimental affect on your score. The most benefit will come from having a high limit and owing as little as possible. At the same time, it is important NOT to close your credit cards. Closing cards can sometimes hurt your length of credit history.

Paying off your credit cards in a systematic and timely manner is great for your credit history. It is important to have as little debt on credit cards as possible. The money you pay in interest could be much better spent elsewhere, such as, investments. If you are in the market to buy real estate or an expensive item, but you can't pay off your credit cards yet, what may help is to spread your debt over as many cards as possible. In some instances, it is in your favor to ask the company to raise your credit limit. However, please note that this could be considered an inquiry that could affect your FICO.

The other three factors that affect your score are these: 15% of your score is derived from your length of credit history - the average length of time you have had credit. The longer the account has been open, the better for the score. That's why it is better to owe nothing on a card, but leave it open. Closing an account detracts from your score. Not using an account also detracts from your score. An inactive account is ignored by credit scoring software, so you don't get the benefit of a positive payment history or the low balance the card may have. Use your cards at least once every six months to avoid having them labeled as "inactive." Just be sure and pay down the amount quickly and regularly.

Often times, what scores of 800 or more have in common are credit cards that are twenty years old or older. Preparing good credit is a slow and time-consuming process where older cards can help. Ten percent of your credit rating comes from the mixture of credit you have on your credit report. While it is not a good idea to close cards, the magic number for a higher score is three revolving credit cards, a mortgage, and a car loan, in good standing. Therefore, don't take out more credit cards than you plan to use. If you have the cards already, leave them alone. In most cases, it is better to owe nothing on a card than to close it. Don't be tempted by all of the credit card offerings that come in the mail. Some can be beneficial and some can cause harm. If you have more questions on that, refer back to the chapter "Plastic Jungle".

And now we are at our last and final factor. Ten percent of your score is obtained from the number of times you apply for credit. When you are applying for a card, companies will contact the credit bureau to inquire about your credit information. The inquiries that damage your credit history are when you personally apply for credit and the store makes an inquiry to the credit bureau about you. Also considered an inquiry that could be detrimental to your score, is asking to raise the credit limit on a card.

You don't need to worry about the unsolicited credit card offers that you get in the mail. They are considered a "credit review" inquiry and do not affect your credit history. Another thing that does not affect your FICO is pulling up your own credit report on line or through the credit bureaus. Federal law allows you to do this once per year from the three major credit bureaus. In this day and time of increased identity theft and credit fraud, it is suggested that you take advantage of this benefit.

If you have a short and limited credit history, you can ask someone to add you as a joint holder or an authorized user to his or her primary account. When you are added, the primary account holder's credit card will appear on your credit report. If the card that gets attached to your credit report has been used for more than 20 years, this could be beneficial to your score, as I explained earlier. It is not helpful to ask someone to put you on their card if he or she has a high balance due on the card. It may not be as beneficial if the card has been used less than five years. Review this before you use this method.

You can also contact all creditors that report late payments and request a good faith adjustment that removes the late payments reported on your account. This sometimes is not easy to do. Be polite and show persistence in speaking to several people at each company. Request their assistance and you may be successful in removing some of the late payments. It never hurts to ask.

You may also need to review your credit report and look in the column, "Past Due." The credit score software automatically penalizes you for keeping accounts with a past due amount. In fact, Past Due can destroy a credit score, so you need to pay the past due amount and then ask to have the credit report corrected by the creditor, or write to the 3 credit bureaus.

If you have charge-offs and liens that are young, that are not more than 24 months old, they can severely damage your score. If you have limited funds, pay the past due balances first. Then pay any credit collection agency that agrees to ask the credit bureaus to remove all references of the charge-offs or liens. If the charge-off or liens are more than 24 months old, there is no credit advantage to paying them off. However, keep in mind the statute of limitations, because the creditor could possibly sue you for the money.

Again, not having the best credit history possible can potentially cost you $500 or more extra each month on your mortgage payment. It could also prevent you from having the best credit card or auto loan rates.

In all aspects of finances, your wealth building is put on hold when you do not have good credit. The extra interest you will have to pay and/or your inability to invest, will over time, cripple your investment impact. That is why if your credit history is poor, it needs to be addressed. If your credit history is good, it needs to be protected.

In closing, this is how a good credit history adds to your ability to attain financial security: It provides the ability to be able to move freely through the economy and purchase goods and services. Good credit also affords you low interest rates that allow you to manage debt at a reasonable level, without becoming financially insecure. Thus, the first step on your journey to financial security is to know your personal credit report, understand how your credit report affects you, and if necessary, know the steps to take to make it better. Once again, let me reassure you, it is never too late to start. Even if your credit rating is not as high as you would like it to be, you can begin to build new credit and rectify the past.

Solution Summary

6: ALTER EGO: YOUR CREDIT IDENTITY

• Establishing good credit is extremely important. Credit can help build wealth and is a great asset.

• Know your credit score and how if affects your credit identity.

• If you do not have credit in your name, begin to establish credit - create a good payment history.

• Be responsible with your credit cards and use a monthly budget to manage your debt.

• Build positive relationships with your creditors and lenders.

• Your bank is the first place to start seeking loans or credit cards.

• In a relationship it is important that each partner maintain separate credit identities.

• Payment history is important in determining your credit score.

• Keep all credit card balances at 1/3 or less of their credit limit.

• To improve your credit rating or to establish new credit, if a friend or family member has a high credit score, ask to be added as an authorized user. You can benefit from their credit rating.

• Once you establish your credit identity always be aware of your credit score, and continue to keep good payment and utilization habits.

Chapter VII

Suit of Armor

PROTECTION AND RECTIFYING IDENTITY THEFT

In today's technology driven, fast paced world, it has become more important to learn how to protect yourself from identity theft. Unfortunately, identity theft is on the rise. There are precautions you can take to lessen the chances that you will fall victim to this frustrating crime. This chapter is going to arm you with a heightened awareness of how to protect your personal information and what procedures to follow if you should fall victim to identity theft.

IDENTITY THEFT DEFINITION AND HISTORY

Identity theft refers to an imposter using another's identity to steal money or to attain other benefits. With the advancement of electronic and computer based asset management and financial access systems, for over two decades the frequency of identity theft crimes has steadily increased. Before the term identity theft came into use, most of these activities were in the categories of fraud and counterfeiting. The good news is there are precautions you can take to protect yourself and your valuable information.

The Federal Trade Commission calculates that up to 8.3 million people in America experience identity theft each year. Identity theft is on the rise and a serious crime. Individuals who are victimized by identity theft may be refused loans for automobiles, homes, and even education. An identity thief harms the victim's credit, and the damage appears on their credit reports. Identity thieves may use the information to obtain a credit card, get an apartment, and obtain a cell phone, etc. The drastic nature and seriousness of the crime is unique, considering a lot of damage can be done before the victim even realizes what is happening. It's usually not until they get notified from a bill collector, law enforcement or one of their creditors that they know something fraudulent has been occurring. In the most extreme situations a person can even be arrested for the criminal activities of an identity thief.

DETECTING IDENTITY THEFT

Detecting identity theft may require that you pay attention to your finances with a little more scrutiny than you have in the past. This requires more effort, but it's worth it and will eventually become a habit. Keep in mind that even though identity theft is a very serious problem, you can take measures to make sure you don't become a victim. Watch for denials of credit that arrive without any action on your part. If an identity thief applies for credit using your identity, chances are some communication from a credit card company might come back directly to you. Watch for unknown credit cards or account statements, statements that don't arrive at all, and correspondence or phone calls about things you did not buy. Watch your credit card and bank statements carefully. If they have purchases or withdrawals that you have not made, contact them immediately. If you are denied credit or see less credit available and it's not making sense to you, be aware. If you normally receive credit card, bank or utility statements and you notice a lapse, check into it immediately. This is a possible indication that someone has stolen them to get your personal information. You may notice some of your mail is missing. It is possible that someone may be stealing your mail to get your personal information. Or maybe you received a notice for your mail to be redirected, and that's not a request you've made. Identity thieves will also try and cover their tracks by changing the billing address. This way you won't discover their activities for a long enough time frame so that they have more opportunity to make purchases and cover their tracks. If you suspect there's an identity thief who has filed a change of address, contact your local postmaster. You can obtain the phone number for your local postmaster by calling 800-275-8777. You can go into more depth with your local postmaster about the address where your forwarded mail is going, or fraudulent credit cards that were sent there. Whenever surfing the web, consider how important your personal information is. Don't click on links in e-mails you don't recognize, and don't click on links in websites you don't trust or didn't navigate to.

HOW IDENTITY THIEVES ACCESS YOUR INFORMATION

This is a story about my client Tom, and this could happen to anyone. Tom resides in Hartford, Connecticut. He has several credit cards and noticed that one of his cards had a transaction that he didn't recognize on the statement. When he reviewed his statement he realized that he had lost the card. Thinking back he realized it happened at a local shopping center, and now someone was making charges on it. Several purchases were made, including an $800 television! Like many people, he found himself frustrated, angry and he didn't really know what to do. For most, credit card fraud isn't something they have had experience dealing with. The first thing I advised him to do was to call his credit card company to report the incident and circumstances and see if he could immediately close his account. Credit card companies will investigate your current transactions and will most likely send another card when your case is cleared. With the frequency of identity theft, everyone should be very cautious with his or her personal credit. Always remember to shred documents that have your personal information, such as your address, social security number, phone numbers, etc.

Another way identity thieves find innocent victims is through the Internet. Some of you may have received e-mail messages from around the world claiming you have inherited a large inheritance or prize. All you need to claim the prize is to provide them with your personal information. Immediately they will respond with the details of how you will receive the money. These are, of course, a small fraction of the scams that are circulating. Please, don't be fooled by these e-mails or information requests. Remember the old adage, "if it sounds too good to be true, it probably is." If you receive an email stating you've won an award there are ways to validate the information without providing any personal information.

If you have a friend or a relative who has been very careful about their personal information, now you know why. Careful management of all your personal records is crucial. Credit card bills, automobile bills, registration documentation, medical information, tax returns, and notices are just a few sources that contain personal information about you where identity thieves can illegally use your identity. Since all this documentation contains personal information it should all be kept in a secure place, and never discarded without being shredded.

Identity thieves can use many different methods to get your personal information. These include:

- Doing research on the victim in Internet search engines, government registers, or public records searches

- Going through your trash seeking documents or any correspondence with your personal information

- Old computers that have been disposed of without properly erasing the personal data contained on their hard drives

- Observing someone in public using ATMS, on phone calls, at banks, etc.

- Using computer based information like Trojan horses (Trojan horses are software programs that fall in the category of viruses that secretly install themselves on your computer when you visit less than reputable websites. They collect personal information from your computer and transmit the information over the web)

- Theft of your personal information like your wallet or purse by pickpockets or purse snatchers

- False advertising, job offers which the applicants will provide full name, bio information, and possibly banking information

- Credit card companies, internet sales organizations or any service where your personal financial information can be compromised

- False changing of your address whereby your bills and personal statements are sent to another address allowing thieves to gather information or delay your discovery of their illegal activities

- Impersonation of one of your existing banking or trusted institutions in e-mail based messages, presenting offers or opportunities which require personal information

- Searching social networks like MySpace or Facebook to gather information from users about other users

IDENTITY THEFT, THE INTERNET, E-COMMERCE, AND SECURITY

Because of the rampant identity theft on the Internet, large banking institutions, department stores, and billing agencies sponsored the development of various secure methods of making purchases using personal and financial information from the purchaser. The http:// in a website address stands for, "hyper text transfer protocol," and is not a secure method of accessing or transferring information on the Internet. This is why https:// was created. The additional 's' stands for secure. This means that the information encrypted isn't visible to hackers and identity thieves. Be aware when you are on the Internet and pay attention to various security notices each website presents you. Your personal information should always be transmitted using a secure process. Internet browsers will offer to "cache" your personal information when you fill out various forms. If your elect to allow them to do this they will create copies of any information you enter. Typically, they will copy address and personal information. All browsers also provide methods to clear this information on a regular basis. I realize that it might be a little more time consuming to do this, but I recommend that you never let the browsers cache your personal information. You should also regularly clear personal data from any browsers you use. One browser, for example, has a feature at the bottom of the tools menu called clear private data. Doing this regularly prevents any personal information from accumulating on your computer. In the event that your computer is somehow compromised, your personal information isn't available.

VARIOUS TYPES OF IDENTITY THEFT

The Internet isn't the only thing you need to consider when protecting yourself from identity theft. I advise everyone to do all that is possible to protect against identity theft, and to adopt a comprehensive plan for protection. Identity theft covers a wide range of criminal activity and relates closely to many other forms of fraud. Many of these are preventable through more secure methods of handling your financial and personal information. These include bank fraud, credit card fraud, check fraud, check washing, lapsed lurker, pharming, phishing, spam, and RFID. All require some compromised information.

ACTION STEPS IF YOU SHOULD BECOME A VICTIM OF IDENTITY THEFT

Credit Cards

If your credit cards were stolen or lost, immediately report the incident to your creditors. In most cases, when fraudulent charges are made, credit card creditors do not hold you responsible for more than $50.

If this happens it is very important for you to make sure that you ask your creditor to put the old account into an "account closed at customer's request" status. This will be better for you than a "card lost or stolen" status. Sometimes when this report goes to the credit bureaus as the card "lost or stolen," new lenders could possibility see this as a derogatory element to your credit report.

Checks and Checking Accounts

If your checks were stolen or if a fraudulent bank account was set up, notify your banks immediately. Secondly, close your accounts as soon as possible.

Before you look into reporting it, be aware that you have to report it in a very specific manner and you also have to make sure your bank reports it very specifically. Fraud can refer to identity theft but it can also refer to illegal activities by the account holder. So, it's very important that you communicate that this is an identity theft and that this is reported properly. Any derogatory reports to the check verification companies could possibly result in you not being allowed to open a checking account for five years. So, I'm sure you can see how this needs to be handled in the right way.

Please do not rely on the bank to automatically take action for you. You can report the information to the following check verification companies. SCAN: 800-262-7771, Equifax: 800-437-5120, ChexSystems: 800-428-9623, CrossCheck: 800-552-1900, NPC (National Processing Co.): 800-526-5380, TeleCheck: 800-710-9898, and Checkrite: 800-766-2748.

ATM/Debit Cards

If your ATM card was stolen contact your bank immediately to cancel it and to order a new one. When you are opening a new account you can ask for a password access only account. When you are canceling the old card, get another one with a new PIN number. You never want to use your old password.

Social Security Numbers

If your Social Security number has been stolen and abused you will want to call the Social Security Administrator (SSA). Immediately report the fraudulent action with your social security number. In very extreme cases, you may want to consider changing your Social Security number. Unfortunately, many people are trying to get new Social Security numbers to evade their bad credit history. In order to get a new Social Security number, the SSA has very specific fraud/victim criteria that you must meet. Also, note that you may want to order a copy of your earnings and benefits statement. You want to scrutinize it closely for any errors. Again, people may be using your SSN to get employment or avoid paying taxes. The website for the SSA is: www.ssa.gov. The phone number is 800-772-1213.

If you have a passport and are a victim of identity theft, contact the passport office to see if anyone recently requested a new one. Check the website: www.travel.state.gov/passport/passport_1738.html

If your driver's license number has been used you will want to contact the Department of Motor Vehicles (DMV) to see if another license was issued in your name. Then put a fraud alert on your current license and request a new driver's license number at your local DMV office. The DMV has a complaint form that is for fraud investigation. You will want to get that form filled out and submitted at your local DMV office.

If you are a victim of identity theft there are four things you should do immediately:

1. Place a fraud alert on your credit reports and review all three credit reporting bureau credit reports. As I've mentioned before, take detailed notes of every person you speak with and any information. Fraud alerts prevent thieves from opening more accounts in your name. You can do this by calling the toll-free number of any of the three credit reporting bureaus. As a rule, credit-reporting bureaus are required to report a fraud alert to each other, so you only have to contact one bureau. As a precaution, I advise you to contact all three. This way you have confirmed with all three and are covered in case the one bureau you report the fraud alert to somehow makes a mistake.

2. Close the accounts that you know, or believe, have been tampered with or opened fraudulently. Contact the fraud or security department of each company. Make sure to document every detail of these phone calls. Following the phone call, while the conversation is fresh in your mind, prepare a written transcript of the call. Send a copy of this to the companies, reiterating the phone conversation. Following up in writing is a very important part of the process. Also, include originals, not copies, of all supporting documents. Send these letters by certified, return receipt requested, so you have documentation of what you sent and when it was received. Keep copies of the letter and the supporting documentation. I can't state this enough - document everything!

If there are fraudulent charges or debits on your accounts, ask the agent to send you the company's fraud dispute forms. If they don't have special forms you can use the sample letter at the end of this chapter. Be sure when you send in the forms or sample letters to send them to the billing inquiry address for the company, not the address for payments. If the account is a new unauthorized account you can file a report directly with the police. Provide a copy of the identity theft report directly to the company. You can also file a dispute with the company. If you prefer to do this, ask if the company accepts the FTC's ID Theft Affidavit. If they don't, ask the representative to send you the company's fraud dispute forms. I advise that you file a report with the police then provide a copy of the identity theft report to the company. This will give you better backup. For instance, if the company has already reported these unauthorized accounts or debts on your credit report, an identity theft report will require them to stop reporting that fraudulent information. You have inherent rights in the identity theft dispute process, and some are directly related to the use of identity theft reports.

When you have completed the process and the dispute is resolved, you can ask for a letter stating those accounts have been closed and the company has discharged the fraudulent debts. If you ever have any errors relating to this account again, the letter is the strongest proof. Years later, the errors relating to this account may reappear on your credit report. This backup documentation will protect you in the event this occurs.

If you've experienced identity theft, you want to make sure it will never happen again. SECURE YOUR IDENTITY! Once you have closed any accounts associated with the fraudulent activity, begin to open new accounts. When you do this, make sure to create new personal identification numbers (PIN's). Don't use consecutive numbers, birth dates or any common numbers like addresses or your license plate number. Basically, don't use readily accessible information.

3. Contact the Federal Trade Commission and file a complaint.
This step will help law enforcement track down the criminals. It also allows the FTC to document and retain information related to the fraudulent activities you experienced. This way they can notify other law enforcement agencies, as well as investigate the companies involved for possible infractions of the law.

The printed copy of your online complaint form can also be given to the police to add to their police report. Remember, the FTC ID Theft Complaint printed for the police constitutes an identity theft report and will provide various protection for you. This includes: blocking fraudulent information from appearing on your credit report, preventing debts from reappearing on your credit report, protecting you from companies attempting to collect debts that resulted from identity theft, and providing an extended fraud alert on your credit report.

A complaint with the FTC can be filed online using the online complaint form. www.consumer.gov/idtheft. You can also call the FTC Identity Theft Hotline at 1-877-ID-THEFT (877-438-4338) or 1-866-653-4261. If you prefer, you can send correspondence to: Theft Clearinghouse, Federal Trade Commission, 600 Pennsylvania Ave., NW, Washington, DC 20580. If anything changes or you notice any fraudulent activity on your credit report immediately follow-up with the FTC updating your complaint information. Here is a sample affidavit found on the FTC website.

4. Contact your local police or the police department in the area where the identity theft occurred. Inform them that you would like to file a report about an identity theft you experienced. You may be required to file the report in person, so be sure and check with them. If this isn't possible, check to see if it can be done via the telephone or their website. Your local law enforcement may not be willing to take the report. If this is the case, request to file a miscellaneous incident report. If that doesn't work you can check the surrounding area for another jurisdiction that may take the report, including the state police. Your state may not require the police to take reports on identity theft. You can always check with the Attorney General's office to see if your state requires this.

Assuming your local law enforcement or the law enforcement in the area where the theft occurred, are willing to take the report, make sure to bring a copy of your FTC ID Theft Complaint form, your cover letter, and your supporting documentation. The cover letter explains why a police report and an ID Theft Complaint are so important to victims.

Ask the officer to attach or incorporate the ID Theft Complaint into their police report. Tell them that you need a copy of the Identity Theft Report (the police report with your ID Theft Complaint attached or incorporated) to dispute the fraudulent accounts and debts created by the identity thief. (In some jurisdictions the officer will not be able to give you a copy of the official police report, but should be able to sign your Complaint and write the police report number in the Law Enforcement Report section.)

Even after doing the preceding steps it still may take some time for the effects of the identity thieves to be corrected. There are many elements to fighting the adverse effects of identity thieves. This will depend on the type of theft, whether the perpetrator sold or gave your information to other thieves, if the thief is caught, and what items appeared on your credit reports.

Monitoring your bank accounts and your credit card accounts is very important. You should also review your credit report every three months. It is even advisable to monitor them more closely. All three credit reporting bureaus provide credit report monitoring services that will send you an email if anything changes on your credit report, or if you take a negative hit because of some new debt or collection.

Finally, be very aggressive when it comes to repairing the damage done to your credit reports. As mentioned before, document all communication and follow-up with all contacts in writing. Reiterate exactly what transpired in your phone conversations. You should keep in mind that identity theft has a snowball effect. The longer it takes you to correct negative, incorrect information the more time it takes to get a resolution.

DO YOU NEED A PROFESSIONAL IDENTITY THEFT SERVICE?

There are many professional services that will, for a fee, help you resolve identity theft. Whether you need a professional service or want to pursue resolution yourself will depend on how much time and work you want to put into the process, and your financial situation. As I've mentioned in other chapters, reputable professional services come to the table with an array of tools and experience that you don't have. However, there is no reason you can't learn it and do it yourself. I suggest doing your research to figure out which way is best for you. The nuances of identity theft repair require a focused and tenacious approach, and diligent follow-up to assure your identity is once again secured. Also, it is important to make sure the correct law enforcement and federal agencies are notified and are processing your paperwork properly.

Here is a list for you to think about:

- Was your driver's license stolen?
- Was your ATM or debit card stolen or compromised?
- Is your mailing address compromised?
- Was your Social Security number accessed and used for illegal activity?

In summary, for dealing with identity theft, keep on top of the situation and in control. This will help you if you have debt collector or collection agencies calling you. You do not have to tolerate harassment. There are laws in place with the FTC that do protect against harassment.

In sharing the stories about my clients, the goal is to help you to avoid or resolve the same issues. A married couple, that are clients of mine had a cellular phone bill that they religiously paid every month on time. They also took pride in themselves for keeping their credit rating high, by paying their bills in a timely manner. Now you can imagine, Joe and Kathy were extremely taken aback when they received a collection notice saying that they owed $290 for a cell phone bill dated back from 2001. The problem, and what alerted them right away was that they had never had an account with this particular cell phone company. They tried to contact the collection agency directly to get this issue resolved, but they couldn't reach anyone. Frustrated, they finally went to a local news network asking for help, and the news network got to the bottom of it. The network contacted the cell phone company. The cell phone company did more research and found out that Joe and Kathy's identity was used to open an account. Kathy and Joe did use the news to help them, however, with more effort on their own, they could have achieved the same results. Contacting the news helped them expedite the process. In conclusion, watch your billing carefully, pull your credit reports regularly, and be on high alert of anything that is suspicious or if there is something you don't recognize. If there is, immediately contact that company and say these magic words, "I think I have identity theft happening. I need you to check into this immediately." This will capture the attention of the company you are dealing with. They have millions of dollars of loss with identity theft and the sooner they catch it the less they stand to lose. Identity theft can be extremely frustrating and time consuming to rectify. The sooner you catch a discrepancy the less frustrating it will be to resolve the problem. This is why I say to stay on top of your credit game and be aware.

Below is a sample letter for disputing charges on existing credit accounts. For more sample letters on existing bank, credit and new fraudulent accounts, visit my website.

Letter for your credit accounts you don't recognize:

DATE

YOUR NAME
YOUR ADDRESS
YOUR CITY, STATE, ZIP CODE

YOUR ACCOUNT NUMBER

NAME OF CREDITOR
BILLING AND FRAUD DEPARTMENT
ADDRESS
CITY, STATE, ZIP CODE

To Whom It May Concern:

I am writing this letter to dispute a fraudulent charge appearing on my statement, relating to the above account number in the amount of XXX. At this time, I am requesting that the charge be removed, and that any finance charges or other related charges to this fraudulent charge be credited to my account. Please send me a corrected statement at your earliest convenience.

I am a victim of identity theft. I did not make, nor did I authorize this charge.

Enclosed, please find relevant information supporting my position (making this specific to your case i.e. police report, credit report with item identified).

I ask that an investigation take place immediately to correct the fraudulent charge (or charges).

Sincerely,

Your Name Here

Encl. (list what you are enclosing)

Solution Summary

7: SUIT OF ARMOR: PROTECTION AND RECTIFYING IDENTITY THEFT

- Protection from identity theft is important.
- Detection requires attention to your finances, with scrutiny.
- Evidence of identifying theft include: credit denials in the mail, unknown credit card statements, missing statements, unknown withdrawals, less credit available than expected on credit cards, lapse in receiving utility bills, mail missing, notice of redirected mail, etc.
- Report unauthorized charges on credit cards immediately.
- Be careful with any documents that have your personal information.
- Use a shredder.
- Keep personal records in secured place.
- Don't allow your computer browser to retain your personal information.
- If you are a victim of identity theft:
  - Place a fraud alert on your credit reports
  - List accounts that you know have fraudulent activity and contact fraud or security department of each company
  - Get company's fraud dispute forms
  - File a report directly with the police and provide a copy of the identity theft report to the company
  - Contact the Federal Trade Commission and file a complaint and submit a copy of your online complaint form to the police - this can protect you from companies trying to collect fraudulent debts
- Continuously review credit reports. Possibly enroll in credit monitoring service that will send an email alert if any changes to credit report occur.

A Piece of American Pie

MORTGAGES

The housing market boom started in the late 90's, reaching an all-time high of profits. This lasted until the crash in 2007, where the market dropped. A large component of the crash was due to the mortgage industry putting loans in the hands of people that could not afford them. Those who would not normally qualify for loans were now the proud owners of a home that was doomed for foreclosure. The banks and the mortgage industry became greedy and were using unethical practices. In some cases they were altering applications, doing anything they could to get a loan approved. Unfortunately, congress and the government never did anything to prevent this and never stepped in. The mortgage and bank industry created new types of loans such as: negative amortization, interest only payments, teaser rates with a balloon payment, etc.

A subprime loan was created for people who had poor credit, low credit scores, or were self-employed and didn't qualify for "A" paper mortgages. An "A" paper loan is granted to those who have great credit and an employment record. There is a much higher interest rate for subprime loans, as opposed to "A" paper mortgages, due to their high risk. In the United States, if a loan doesn't meet Fannie Mae or Freddie Mac qualifications, the loan is considered subprime.

In various cases, lenders were sued or even lost their jobs over their unscrupulous practices. Brokers' quick fix greed foreshadowed the borrowers long-term ability to repay the loans. Homeowners were enticed by low monthly payments and teaser interest rates. Some lenders never told the homeowners that these terms would never be paid off. They were also never told that even if they made the advertised payments it would actually lead to an increase in the loan balance. A Negative Amortization (or NEG AM loan) is a mortgage where you pay a low interest rate but your balance increases. There were also allegations in the lawsuits that stated that the brokers misused weak underwriting standards to get homeowners into complex mortgages. Loans were given to borrowers without checking for documented proof of their income and assets. In most cases it was not the borrowers fault. In many cases when people were buying a first time home obviously never having done this before, and they were relying on the expert, the mortgage broker or banker to give them correct information. They're trusting this information to be true. So, when they were told, "Why pay rent when you can afford a mortgage?" (Which really wasn't the case in the long term, which, of course was not explained to them). These people were taken advantage of. Now, there is also the flip side of the coin of the savvy investor or person who is less ethical. The ones who acted more out of greed, who knew exactly what they were doing, and taking advantage of the system to turn a quick profit.

Often times the homebuyer had no idea what type of problem they were getting into. They just wanted a piece of the American pie; to own a home. Can you blame them for wanting a home to help build their future? Who is to blame? In my opinion, the lenders and the lack of government intervention. The lenders were making billions on these loans and they are still taking every last cent from some people. What can we do now? Never get taken advantage of again by lenders. Know what you are getting into with a loan, and if it sounds too good to be true it probably is!

This chapter is designed to help you know what types of mortgages are available to you and how to save money on your loan. For the majority of you, a home is the most important decision and most expensive purchase you will ever make. It can seem intimidating, but it can also be the most exciting purchase you will ever make. The purchase of a home can also be instrumental in building wealth.

My advice is to be cautious, and not be fearful of buying any real estate. If you do your research you can buy in confidence.

IS A MORTGAGE RIGHT FOR YOU?

If you are considering a mortgage you should be confident that you are ready to take on a financial commitment that can possibly last for a few decades. Do you have a secure job and income and are you the type of person that will be content with a grounded and long-term situation, such as buying a home? Have you set aside any savings that you could use as a buffer, in case you find yourself with employment problems or financial issues? You ultimately will have to make the final decision on whether being a homeowner is right for you now, or you may gather all of this information to be ready for the future.

There are many ways you can utilize this chapter and mortgages:

1) If you are purchasing a new home
2) If you are refinancing your current home
3) If you would like to take out a home equity loan or line of credit (HELOC)

First, you will want to search out the best and most reputable companies to give you quotes. I suggest asking friends, family and co-workers for recommendations. Also, search the internet, newspapers and ads for different offers available. Realtors sometimes can be a good resource for knowing where to get a good mortgage. Be sure to not just take their recommendations, but to get others. Remember they may have their own best interests at heart, wanting to sell the house at any cost to you. Talk to your bank as well as the banks of your friends, family and co-workers or random banks. If you are not familiar with the institution you are dealing with, you can check the BBB to be sure they are reputable. My rule is, always get 3 separate quotes on any purchase.

Always take notes and be sure to get everything in writing before ever committing to any purchase. The interest rate certainly is a large factor, however, a lower interest rate may be a bad deal in the long run. This depends on other fees, so don't base your decision as a yes to a lender, solely on the interest rate. Often times the lenders will use low interest rates to get your business, and then there are hidden fees. That could be to the tune of thousands to even hundreds of thousands of dollars over the life of a loan. Always verify if the interest rate is based on a fixed-rate or adjustable-rate mortgage. If the rate is adjustable be sure to gather all information on the increases and specific terms. Do not let them just gloss over this one! Get in-depth details. Be sure to compare all fees from each quote you receive. Some fees to watch for are: underwriting, origination, appraisal, broker fees, doc fees, and doc transfer. You want to be clear on all closing costs. Ask if there is a prepayment penalty and if there are any points attached to the loan. If they are attaching points, be sure to ask them to translate that to dollars so that you may have a better understanding. Get all details on the points. Ask if a private mortgage insurance is required, and what the cost is. Lastly, always look at the down payment and requirements. They can vary from 0 to 20%. With the mortgage crisis it is very rare, except in extraordinary cases, that they will offer a 0% down. Depending on your credit history and income, they may ask for more then 20%. Sometimes the larger the down payment the lower the interest rate offered. I once got a mortgage that gave me a lower interest rate if I signed up for auto pay, each month, from my bank. Be sure to ask if there are any fees attached to any service they are offering you. If a mortgage company or bank is not explaining the loan process to you, move with caution. Remember, you are the customer and they are making money on your loan. They should be willing to explain and answer any questions you may have, so that you have a thorough understanding of the terms in your contract. If you want more flexibility with your loan you may choose an open mortgage, however, that may have higher interest rates compared to a closed mortgage.

After reading this chapter, if you have a current mortgage you may want to consider refinancing to get a better deal on your terms and rates. This could save you thousands to hundreds of thousands of dollars over the life of your loan. Another way that could save you the same large dollar amounts is to choose a bi-weekly payment program.

BI-WEEKLY PAYMENTS

On a 30-year fixed mortgage you can possibly reduce your loan by seven years when using a bi-weekly program. Be sure to ask if your lender offers this program and if there are any fees attached. The way this works is you will make 26 half payments per year, or 13 full payments per year. Inquire about prepayment penalties for your loan. Also, be clear on their procedure for the additional amount to be applied. Be sure that this is only applied to your principle balance and not the interest. You can also save by making extra payments towards the principle. If you apply any extra cash, income, tax refunds, inheritance or bonuses towards making extra payments, you could shave years off of your loan. If you calculate paying only one extra payment per year, you will usually reduce your loan by seven years.

A client, Sherry, was about to graduate from college. She was starting to seriously look at her financial situation and future, because she was going to be graduating in two months. Sherry was getting her bachelor's degree in Medical Technology. She felt that it would be a secure profession and she was now considering buying a home. As a mother of four, her desire to own a home was centered on her children and providing a stable home environment. Previously, she had been moving every six months to a year, and living in leased homes or apartments. She was researching various mortgage plans but wasn't able to decide which plan would benefit her family the most. Her take home salary was $43,000 and she was planning on it increasing once she concluded college and received her bachelor's degree. Her husband's income was roughly the same, about $40,000 after taxes. While she was pursuing her degree, she and her husband were also able to set aside a little money to put down as a down payment on their home. They were even considering building a small to medium sized house on a property they had purchased a few years earlier.

We were working on a structured plan to help her. I advised her that the mortgage plan she should choose was directly related to her and her husband's combined incomes, along with the needs and size of her family. I reminded her to think about the duration of the mortgage. Mortgage terms vary and are based on the amount of the down payment, the total of the loan, and the amount of time she wanted to repay the debt. If her family was capable of paying a higher monthly mortgage payment, then she could look at a 10 to a 15-year mortgage. If the length of the mortgage wasn't of much importance to her, she could get a 30-year mortgage. Then she could have lower monthly payments, which would leave more money for the day-to-day expenses of raising a family. I discussed with her that building a home on property she owned was a great idea. One thing for her to consider was all the elements involved in building her own home. Choosing the design, hiring a contractor, a builder, and dealing with the cost overruns and inevitable schedule extensions involved. This can be a frustrating experience, especially if there are comparable and desirable properties available that are meeting her family's needs. We talked about her leasing a home while she was still in the planning and building process of the home she wanted to build on her own property. The obvious advantage to building a home on your land is that you own it, and the investment in the land has already been made. The drawback is the amount of planning and preparations that go into home construction. As Sherry was house and mortgage shopping, she found the best way to go for her family was to build. She has a friend who is in the construction business who gave her a good deal, and she could trust him reducing the stress levels a bit. Ultimately, she decided to continue to rent while the house was being built so she could keep her kids in their same schools.

No matter what your motivation, owning a home is a great way to build your assets. However, be sure to make the best lending choices for your personal needs. When you own a home through a mortgage you not only benefit from the investment and financial advantages, but you also benefit from the tax benefits. In most cases, mortgages allow the debtor to deduct mortgage interest on their federal tax return, as well as, property taxes. I advise you to check with your tax professional.

MORTGAGES

Mortgages are loans made by lenders that are secured with the debtor, pledging the property as collateral. The lender has lien on the home or property that secures the loan, and this loan is repaid over time based on the specific conditions of the mortgage. Mortgages exist throughout the world in most countries as a means for home purchases. There are numerous types of mortgages and each has its own benefits and drawbacks.

Fixed-Rate Mortgages

Fixed-rate mortgages are extremely common. Homebuyers making their first home purchase typically choose a fixed-rate mortgage because of the predictability. The payments of a fixed-rate mortgage stay the same over the entire length of the loan and come in various lengths, including:

- 15-year loans
- 20-year loans
- 30-year loans
- 40-year loans

Their benefits include protection from inflation. Fixed-rate mortgages cover you if interest rates rise and prevent the monthly payment from rising. The longer the duration of the loan, the more this element of fixed-rate mortgages comes into play. There tends to be reduced risk with fixed-rate mortgages since you will always be able to plan for the payments. This also allows you to do long-term planning. After all, you know the entire duration of the loan and the exact payments that you need to make. There are no surprises, and this strong structure is great for people who need this type of process and planning.

All the benefits stated above also mean that with a fixed-rate mortgage you don't have the ability to get a lower interest rate if interest rates drop. If there are increases in your taxes or insurance, fixed-rate mortgages may adjust. This will add payments on the back end to cover the additional costs, while still honoring the commitment to keep the monthly payment the same. Also, since the interest rate is set and won't change, lenders may not qualify you for higher loans when applying for a fixed-rate mortgage.

Fixed-rate mortgages come with an interest only option. This option splits the mortgage into two time periods. While you are in the first period of the loan your monthly payment is lower because you are only paying the interest and not the principal of the loan. Then starting in the second period you begin to pay both the interest and the principal. This option is available in various durations just as the regular fixed-rate mortgage. The benefit and drawback of this option is clear. You pay much lower payments for the first period of the loan and consequently much higher payments during the second period. If you are seeking a way to make more funds available during the beginning of a mortgage this loan will work but you need to remember that you aren't making any payments towards the principal. You will have to make much larger payments during the second period and also need to qualify for this type of loan. You must have the means to cover the second portion of the loan.

There are also bi-weekly mortgages that break down the monthly payments of regular fixed-rate mortgages into two monthly payments. For many people this type of payment arrangement is a huge asset. Some people have a very hard time budgeting on monthly or yearly scales, but being able to make mortgage payments bi-weekly allows them more freedom to budget in a way that is more comfortable to them. Basically keeping your money closer to the vest and requiring a little less discipline is preferable to some of you. Another advantage of a biweekly mortgage is that the lender pays off the mortgage sooner. They end up making one more payment a year, or 26 mortgage payments instead of the conventional 12 monthly mortgages payments. If you are interested in a bi-weekly mortgage, you will need to shop around to various lenders. Not all lenders will offer this type of loan. Additionally, for a fee, some lenders may offer to change a fixed-rate mortgage to a bi-weekly mortgage. If you think this would benefit you I recommend you enter this type of loan from the start. It would be a better option than for you to try to change the loan with your bank later on. If you try to switch over later there will probably be a fee, which you could have avoided if you pursued this type of loan from the beginning.

Adjustable Rate Mortgages (ARM)

The aptly named, adjustable rate mortgages, are mortgages that have interest rates that change over the duration of the loan. They typically start with the best interest rate available at the time the loan is secured, but are based on the flexibility of the interest rate being able to change. Adjustment periods are built into an ARM that establishes when and how frequently the interest rate can change. During the beginning of the ARM there is an initial period where the interest rate doesn't change. Varying anywhere from six months to ten years, during this time period the lender cannot raise the interest rate. Following this period the lender is free to adjust the interest rate of the ARM and will do so at various times throughout the remainder of the loan.

Indexes and Margins

Banks decide the interest rate based on what are called indexes and margins. After the initial time frame where the interest rate is unchanged, lenders then review the published index. The published index basically outlines the current financial situation at the time. There are various sources for this information, including, the U.S. Constant Maturity Treasury or CMT, or the London Interbank Offered Rate or LIBOR. The lending institution then applies the indexes based on the margin, which is generally the percentage that can be added to the index in calculating your new interest rate. As the adjustable rate of your mortgage increases, so will your monthly mortgage payment.

Caps, Ceilings, and Floors

All adjustable rate mortgages have a limit on how much the interest rate can increase or decrease, during each adjustment period, and also over the entire duration of the loan. This is called the cap, ceiling, or floor. This is where the lender will determine when the date of the first adjustment will be. They will also figure out how much the interest rate can go up or down for that adjustment period, and the life of the loan.

Hybrid Adjustable Rate Mortgages (ARM)

A Hybrid ARM has a fixed interest rate for a set period of time with adjustable-rate characteristics. The interest rate will adjust for the rest of the loan, the same as a normal ARM. A Hybrid ARM comes in many forms, with the initial time frame varying. For example, in a 10/1 you will have a 10-year term where the interest rate doesn't change. Following that is the subsequent 1-year interest-rate adjustment period. This is the reset period where hybrid ARM shifts from a fixed-rate payment schedule to an adjusting rate payment schedule.

Adjustable-rate mortgages tend to allow the debtor to qualify for a higher loan because the interest rate is lower than a fixed-rate mortgage. If interest rates are high at the time and you opt to go with an ARM, thinking it might be lower and your payments will go down, be careful, reductions aren't very common. However, ARMs do provide savings if the interest is low and the initial adjustment period is greater than 5 or 6 years. Generally, an ARM's interest rates will adjust to higher rates some time in the duration of the loan. So, be prepared for higher monthly payments.

Reset Mortgages (Balloon)

These types of mortgages are considered two-step mortgages. They are monthly mortgage payments that are based on a 30-year amortization schedule with the entire balance due at the end of the 5 or 7-year term. They are called reset mortgages because the borrower, at this time, must either pay off the balance of the mortgage or exercise their right to reset the mortgage. If the borrower chooses to reset the mortgage the interest rate is reset at the current market rate for the remainder of the amortization period. Lenders may have other conditions that must be met to qualify for the reset. This includes, paying the mortgage on time for a minimum of one year to the balloon maturity date, there must be no liens on the property, and you are still the occupant and owner of the home. In some instances, it is also possible to refinance or reset a balloon mortgage.

Balloon mortgages typically come with a lower initial interest rate than fixed-rate or adjustable rate mortgages. This helps qualify you for a larger loan than the other mortgage types. Keep in mind, if you are planning on selling your home before the maturity date of the reset mortgage, this is a good way to go and allows you to pay off the loan. If you change your mind and decide to stay, you will need to reset the mortgage. If during the course of your balloon mortgage the interest rate goes up considerably, you will have a much higher payment if you decide to reset the mortgage.

Many banks and mortgage companies are currently offering refinancing and restructuring options. I highly suggest always keeping on top of your mortgage and never just letting it go by the wayside and paying it, but continue to search out possible better options. In fact, I just got a phone call the other day from a large well-known bank asking me how I was doing with the economy, and they're just touching base with their mortgage customers while they are in good standing to see if things are tight for them and if there's possibly a better option for them to move into a different mortgage. It never hurts to keep in contact with your bank or mortgage lender checking to see if they have a better option or offer. It's well worth your while to take the time out to make phone calls to their competitors seeing if they have a better offer. With the mortgage crisis, lenders are more willing to look at options than ever before to keep you from falling into foreclosure. I suggest taking advantage of any beneficial offers that may be available.

Solution Summary

8: A PIECE OF AMERICAN PIE: MORTGAGES

- Purchasing a home is one of the most important decisions you will ever make.

- Real estate ownership can be instrumental in building wealth and a great way to build assets.

- Real estate ownership can have tax benefits and in most cases you can deduct the mortgage interest and property taxes on your tax return.

- A mortgage is a secured loan - the home is the collateral.

- Do your research and buy in confidence.

- When considering a mortgage, make sure you are ready, have a secure job, adequate savings and are content in a grounded long-term commitment.

- Refinancing an existing loan can save thousands to hundreds of thousands of dollars over the life of a loan.

- A bi-weekly payment program can save over the life of loan - know if there are any fees associated with this option.

- You could shave years off of your loan by making extra payments towards the principle. One extra payment per year, usually will reduce your loan by seven years - be sure any extra payments that are made are applied to the principle only.

- Fixed-rate mortgages have a reduced risk, as payments are the same over length of the loan even if the prime interest rate goes up.

- When seeking a mortgage or refinancing:

  - Research reliable companies, ask friends, colleagues and family for recommendations on banks and mortgage companies

  - Check with the Better Business Bureau

  - Get 3 separate quotes for any purchase

  - Takes notes - get everything in writing before committing to any purchase

  - Don't get a loan solely based on a low interest rate

- Know if your interest rate is based on a fixed rate or adjustable rate
- Compare all fees from each quote you get
- Compare closing costs
- Review down payment requirements - a larger down payment might secure a lower interest rate
- Be sure to ask if there are fees associated with any service that is provided
- Ask if there is a prepayment penalty for your loan
- Get explanations and answers for any questions you have

The Great Escape

FORECLOSURE

If you are facing foreclosure, you are not alone. The foreclosure crisis has hit more than 2 million American families in this country. In today's world, the following stories are all too common. Foreclosure does not discriminate. It affects all age groups, races and economic backgrounds. Sketchy lending practices and manipulation into believing that we can afford things that we can't, are all too common. As you read in the previous chapter, the subprime loans have really affected our entire country on many levels.

It is easy to see how this foreclosure trap misled millions. It even happened to someone very close to me. A few years back, everything was going Joe's way. He had a construction company that was growing and business was booming. At home he had a loving wife and a daughter attending private school. With his hard work having paid off, he decided to expand his home to 8,000 square feet. Joe was living the American dream. In 2001 he began to expand his investment portfolio, and with the boom in the real estate market, buying property seemed like a natural progression. And since construction and home building were his area of experience, this seemed like a good move. If you have a successful construction company, why not be profitable in real estate? It made sense. So, Joe embarked on his new investment opportunity and bought a nine-acre farm, an apartment building, a rental home, and he and I even invested in a home together. We expanded a 900 square foot home to 3,500 square feet, and turned around and sold it for a hefty profit.

As you can imagine, in order for Joe to get into all of these properties he had to have several different types of mortgages for each one. When he first began to invest, his credit score was less than stellar. His mortgage broker was working with him to get his credit score raised, so that in the following year, Joe could move into a better mortgage rate. Everything was going according to plan. Within one year he had a better credit score and was able to qualify for better mortgages and interest rates. When Joe was on a roll in purchasing these properties, he got caught up in the teaser rate syndrome. He had several teaser rate mortgages that after one, two, or three years, would explode into incomprehensible mortgage payments. His mortgage broker's plan was to get him re-financed and moved out of these mortgages and into better mortgages in one to three years time. Joe, trusting his mortgage broker, never looked back. After all, he had gotten him into these four properties. It can't be all that bad, right?

As fate turned out, his broker had an illness in the family, which distracted his focus away from his business practices. Suddenly, Joe found himself slammed into one after another-skyrocketing mortgage rates that he could not keep up with. He and his wife were now working day and night just to pay the mortgages. Joe found himself unable to keep up his payments and began missing payments. His mortgage broker had dropped the ball, overwhelmed with his own personal crisis. Joe's efforts to raise his credit score now turned into a downward spiral. He scrambled to get new mortgages to fix the situation, but with his credit score in the tank, it was impossible to find options. All he could do to stay above water was to continue on the hamster treadmill. The next thing he knew, he was faced with foreclosure on all of his properties. The hole he had dug for himself kept getting deeper and deeper. Joe was helpless, watching his years of hard work and money go down the drain. And to make matters worse, the sheriff was about to show up at his home that Monday morning to take possession of it.

Just when he was about to throw in the towel and didn't know what else to do, he called me. I told him to never give up. I told him to speak to a higher-level person at the mortgage company than he had been speaking to. And if that didn't get him somewhere, to go to the person of even higher ranking. But don't just give in. Ask for the next supervisor, to the next supervisor, and talk, talk, talk to anyone you can at the mortgage company or bank. In most cases, the banks and the mortgage companies will negotiate with you. The key was to get to the right people. It was 4 pm on Friday, and the clock was ticking. The banks were closing at 6 pm, and the following Monday morning the Sheriff was due to arrive at his house. With the pressure on he used the guidance and encouragement I gave him to pull himself together and to physically go down to the lending institution. I told him he had no time for depression, and no time to feel sorry for himself. Right now he needed to put all emotions aside and save his property. When he arrived, he asked to speak to the supervisor in person and made an arrangement for a forbearance agreement. This gave him time to either sell the properties or get into a different loan program. In the twelfth hour he escaped foreclosure and you can too! I do not suggest waiting until the last minute to do this, just know there is hope and that you have options. A forbearance agreement is not always the best option. It may end up being more costly. After gaining knowledge about your options you need to make the best decision for your personal situation.

SOLUTIONS FOR FORECLOSURE

When under the gun with a situation like Joe's, first and foremost, you must COMMUNICATE! Put your pride aside, get out of denial, and be honest. This is not the time to play the hero. In some cases this is not your fault, and no one can help you if they don't know that you need help. Family and friends are the best place to start. Opening up to them can help you realize that you are not alone in this fight. You have a team behind you that is rooting for you. Holding a big secret like this inside will only create stress, not to mention, hurt your emotional and physical health. Even if they can't help financially, being able to vent without judgment can lift a huge weight off your shoulders. Then you can use this momentum to plunge forward with your next step. This is not an easy thing to do, however, it is extremely important to share and tell them how you got into this position.

When unseen health issues arrive, foreclosure can also happen. Michael was brought up with strong money values and was responsible his whole life. He graduated from college and then worked really hard to build his small accounting business. Feeling secure in the path he had built for himself, Michael bought a house and had a nice car, always making his payments on time. Unexpectedly, he got into a car accident and hurt his back. He was forced to take time off work, and since he worked for himself, he didn't receive a paycheck while he was recovering. His business started to suffer and eventually went under. He was also now faced with the weight of unexpected medical bills. Michael was in a lot of pain, and depression set in when default notices started arriving at his house. Unless he did something to get back on track, foreclosure was in his future. Michael went to his mother to see if she could lend him some money to help him get up to date with his payments. At this point it was not only important to help save his house, but his credit score, which was quickly plummeting at a dismal rate. Michael's mother knew he was responsible with money and felt comfortable stepping in to help.

Whenever you get financially involved with a family member or friends, I recommend creating a contract between all parties. This documentation will spell out all the expectations and responsibilities of everyone involved. This also offers reassurance to family and friends that you have the best interest of both parties. Other ways to encourage family and friends to get involved is to solicit their help as an investment. Offer to give them a part of the profit when you decide to sell someday. You want to give them every reason possible to say yes. There are so many ways to make things work. By thinking outside of the box you are bound to come up with several solutions. One person's nightmare could be another's good fortune, making solutions win/win for everyone.

For example, Michael's mother was semi-retired, owned a home where her mortgage was paid off, and had a part-time job to keep active. Michael suggested that his mom open a HELOC. This would allow Michael to catch up on his mortgage payments, pay off medical bills, build his credit score, and focus on his continued recovery. In fact, he was able to rehabilitate himself enough to get a part-time job with an accounting firm. As he began to feel better, they allowed him to work towards full-time status. Since Michael had been responsible his whole life and now had a form of income, his mother knew he was a risk worth taking. She knew he would be able to make all payments on the loan and cover the interest. The interest on a HELOC is tax deductible for his mother, so this transaction turned out to be a win/win situation for both Michael and his mother. Michael was never late on his payments and he was able to save his house from foreclosure. His mother received all the tax benefits from the HELOC, while working part-time. She had been concerned about having enough tax deductions from her part-time job, but now with the HELOC, she had tax benefits that saved her from paying extra taxes. Everyone wins!

If you are late on your mortgage, chances are good that you are late on other payments as well. If credit card companies and collection agencies are calling, don't spend your time on them just yet. You can take the time to worry about your credit score when your foreclosure situation is figured out. You need all your energy put towards saving your house. Credit cards are considered unsecured debt. This means that they can't take back the items that you purchased with the card. A car or a home loan is considered secured debt, and they can take over possession of either if they're not paid. Many people who are faced with foreclosure feel they are going to lose the house anyway, so why bother paying the mortgage? They just worry about the credit cards, thinking, if they can't keep the house, at least they can buy food or other things for the family. When actually, this could be the wrong thing to do. I always suggest paying secured debt first and really work out the numbers to see if it's most advantageous for you to save your home or let it go by selling or one of the options below. There are always options, so do not give up so easily!

Building relationships and connections will assist you in having more options and solutions. If going to a family or friend is not an option for you, the next step is to talk with your loan officer. The best way is to set up an appointment to meet in person. Talking over the phone is not as effective as a face-to-face meeting. Foreclosure produces a lot of extra paperwork for them, so they want to help you avoid it. If they can't fit you in right away, go to their office and tell them that you will wait until they have time, or meet with a different loan officer that can help you. This may seem like a scary thing to face, but remember, this is nothing to be embarrassed by and there are millions in this situation. You are not alone. There is no need to dwell on the past; you need them to help you find a solution now. If they still won't help you, try a different bank and talk with one of their loan officers. Competitors are always ready for your business and may be able to help you refinance. Just be sure not to make the same mistakes and get yourself back into hot water.

The bank may be able to make modifications to your current mortgage. This can result in changing terms or interest rates. In the long run, it will cost you extra in fees or interest, but the payoff is that you get to keep your property. It also allows you to stay calm and resolve other issues in your life that were brought on by the foreclosure process. Another option is forbearance. This allows you to stop making payments for a few months until you can get back on your feet. During this time, interest is still being charged.

Remember, any change you make with the bank to your mortgage will still cost money. If you think you will be unable to keep up with the payments even after changes have happened, you might need to consider selling the house. If you can make payments for a few months, hire a real estate agent to sell it in a timely manner and help you get the most money for your house. If you have no time, you should consider a short sale. The bank will allow you to sell the house for less than you owe them.

The most important thing is to never GIVE UP. If one suggestion doesn't work, try a different one. When that doesn't work, try a new approach. This will take effort and diligence on your part, but the payoff will be worth it! You worked hard to get where you are. You owe it to yourself and your family to do everything possible to keep your home.

Sometimes, you may decide that there is too much emotional baggage in your house and you want to get rid of it and start fresh. When divorce occurs, this is common. Often, two incomes are needed to pay a monthly mortgage. When the split occurs, it can become near impossible for the bills to be paid on one income. When Mary was faced with divorce, after months of messy divorce proceedings, she felt like she didn't have any fight left in her. In the settlement she got the deed to the house. Immediately, she was falling behind on payments and the bank was sending her notices. To correct the situation, Mary spent a lot of time talking with her friends, family, and even the bank. She felt that all the fighting from the divorce resulted in negative energy in the house and she wanted to sell it and have a fresh start. A good approach is to talk to a reputable real estate agent that understands the local market and your urgency to sell quickly. Another option is a short sale. This is when you sell the house for less than the outstanding balance and the lender agrees to accept the lower payment for the remainder of the balance. Both allow you to become free of the property and avoid foreclosure, but the first option is to refinance, get a different loan or a loan modification.

Cheryl, my client, is a 43-year-old woman who was unemployed, with two teenage children to support. She has been happily married for 15 years and owns some property, including the home she currently lives in. Three years ago she purchased her home in New Haven, Connecticut for $250,000. Then, she was laid off from her job where she had been employed for years. Cheryl was worried that because of her loss of income, she might lose her home. She was seeking alternate employment opportunities. However, she was uncertain if she would get a new job before her next mortgage payment was due. Cheryl did not have adequate savings set aside, so she was beginning to feel the stress and pressure of the situation. It is recommended to always have enough liquid cash saved and available to cover your monthly expenses for six months. You never know when an unexpected tragedy may hit, and it is best to be safe than sorry. Cheryl's situation is unfortunate to hear about, but as surprising as you may think, this sort of thing happens to hard-working individuals, every day. Just realize that there is help out there. I suggested to Cheryl that she contact her lenders as soon as possible, before her situation had a chance to get worse. Her lender may be able to postpone a few payments and decrease the amount due until she was able to find another job. In regards to this situation, it would also be a good idea to also provide proof. Every state has laws specific to their region about unemployment and foreclosure. This law may work in your favor by granting you 6 months to resume paying your mortgage.

FORBEARANCE AGREEMENT

Here's another story about foreclosure. One of my clients was going to get into a forbearance agreement to stop the foreclosure sale of his home. This is an agreement made between the two parties that says, the lender will delay his right to exercise foreclosure if the borrower agrees to a mortgage plan that will be paid off over a certain amount of time. The time period and the payment plan depend on the details of the agreement.

A forbearance agreement stops the trustee sale but it doesn't get you out of foreclosure. It is basically an agreement you sign with your lender that states the lender will still be due the amount you owe, but at a later date. The duration varies depending on the lending institution. There is a down payment and a reduced monthly payment schedule, which is negotiated in the forbearance agreement.

The forbearance agreement is a much better option than going into mortgage foreclosure. You can delay your monthly mortgage payments for the short period of time granted from by the lender. When you resume payments at the end of your extension period, interest will have continued to accrue, while the principal and the respective payments will have increased. Forbearance agreements are only recommended if you are facing foreclosure. You will still need to resolve the core of your financial problem, and the forbearance agreement is designed to give you time to do this, if you decide it's the right option for you. If you have a mortgage payment of $2,500 and have a forbearance agreement for four months, you now owe the additional $10,000 in missed payments, plus accrued interest. This additional amount is added to your principal and your monthly payments increase.

During the application process your lender will go through your financials to evaluate your entire financial situation. In my client's case, he was at the point of a sheriff's sale of his property. You have to agree to the terms of the agreement in order to stop the sheriff's sale. When trying to negotiate a forbearance agreement, the banks are on your side. Reason being, they will make more money in the long run and they have a commitment from you to pay everything back. Banks don't want to foreclose on borrowers. They will incur legal expenses and then have to sell the property. And on most occasions they will lose money doing this. They are in the business of lending money, not in selling houses. It is in their best interests to approve a forbearance agreement.

If you decide to seek a forbearance agreement make sure you are talking to the right people. Debt collectors are not the first people you should approach when seeking forbearance. They can't do anything to help you change the loan. This is where working with real estate lawyers and/or mortgage loan professionals will become an asset. They can help you navigate the lending institution bureaucracy to get to the people that can help you.

LOAN MODIFICATION

Loan modification means you pay a down payment and then they put the rest of the arrearage at the end of the loan, and redefine the terms of the loan. This should be something you can handle. Depending on the size of the loan, it may raise your monthly payment. More than likely, it will be less of an increase than if you went with a forbearance agreement. If the monthly payment does increase, it could increase anywhere from eighty to one hundred dollars, where the forbearance agreement would be much more.

In order to get a loan modification, you need to talk to a loan modification company. It is hard to negotiate a loan modification by yourself. A loan modification requires an acute knowledge of the entire process and the players involved. You also have to be very careful about what company you hire to do it. You want someone who is seasoned and well versed in modification. If the borrower is having financial problems and isn't able to acquire different financial solutions, the lending institution will be willing to negotiate. A loan modification company communicates with the lender and presents why they should consider working out a deal with the borrower. The lender will then change terms either by lowering monthly payments, lowering the loan interest rate, or anything necessary to prevent foreclosure.

In looking for a loan modification company, you should interview a lot people. Be careful of going with someone who is only telling you what you want to hear. It might be a good idea to do some research through government agencies to find reputable people. You should go with a company who specializes in loan modifications. Review their credentials and references, as well as copies of their proposals and contracts.

When you work with the right loan modification companies they help you navigate the process. When you get a loan modification your loan goes through what's called, "Climbing the Ladders." Instead of going through the offshore phone tree, it goes straight to the loan modification people. These are the higher up people who can track back and look at the loan's history and see that before you went into foreclosure, in seven years you never had a single late payment.

There are laws and legalities that loan modification companies must follow. Loan modification companies can help you with unfair practices. Most lending institutions want to get the loans off their desks by foreclosing, re-modifying the loans, or by forbearance. They want to do whatever they can to make the most money. Forbearance is typically where the most money is made. Many lending institutions are now offering loan modification directly. If you feel comfortable enough working on the loan modification yourself, you certainly can do so. Some of my clients have hired attorneys to handle the loan modification process for them.

A loan modification changes the payment terms and the interest rate of the borrower so they can obtain a fixed rate. The reduction in payments and rates is achieved without obtaining new surveys, appraisals, legal charges, and taxes. A new closing isn't necessary to achieve a loan modification.

Loan modification companies will mediate your situation and will present as much information as possible to achieve results for you. Be ready to present your entire situation, including any hardships you have experienced, that have played a part in your current financial situation and mortgage delinquency.

These may include:
- Loss of job
- Business failure
- Reduction in salary
- Illness
- Job relocation
- Death of co-borrower or spouse
- Incarceration
- Marital separation
- Divorce

- Medical bills
- Military duty
- Damage to property (natural disaster)

If you obtained a forbearance agreement and are now considering a loan modification, you might be able to use the terms of the forbearance in your argument for a loan modification. If you put a substantial amount of money down for a forbearance agreement, the loan modification company can argue that you qualify for a loan modification, which gets you out of foreclosure. Once again, you need to find someone who is well versed in all aspects of making this happen. The first thing they will tell you to do is to put your money aside, even if this means stopping to make payments on your forbearance agreement. You will need the money for the loan modification. Without it, it will fail. My client used this method with great success and managed to get out of foreclosure.

BANKRUPTCY

This same client also thought of filing for bankruptcy. You need to have less than 1.1 million dollars in secured debt, so this was not a solution for him. Secured debt is a house mortgage or a car loan. Loans that are backed with collateral are secured loans. My client had 1.3 million in secured debt, which did not allow him to file Chapter 13, which is re-organization. The next thing that would help him in his dilemma would be to file Chapter 11. This also didn't work for him because, although it would reorganize his debt, it would also cost $15,000, as opposed to the $1,500 it would cost to file Chapter 13. Aside from the high cost to file Chapter 11, there is no mortgage protection. If you can't make your mortgage payments during the reorganization period along with all the other unsecured debt, you may be taken to bankruptcy court. There the judge could force you into a Chapter 7, which is a total liquidation of all of your assets. Eighty-five percent of all bankruptcies fail. People think they will get some relief from their financial situation, but more times than not, bankruptcy does not cure their problem.

Lawyers typically want to do Chapter 13 because it is a quick $1,500 in their pockets and only requires a couple of filings. Chapter 11 is usually set up for businesses, so an attorney for a personal case can be hard to find. In Chapter 13 and Chapter 11 you are not wiping out the debt, you are re-organizing it over time. This can be anywhere from one to five years of paying the arrearages on the debt. The only way that you can qualify for these types of bankruptcies is if you can prove your income, along with several other criteria. Otherwise, you can be forced into a Chapter 7, which is a liquidation of assets to pay back the creditors. If anything remains after the creditors are paid, what is left over goes back to the original owner. If at all possible, I want to discourage you from choosing the path of filing for bankruptcy.

REVERSE MORTGAGE

A reverse mortgage is an option for homeowners who are 62 or older. With the current economy, reverse mortgages have become more popular across America. The federal government insures about 350,000 reverse mortgage loans - 107,000 occurred in 2007 alone. When life is plagued with high medical bills, expenses, or social security isn't meeting the needs required to survive, a reverse mortgage can be an option for seniors. Be leery that this is a risky option. As more Americans approach retirement age, some financial institutions are aggressive in pushing the reverse mortgage as an easy, cost-free loan. With a reverse mortgage the homeowner can convert the home equity into cash, and there will be no interest or principal payments during the life of the loan. It is what is called a "rising debt" loan, where the interest is added to the lien on the property.

The need for cash to afford a certain lifestyle or to avoid foreclosure is understood, but keep in mind that a reverse mortgage is a serious decision that should be carefully examined to see if it is right for you or someone you know. Especially, when you consider that a home is typically your most valuable asset and often an important source of one's retirement security. Not only does a reverse mortgage have high up-front costs, but there is also the possibility of becoming ineligible for different benefits, including Medicaid.

A reverse mortgage is due when the homeowner dies, leaves or sells the home. If the homeowner was to leave to go to a nursing home, they may find that they have little left over in their equity to pay for long-term care. The Financial Industry Regulatory Authority (FINRA) is carefully monitoring brokers who recommend homeowners to get a reverse mortgage in order to invest in other financial products that could result in possible harm to the homeowner's financial future.

For some, they need money now, or need to escape foreclosure and they are not worried about the future issues of Medicaid. This should be used as a strategy when other options do not exist or if the homeowner fully understands the proper use of a reverse mortgage and are able to meet its requirements. Before engaging in this type of loan, seek counseling from a third party financial institution from a source that is approved by the Department of Housing and Urban Development (HUD).

SHORT SALE

Lastly, my client considered a short sale, which is a new phenomenon. A short sale is when a lender, investor or an attorney accepts an offer from a buyer who offers less money than the home loan is worth, as opposed to the home going to a trustee sale. A trustee sale is when your home is put up for auction. You want to avoid being foreclosed upon and going to a trustee sale. If your home is auctioned off, not only will you lose your home, but you will also get a debilitating mark on your credit score. A short sale works something like this. Say, for example, a person has $600,000 in debt on their house and they have $590,000 in mortgages. $90,000 of it is a second loan, where the lien holder will accept ten percent in repayment and then go away. The remaining $500,000 of debt remains, and the buyer has made an offer of $380,000. The second lien holder will get ten percent in a short sale, and the first lien holder will usually receive at least 50% or more. In order to do this you need to be able to prove that you can't do various other things first. There is a lot of paperwork involved and a lot of time. Short sales also have an adverse affect on the local real estate values. If a home valued at $600,000 is sold in a short sale for $380,000, then the buyer(s) turns around and sells it for $450,000. This negatively affects the resale value of all the homes in the neighborhood. Short sales are harmful to our economy.

Solution Summary

9: THE GREAT ESCAPE: FORECLOSURE

- Immediately contact lenders when problems arise. Search out all of your options and remember that a lender typically does not want to foreclose.

- Realize that you are not alone.

- Know your rights. Each state has local jurisdiction rights when it comes to foreclosure.

- Contact the loan officer with your lender as soon as possible to seek refinancing.

- Try refinancing your mortgage with a different lender and lower interest rate.

- Seek help from family and friends. If you secure assistance from family or friends, create a contract. If you sell the property, offer them a percentage.

- Try to reinstate your mortgage. Paying a lump sum of money to cover all past due bills and fees will solve this. Then you can continue on with normal payments. If you don't have a large sum to cover this or if you can't find one quickly, a reinstatement can be near impossible.

- Try to make a mortgage modification by changing the terms or the interest rate.

- If you are a senior, consider a reverse mortgage. Instead of making payments the bank sends you payments from the equity built into the home.

- Forbearance is also an option. It allows you to stop your payments and get back on your feet. The bank continues to charge you interest during this time.

- File a demand to delay the Sheriff's sale. Any delay will help you stall time so you can find a solution.

- Consider offering the bank a deed in lieu of foreclosure. This gives ownership of the property back to the bank. You are now cleared of any amount you owe and any amount of equity you have in the house.

- See if your bank has a Loss Mitigator. They can help you avoid foreclosure and make sure the bank loses the least amount of money possible.

- Be careful of predatory lenders that are just waiting to take advantage of you with your current situation. Do your homework and shop around.

- Hire a real estate agent to help you if you need to sell your house.

- A short sale is also an option. This is when the lender allows you to sell the house for a value less than the outstanding balance. The profits from the sale go to the lender.

- Pay off your secured debt (mortgages/cars) before you worry about paying off your unsecured debt (credit cards).

- Consolidate your debts.

- Have a garage sale, take items to resale stores, or sell some possessions on the Internet to get some quick cash.

- Get a part-time job or look for another way to bring in some extra income each week.

- Budget your current expenses. Cut out unnecessary costs: cable service, dry cleaning, entertainment, eating out, sell your car for one that is less expensive. Downsize your life style.

- Hire a debt/credit counselor. They can help you figure out a budget and also negotiate repayment options with creditors.

- If family members are willing and can qualify for a HELOC (Home Equity Line of Credit) loan, this can be used to consolidate debt and allow you to get back on your feet. In the meantime, they get the tax benefit of writing off the interest with no out-of-pocket expenses of their own.

- As a last option hire a bankruptcy attorney and find out if that is your best option. There are ways to get rid of debt or reorganize debt. Only a qualified lawyer can direct you to your best solution.

- Realize that your self-worth is not defined by your possessions. Life goes on and so can you.

- Learn from your mistakes and make positive changes. Remember to not make the same mistakes again.

Chapter

To Claim or Not To Claim

BANKRUPTCY

I know the thought of this chapter is difficult. If you or your loved ones are financially distressed enough to be considering bankruptcy. This chapter is designed to help you make the decision, whether or not to file for bankruptcy. Filing bankruptcy must be your last resort. First attempt to exhaust all other measures and never consider bankruptcy a quick fix.

FINAL CONSIDERATIONS BEFORE FILING BANKRUPTCY - THE ALTERNATIVES

The first line of action is to try to consolidate your debt. If you have a home, try to take out a home equity loan if you can. Another option is to try to do a cash-out refinancing. Try refinancing your car. Try to get a personal loan. Ask family or friends for help. If you are 62 or older and own your home outright, a reverse mortgage might be right for you, call all your creditors and negotiate better terms on your own.

If you're in a situation where you're tens of thousands of dollars to even hundreds of thousands in debt, and you have no hope in mediating payment arrangements, or finding outside help, then you may consider filing bankruptcy. There are no specific guidelines outlining how much debt and how much income one should have prior to pursuing bankruptcy. You must be in a very serious financial situation to consider filing bankruptcy.

Some may feel that filing for bankruptcy is humiliating and beneath them. If you have reached a point where you are filing bankruptcy, you are utilizing a process that is set forth in the United States Constitution that has helped many individuals and companies. America's foundation is built on the principle of a second chance. Rest assured, if you have come to the final decision to file for bankruptcy, you are not alone. This situation can happen to anyone. There are even some famous Americans who have filed bankruptcy: Walt Disney, Mark Twain, Henry Ford, Abraham Lincoln, Kim Basinger, Kathy Lee Crosby, Larry King, Cyndi Lauper, Jerry Lewis, Burt Reynolds, Donald Trump, Oscar Wild, Willie Nelson, Ulysses S. Grant, P.T. Barnum, and Frances Ford Coppola. You can see from this list that many have gone on to do great things with their lives. And like a phoenix rising from the ashes, you too can bounce back from the setback of bankruptcy and do wonderful things with your life.

CONSOLIDATING YOUR DEBT

Start by compiling all of your information. As a reminder, gather all your financial statements, including all your bank statements, investment accounts, utility bills, and anything associated with income or expenses. As I've mentioned before the importance of creating a budget, and I still hold true to that. Create a budget. If you are the type of person who doesn't really do this, it can seem tedious. However, it is well worth the effort. By creating a budget you will have a realistic view of what you are spending each month. From there you can start to work the numbers to see what kind of monthly payment you might be able to make. This entire process is crucial before you start negotiating with your creditors. By starting here you will be able to accurately work with them and come up with a solution. This budget will also allow you to start looking at the incidentals you are spending money on each month, and if necessary, you will be able to make sacrifices to get into a reasonable payment arrangement with your creditors. Whether you do it yourself or hire a debt consolidation company, the key here is communication. The creation of a detailed budget will also serve as an explanation when making payment arrangements, to prove why you are only able to pay a certain amount towards your debt.

DEBT CONSOLIDATION COMPANIES

If you don't want to mediate your debts on your own, you can pursue assistance from a nonprofit credit or debt-counseling agency. They will work with you to aid you in repaying your debts and improving your financial picture. Debt counseling agencies provide a liaison between you and your creditors and help manage the vast information and expertise needed to get results. Information about agencies in your area is available at the United States Trustee website at www.usdoj.gov/ust. Click "Credit Counseling and Debtor Education," and this will take you to a state-by-state list of agencies the Trustee has approved. It is now required to complete this before filing for bankruptcy.

A debt consolidation loan is not the easiest to get. Lenders know that when people are in the position of needing a debt consolidation loan, they're having financial issues, high balances, missed payments, late payments, etc. Because of this they will charge a high interest rate, since you are considered a risk to loan money to. Fees will also be involved. Your monthly payments may be lower, which could reduce your stress for the moment. However, in the end you will be paying more. You will want to assess if this is the right choice for you.

When you enter into a debt management program your credit report will have a notation that states that you are paying an account through a credit counseling, consolidation, or settlement agency. This statement will stay on your credit report until the account is paid in full, and this is visible to any creditor who has access to your credit history. There are many contributing factors as to whether or not this type of notation affects your credit score. There will be a derogatory mark left for the lender or creditor to make a judgment call.

If you are deciding to go this route you may want to consider this. If you are meeting with a debt consolidation or debt settlement company, most likely, your credit score is on the low side already. What you will want to consider is that you will have a negative effect on your credit history for a shorter amount of time. If you didn't go this route your derogatory payment history and high debt ratios could last many more years, sometimes even up to 20 plus years. Reduced stress and avoiding the possibility of bankruptcy are the obvious benefits.

WHAT EXACTLY IS BANKRUPTCY?

Bankruptcy means that you are legally and voluntarily making the claim that you lack the ability to pay your creditors. A person or organization may declare bankruptcy under one of many chapters of the federal bankruptcy code.

When you file for bankruptcy, you won't have to explain the reasons for your need to file. However, you will have to provide your salary, assets, and expenses. Typically, financial problems arise from medical bills, losing your job, divorce and poor financial habits and/or planning. None of this is a concern to the bankruptcy court. The specific reasons and pitfalls you have experienced aren't relevant in bankruptcy court proceedings. You need to have interacted honestly with your creditors, making attempts to resolve your debt before you can file for bankruptcy. There must be an acceptance of reality that you cannot pay your debts based on your current income. Your income is calculated by averaging your salary over the last six months. In a majority of bankruptcies you can keep your belongings. The United States Constitution outlines that you are allowed to keep some or all of your property. There are exemption statutes that will help you protect your property.

Under the U.S. Constitution, bankruptcies are under Federal jurisdiction. Bankruptcy cases are always filed in United States Bankruptcy Court but are also dependent upon state law, which influence claims and exemptions. In regards to bankruptcy law, you will need to follow the specific guidelines that are set for the state of your residence. Bankruptcy cases cannot be filed in state court. Prepare yourself, because you will need to become versed in federal and state laws in regards to bankruptcy. You will also need to know the guidelines that are specific to the state where you are filing.

Here's a story about my client, Francis. Francis felt like she was swimming in credit card debt. Because of her excessive credit card balances, she felt like she had no control over her finances. Debt and financial mismanagement tend to merge in a negative downward spiral, and it became gradually more difficult for her to balance her budget and to reduce her credit card balances. Francis' debt was $12,486. She found herself in a situation where she wasn't able to pay down the debt. She began to think that bankruptcy was her only solution. She knew the only other solution was to pay the balance entirely or make a high monthly payment. She felt confused and frustrated and was seriously considering filing bankruptcy to get out of debt and start fresh. When she shared her concerns with me, I told her there was hope. I began by presenting to her alternatives to bankruptcy.

One option was finding a financial adviser to review her finances. Someone with a professional opinion that could come up with solutions that she may not have thought of. Debt consolidation companies are a good way to settle and maintain your debt payments. One way they can do this is by a debt consolidation loan. If the person has a home or car, they will issue you a secured loan at a lower interest rate, using the home or car as collateral. I explained to Francis that by using the services of a debt consolidation company, there would be a negative mark on her credit report. This is by far, less destructive to her credit report than filing for bankruptcy. And although she would get a negative mark on her credit report, it would also indicate that she sought help, and that she is committed to paying off her debts. The solution to her problem involved tracking her spending history. In this case, it was the key to paying off her debt.

If you tracked every single expense you had during a week, you would be amazed by the different incidental expenses you didn't pay attention to. Whether you take the initiative and do it yourself, or if you contact a debt consolidation company, this is the start to becoming more financially responsible and accountable of your spending. For many of us our spending habits are a foreign subject. Most people are in the category of not knowing what they spend on a day-to-day basis.

It is possible to settle your own debt. You don't need to use a debt consolidation company. Like credit repair, identity theft, and most of the topics in this book, you can do this yourself! It just requires action, discipline, patience and a commitment to seeking out all the resources and guidance you will need to do it successfully.

THE AUTOMATIC STAY

A part of filing bankruptcy is a court order called an automatic stay. After filing bankruptcy the court orders an automatic stay. The automatic stay prevents many of your creditors from taking any action to collect debts from you. The only way they can restart the debt collection process is if the creditor motions the court and the court lifts the stay.

Following the filing of your bankruptcy the automatic stay is your strongest ally preventing bill collectors from ongoing pursuit of your debts. It immediately ceases all lawsuits filed against you and a majority of the actions pending against your assets by all creditors, collection agencies, or government agencies.

If you are concerned about the possibility of being foreclosed on, or losing simple resources such as utility services, welfare, unemployment benefits, or your job or wage garnishments; the automatic stay is a very important and positive part of bankruptcy. It provides protection and allows you the benefit of restructuring your life and getting back on your feet.

If you are facing eviction from your apartment or home the automatic stay can possibly provide some help. Though, the new bankruptcy law still makes it possible for landlords to proceed with evictions. The automatic stay may buy you some time, but probably won't prevent eviction. If your landlord already has a judgment of possession, the automatic stay won't stop the eviction. If your landlord alleges that you have been using illegal substances, this is another situation where the automatic stay isn't much use. So, if you are facing eviction, even if you file bankruptcy the eviction will eventually run its course.

Bankruptcy does stop wage garnishments. If you are being threatened with one or more wage garnishments, bankruptcy will resolve this for you. You will be able to take your full salary and possibly discharge the debt associated with the garnishments.

If you are behind on utilities and the utility company is threatening to disconnect your electricity, phone, gas or water, this is another situation where the automatic stay will have some effect, delaying service disconnections for 20 days. If this is your only debt concern there are many ways to resolve this without filing bankruptcy.

The automatic stay temporarily stops the processing of foreclosure on your home but the creditor will eventually be able to continue processing the foreclosure. In this case, Chapter 13 or 11 bankruptcy is what you need to file to protect your home.

If you have received overpayments of public benefits, typically the government agency is allowed to collect the payments out of your future paychecks. The automatic stay prevents this collection process. The automatic stay does not, however, protect your public benefits. The agency will evaluate your eligibility for benefits and can terminate them if your eligibility changes.

The automatic stay won't stop various tax debt action. The IRS can still audit you, issue notices, and demand tax returns. They can issue tax assessments, but it will stop them from issuing a tax lien and/or seizing your property or income. If you are in a bad debt situation with the IRS and have a lot of IRS debt, then bankruptcy does provide you with some meaningful protection.

The automatic stay doesn't affect support actions. It will not stop a paternity suit that is filed against you or someone that is trying to establish, modify or collect child support or alimony payments. If you have pension loans, money can still be taken from your salary to repay the loan. This all depends on which type of pension the loan is drawn on. This includes most job-related pensions and IRA's. If there are criminal proceedings currently pending against you, these can be separated into their debt and criminal portions. The criminal portion of the proceeding will continue even though there is an automatic stay in effect. If there is a community service element to your sentence, along with other payments, such as, fines, the community service element will still be required.

Keep in mind that if you have already filed a bankruptcy in the previous year, this will cause the stay to terminate in 30 days. The only way this will change is if you, one of the trustees, or the creditor, requests that the stay continue, and supports you in presenting the current bankruptcy filing as being pursued in good faith. When you file bankruptcy cases, you must be careful to make sure you are not violating bankruptcy law. Any violation of bankruptcy law will be considered an act of bad faith, and the automatic stay will be lifted because of negligent processing.

If you are relying on the automatic stay as protection and as your merit in filing bankruptcy, you should be knowledgeable in all its powers and limitations. Creditors will still try and find ways to pursue their debts with you through loopholes, and their experience in getting around the automatic stay. If it is felt that the automatic stay is not serving the intended purpose, creditors can request the bankruptcy court to remove it.

In cases of foreclosure, the creditor may be able to get the automatic stay lifted if you file a bankruptcy close to the foreclosure of your home. They will look at whether you have any significant equity in the home and are able to pay all the debt on your mortgage in arrears. If it appears that you have no equity, and no ability to pay all the debts on your home, the bankruptcy court may rule against you and lift the automatic stay. As you can see, even elements of the automatic stay have many variables and nuances that require strong knowledge of the bankruptcy process.

There are debts that bankruptcy courts will not discharge. These debts will continue even if you file for bankruptcy. Student loans, for example, require that you prove that repaying the debt would be a hardship. Proving this is very difficult and there is no real known method for achieving this ruling. If you owe back child support or alimony, both of these debts are not easily discharged. If you have tax debt, there are only certain kinds of tax debt that will be discharged through a bankruptcy filing.

There are six types of bankruptcies called Chapters:

Chapter 7 – basic liquidation for individuals and businesses

Chapter 9 – municipal bankruptcy

Chapter 11 – rehabilitation or reorganization, used mainly by business debtors, but also occasionally by individuals with large debts and assets

Chapter 12 – rehabilitation for family farmers and fishermen

Chapter 13 – rehabilitation with payment plan for individuals with a steady source of income

Chapter 15 – ancillary and other international cases

The most common of the six types of bankruptcy are Chapter 7 and Chapter 13, which will be covered in this chapter.

In Chapter 7 bankruptcy you are appointed a trustee who gathers all non-exempt property, sells the assets, and distributes proceeds from the sale to appropriate creditors. Also, the debtor doesn't make a payment to the trustee. Under Chapter 7 bankruptcy there are 19 classes of debt that are discharged. The most common are a majority of taxes, and student loans. The benefit of this Chapter of bankruptcy is that the debtor can continue to pay a home mortgage and/or a car loan. Part of the United States Government Bankruptcy code states that a debtor can be allowed to retain some or all of their property.

Chapter 7 starts with the applicant filing a petition. The petition is filed in the bankruptcy court in the area where the individual lives, where the business debtor is organized, has its principal place of business, or principal assets. Additionally, the debtor must also file with the court:

- Schedules of assets and liabilities
- Schedule of current income and expenditures
- Statement of financial affairs
- Schedule of executory contract and unexpired leases

Also provided to the trustee is:

- A copy of the tax return or transcripts for the most recent tax year
- Tax returns or transcripts for prior years not filed when the case began

Individual debtors with primarily consumer debts must also file:

- Certificate of credit counseling

- A copy of any debt repayment plan developed through credit counseling
- Evidence of payment from employers, if any is received 60 days before filing
- Statement of monthly net income and any anticipated increase in income or expenses after filing
- Record of any interest the debt has in federal or state qualified tuition accounts

A Chapter 7 bankruptcy typically takes three to six months.

In Chapter 7 bankruptcy you will negotiate what will be liquidated. This type of bankruptcy is contingent on some of your property being liquidated to lower your debt. Consequently, most or all of your unsecured debts (debts not backed with collateral) will be erased. You get to keep exempt property. Exempt property is classified as exempt under the state or federal laws applicable to your state and Chapter 7 bankruptcy (such as your wardrobe, automobile, and household belongings). The ability to retain most of your belongings is a definite positive to Chapter 7 bankruptcy, especially for individuals.

For secured debts, Chapter 7 bankruptcy works like this: if you owe money on a secured debt (for example, an automobile loan where the car is collateral to guarantee payment of the loan), you can choose to allow the creditor to voluntarily repossess the property; continuing your payments on the property under the contract (if the lender agrees). You can also arrange to pay the creditor a lump sum amount equal to the current replacement value of the property. Some types of secured debts can be eliminated in Chapter 7 bankruptcy.

CHAPTER 13 BANKRUPTCY

Also called a wage earners plan, Chapter 13 bankruptcy empowers those with annual salaries to create a plan to repay all or part of their debt. In Chapter 13 bankruptcy the repayment plans are set to have installments paid to creditors in a time frame of three to five years. The state median income comes into play and if the bankruptcy filer's income is over the median the duration of the repayment is less than three years. In order to extend it the bankruptcy court calls this, "for cause," and must approve the longer time frame of five years. Five years is the longest a Chapter 13 bankruptcy is allowed to extend. A benefit of Chapter 13 bankruptcy is that during this period creditors are not allowed to initiate collection proceedings of any kind.

To qualify for a Chapter 13 bankruptcy the applicant must not exceed the amount of $306,675 in unsecured debts and secured debts are less than $922,975. Be sure to check with your attorney to know the latest numbers pertaining to your area. Adjustments to these amounts are made over time to allow for variations in the consumer price index. Chapter 13 is only extended to individuals and is not available to corporations or partnerships.

Bankruptcy courts are very strict about procedures and they restrict the filing process to prevent duplicated filings to exploit benefits of the system. If a bankruptcy petition has been filed, individuals must wait 180 days before they file again. A debtor cannot file again if they purposely did not appear before the court or comply with orders of the court. They also cannot apply if their bankruptcy petition was dismissed, following the action of creditors who pursued relief from the bankruptcy court to try and recover property that already had liens.

A more recent addition to bankruptcy law is the requirement that the filer has received credit counseling within the first 180 days of filing a bankruptcy. There is a listing provided by the bankruptcy court of approved credit counseling agencies. The filer must get counseling as an individual or as part of a group. Part of the process is the creation of a debt management plan. There may or may not be a plan. If one is created it is required that it be filed with the court as well.

The most appealing benefit of filing Chapter 13 bankruptcy is allowing debtors to save their homes from foreclosure. When filing a Chapter 13 bankruptcy debtors can cease foreclosure proceedings. This is obviously a huge benefit if you are seeking bankruptcy to save your home. Another benefit is the ability to catch up your delinquent mortgage payments over a period of time. The thing to keep in mind is that Chapter 13 doesn't free the debtor from making mortgage payments. If you file Chapter 13 you will still need to make your mortgage payments on time, as laid out in the Chapter 13 plan. Chapter 13 can also help co-signers. There is a special provision that protects third parties who are liable with the debtor on consumer debts. Chapter 13 also allows the filer to be able to restructure their debts and it acts as a consolidation loan, buffering the filer from creditors. Debtors will have no contact with creditors during the duration of their Chapter 13 protection. Payments are made to their trustee who then makes payments to the filer's creditors.

To start the process you will file a petition with your corresponding bankruptcy court in the area where you live and/or own your home. Based on direction from the court you will file:

- Schedules of assets and liabilities
- Schedule of current income and expenditures
- Schedule of executory contracts and unexpired leases
- Statement of financial affairs

Additionally, the filer must provide:

- Certificate of credit counseling
- A copy of any debt repayment plan developed with the credit counseling company
- Evidence of payment from employers (received 60 days before filing)
- Statement of monthly net income (including any anticipated increase in income or expenses after filing)
- Interest the debtor has in federal or state qualified education or tuition accounts
- A copy of the tax return or transcript from the most recent tax year
- Tax returns filed during the bankruptcy filing (including copies of tax returns for prior years that had not been filed when the case began)
- If married, you can file a joint petition or individual petitions

Charges approximately include a mandatory $235 case-filing fee and $39 miscellaneous administrative fee. Be sure to check with your attorney for current fees. Fees must be paid to the clerk of the court at the time of filing. With the court's permission, it is possible to make installment payments of the case-filing fee. The installment payments are limited to four, and the final payment must be made within 120 days after the petition filing. If you are experiencing real hardship and prove "cause shown," the court may extend the time of the installment payments, as long as all payments are made within 180 days of the filing of the petition. If you fail to make these payments your case may be dismissed.

Official bankruptcy forms that make up the petition require the following information:

- List of creditors, the total debts and origin of their claims
- Debtors income, including pay dates
- List of the debtors monthly living expenses, including: food, shelter, utilities, transportation, housing, taxes, medicine, incidentals, etc.

After you file the petition there will be a meeting of creditors held by the trustee assigned to your case. This may occur anywhere from 20 to 60 days after the debtor files the bankruptcy petition. This depends on whether the trustee or bankruptcy administrator schedules the meeting and various administrative staffing issues relevant to your case. In this meeting you will be placed under oath and there may or may not be questions from the trustee or creditors. Attending the meeting is mandatory. There you can answer questions regarding your financial situation and questions about your financial plan. If you are married and have filed the petition jointly, both partners must attend the meeting to answer questions. No bankruptcy judges will be present at this meeting, as this might prevent them from ruling impartially on your case.

As I've stated throughout this book, and I will say it here again, communication is the key. Here, communication can be a great asset to you. Before you meet with the trustee assigned to your case and your creditors, you can consult with your trustee to make sure there are no issues or problems with your plan. The trustee who is handling your case has a lot of knowledge that can help the entire process run smoothly. This is why it is in your best interest to contact him or her. Review whatever details you may have questions about. This will help you to get some guidance in the process and alleviate some stress.

You have 15 days after you file your bankruptcy petition to file a repayment plan with the court. The court must approve the plan and outline fixed payments that will be made to the trustee on a consistent basis. These are usually bi-weekly or monthly. The trustee will distribute the payments to your creditors, based on the plan.

Claims are broken down into three categories: unsecured, secured and priority claims. Bankruptcy law gives special status to priority claims including the costs of the bankruptcy proceedings and taxes. Unsecured claims have no real property associated with them and the collector cannot repossess any property associated with them. Secured claims allow the creditor to take back certain collateral.

Pending certain circumstances that can influence the claim, priority claims must be paid in full. In instances of secured claims the debtor may be able to keep their collateral as long as the creditor receives the value of the collateral. In terms of loans where the collateral is used to secure the loan, the creditor must receive the full payment of the debt. This would apply to automobile loans, recreational vehicles, etc. In the case of a home loan, the debtor can repay the home loan based on the payment schedule of the mortgage, as long as any arrearage is paid during the bankruptcy plan.

Unsecured claims do not have to be paid in full. The stipulation is based on disposable income and the applicable commitment period. The debtor must be paying all their disposable income in their bankruptcy plan towards their priority, secured, and unsecured claims. In Chapter 13 bankruptcy, unsecured claims pay the creditors what they would have received if the debtors assets where liquidated under Chapter 7 bankruptcy proceedings.

Disposable income is calculated in Chapter 13 based on the debtor's income. This does not include child support payments that are due to the debtor, minus reasonable amounts essential to provide the support of the debtor or dependents. Charitable contributions are also deducted from the disposable income amount up to 15% of the debtor's gross income.

If the debtor is a business owner, disposable income does not count as expenses essential to the operation of the business. Just like in Chapter 7 bankruptcy, the duration of the bankruptcy agreement is three to five years and is based on the median income calculation.

See Chapter 7 bankruptcy. The applicable commitment period may be less and it relies on the unsecured debt being paid in full over a shorter period.

Payments to the trustee must be paid within 30 days after filing the bankruptcy petition with the court, even if the court hasn't yet approved the bankruptcy plan. This includes payments on secured loans, like home and car payments. If the plan hasn't been approved before a payment comes due, the payments need to be made directly to the leaseholder or secured lender, then deducted from payments due to the trustee.

A confirmation hearing held by a bankruptcy court will occur within 45 days following the meeting with the trustee and creditors. They will evaluate the plan and decide if it's acceptable and conforms to standards outlined in the bankruptcy code.

A 25-day notice of the hearing will be sent to creditors who can object to the confirmation. There are a number of different objections that can be made by creditors, including the claim that the payments being made to the creditor don't match or are less than the amounts they would receive in Chapter 7 liquidation. The creditor may also object to the disposable income being committed from the debtor, alleging the amount isn't all of the debtor's disposable income.

With the acceptance of the bankruptcy plan by the court, the trustee will begin to make payments as described in the plan. The court, however, may decline the plan. If this occurs, the debtor can make changes and file the modified plan for approval. At this time, the debtor may also change the case to a Chapter 7 and liquidate their assets. Lastly, the court may dismiss the case after the modified bankruptcy plan is reviewed.

A Chapter 13 bankruptcy plan can also be modified after confirmation. This can occur when a creditor objects to a plan or another creditor appears who was not listed on the plan. The new creditor can be added by modifying the plan.

Once the plan is confirmed, all provisions are set. The debtor must meet the set payment schedule and all creditors must also abide by the plan. The debtor must now manage their finances on the fixed budget outlined in the plan for the duration of the plan. The debtor gets to keep all property and move towards resolving their debt and delinquencies without any threat of repossession of property and direct contact from creditors. Now their second chance begins. Beyond maintaining all payments and living on the fixed budget, the debtor must not incur any new debt without consulting the trustee. New debt can change the debtor's ability to complete the plan and is under the discretion of the trustee.

It is possible to get Chapter 13 discharged once you meet the following criteria:

- You have completed all payments under your plan and certify that all domestic support obligations (child support, alimony) that are due during the plan are paid
- You haven't had prior Chapter 13 bankruptcy cases discharged within the last two years, or Chapter 7 cases within four years
- You have completed an approved financial management course (if your trustee or bankruptcy administrator determines they are available in your district)

If all these criteria are met the only element considered by the bankruptcy court is your homestead exemption. Chapter 13 will be discharged as long as the court hearing determines that there is no reason that pending processing could influence your homestead exemption. This means, the debtor is released from all debts outlined in the bankruptcy plan and the creditors cannot take any legal action to collect discharged obligations.

If you are considering bankruptcy, my hope is that you now have more clarity on whether to claim or not to claim.

Please note: this is not meant to be legal advice, it is information given to you allowing you to make the best decision with your attorney.

Solution Summary

10: TO CLAIM OR NOT TO CLAIM: BANKRUPTCY

- Consider debt consolidation.
- Professional debt consolidation companies act as a liaison between you and your creditor, and they will work with your budget to reduce your overall debt.
- If you are a homeowner consider taking out a home equity loan or a cash-out refinancing.
- If you are over 62 consider a reverse mortgage.
- Be aware of your legal options and the types of bankruptcies called Chapters.
- If filing for bankruptcy, you have to provide your salary, assets, and expenses.
- In bankruptcy there are exemption statutes that can help protect your property.
- Hire a professional attorney to assist you if claiming bankruptcy is a consideration.
- You and/or your attorney need to be versed in Federal and State laws and bankruptcy guidelines specific to your state of residence.
- One benefit of bankruptcy is automatic stay. An automatic stay stops creditors from pursuing debt collection and ceases all lawsuits filed against you.
- Automatic stay will delay eviction, but if it is not brought current the court will lift it and you can still be evicted.
- Bankruptcy doesn't stop wage garnishments.
- Bankruptcy does not stop IRS action.
- Bankruptcy won't discharge some debts, such as, student loans. You must prove that repaying the debt would be an undue burden.
- Child support and alimony payments are not discharged by bankruptcies.
- Bankruptcy courts are very strict about filings.

Get Your Head Out of the Sand

TAX DEBT

Managing your taxes can be beneficial or it can be a huge problem and a source of stress. First and foremost, you must face your tax debt and to do something about it! Depending on your situation you can handle the problem yourself, or you may need to hire a tax professional. The general rule of thumb is if you owe the IRS less than $10,000, consider handling your tax debts yourself. If you owe the IRS around $11,000-$25,000 or more, a tax professional is advised. A tax professional can recommend a payment plan that is right for you so you will not default. This could end up saving you money in the long run. They can also review your deductions to make sure you are receiving the most benefits from them. If you owe the IRS more than $25,000, I strongly suggest working with a tax professional, and that you have a specific plan for your individual needs. The more competent and qualified a person is in their profession, the more you benefit from their services. This is definitely true for tax professionals. If you have a tax debt of $11,000-$25,000, or even higher, you may feel like your situation is beyond repair. It isn't. The IRS has a process called, "Offer in Compromise," where the IRS will work with you. They will possibly accept an amount that is considerably less than your debt, and then wipe your slate clean. Seasoned tax professionals and IRS employees, both have had documented success using this process. If this is the solution you seek, working with a professional who has experience with this process would put you at an advantage.

When searching for a tax professional, conduct a detailed interview process to assure they are qualified to help you. Work history, references, and their rate of success are a good place to start. They should either be an enrolled agent, tax attorney, or a certified public accountant, all of which, are allowed to practice before the Internal Revenue Service. Be sure to ask for rates and see if they will provide any guarantees of their work.

Whether you decide to work with a tax professional or decide to go it on your own, you are not alone! Many people have found themselves in the same situation and have found a successful way out of their tax debt.

If you are in tax debt, it is possible you made some miscalculations along the way. You may have made some irresponsible decisions with the intention of catching up, and resolving your debt before it became an issue. Whatever the reasons, here are some basics that will help you.

Accuracy is crucial. Always recheck your tax returns to make sure you have not overlooked some deductions. This could save you a lot of money and adjust the amount you owe the IRS. In many cases, clients were not completely sure about the deductions they could qualify for. I will list some suggestions, however, a professional tax advisor can assist you best with your specific needs.

Learn to maximize your tax deductions. There are many benefits to itemizing your tax deductions. Do you own a home? Do you pay property taxes? Do you make charitable donations? The list below contains the main categories you may be able to claim as deductions:

- Home Ownership
- Taxes
- Charitable Donations
- Medical Expenses
- Miscellaneous Expenses

Fill out Schedule A from your tax form, so you can compare what your standard deduction would be in comparison to your potential itemized deduction. If your itemized deduction is higher than your standard deduction, you should claim that.

The basic standard deduction amounts for the 2007 tax year are:

> Single taxpayer - $5,350
> Married taxpayer, filing a joint return - $10,700
> Head of household taxpayer - $7,850

If you're 65 years or older, or if you are blind, you may increase your standard tax deduction by $1,050.

The objective, if possible, is to use itemized deductions so you can claim more than the standard deduction. If you have been spending more money that could possibly have been used as itemized deductions, and you have not claimed the deductions on your previous return, you have been giving the IRS more taxes than you should. Over the course of your life this really adds up.

If you own a home you should review your 1098 to see if the mortgage interest you paid in the previous year is more than your standard deduction. If the mortgage interest is more, you could definitely itemize. So far, you are already doing better than the standard deduction, and you haven't even counted in real estate taxes, or local income taxes. Also deductible are (PMI) premiums for mortgage insurance. You don't need a home to benefit from itemizing. If your federal and state taxes total more than your exemption, it is best to itemize.

Any donations you made can only be deducted if you itemize. This includes furniture, clothing, and household items. These are items you don't normally think of or remember when it comes time to do your taxes. Charitable contributions of $250 or more require a receipt.

Medical expenses are deductible, but few taxpayers get to deduct them. The reasons are:

- Expenses must exceed 7-1/2% of your adjusted gross income. If your AGI is $25,000 the first $1,875 does not count.

- Deductible Medical Expenses Include:
- Health insurance coverage
- Doctor fees
- Dentist fees
- Chiropractor fees
- Lab fees
- Contact lenses
- Glasses
- Prescription drugs
- Medical supplies

MISCELLANEOUS TAX DEDUCTIONS

Here are a few qualifying miscellaneous tax expenses that you could possibly deduct:

- Union or professional organization dues
- Magazine subscriptions and other publications that are related to your work
- Business liability insurance premiums
- The cost of protective work clothing, such as hard hats, safety shoes and glasses, and the cost of uniforms you're required to wear to work
- Tools and supplies used in your work
- Medical examinations required by an employer
- Tuition for classes that maintain or improve the skills required for your present job
- Expenses you incur while looking for a job in your same line of work (examples: resume costs, career counseling, and employment agency fees)
- Depreciation on your computer or cellular phone - only for the time you use them to keep track of your taxable investments (stocks, bonds, mutual funds), or for your job, if it is required by your employer
- The fees you're charged by your financial institution to maintain your IRA account - only if you pay them from funds outside of your IRA account (if your financial institution just deducts the maintenance fees directly from your IRA, you can't deduct them)
- Safe deposit box rental fees – only for the use of storing stocks, bonds, or other investment-related documents (storage of jewelry and personal items are not deductible)

- What you pay to get your taxes done, whether it's by a professional or with tax preparation software, including books or publications to help you prepare for it
- Legal fees paid to protect your taxable income, or to produce your taxable income (This includes fees for legal assistance for helping you keep your job, for tax planning or investment counseling, and for handling an audit on your tax return. Legal fees for divorces aren't deductible, except for any portion specifically related to helping you collect alimony payments or for advice about the taxability of your alimony. You can only deduct legal fees that you pay in your efforts to collect income that's taxable to you)

MISCELLANEOUS DEDUCTIONS NOT SUBJECT TO THE 2% RULE

The two percent rule states that an individual is not allowed to take a miscellaneous deduction (either in entertainment expense or other expenses) that exceeds two percent of their adjusted gross income.

- Amortizable bond premium
- Gambling loses
- Federal Estate Tax on Income in Respect of a Descendent
- Tax preparation fees
- Tax preparation software

I have a client who owed the IRS $4,600 in taxes from the previous year. He didn't want to file bankruptcy and was concerned about how this was affecting his credit score. I told him he had a few options to eliminate his burden. You can offer to settle on a lower amount than what is due, pay the total amount with a partial payment, or pay off your debt in monthly installments. Judging from his circumstances, I advised him to try and pay monthly installments to lower the overall balance. I suggested he contact the IRS and negotiate a payment plan. He was amazed at how easy it was to negotiate a payment plan with the IRS. He couldn't believe how close he was to claiming bankruptcy over something that was so easily rectified.

When dealing with tax debt, communication is key! There are ways to handle your tax debt and lower or eliminate it altogether. An Installment Agreement is one way to pay off your debt with the IRS.

This is a monthly payment plan that is fairly simple for either you or your tax professional to arrange. It should only take a couple of hours of your time - you can set up an installment agreement by calling the IRS at 1-800-829-1040. They usually will set up a payment plan over the phone. You can also fill out a 9465 form, which is an Installment Agreement Request. Go to the IRS website to learn more and go to forms at www.irs.gov/. These are some general rules, however, it is best to check with the IRS for updates and specific individual information. If your tax debt does not exceed $10,000, you can possibly qualify for an installment agreement. Within three years it is likely your monthly installments will have paid your debt in full.

When you call or log on to the website, have copies of your tax returns on hand. Know how much you can afford to pay each month. Figure out if you want to set up an automatic withdrawal for your payments, and if so, you will need to have your banking information handy. When setting up a payment plan with the IRS, **DO NOT DEFAULT ON YOUR PAYMENTS!** To ensure that they receive the payment on time, send the payments ten days before they are due. Set up a payment plan that you can afford, and keep up with that commitment.

In January 2005, the IRS made a Partial Payment Installment Agreement available. This allows you to have a reduced payment plan. With this agreement the taxpayer's payment does not pay off the tax debt in full. However, the taxpayer does make agreed monthly payments, and when the term is completed the outstanding tax debt is forgiven. For this you will need to hire a tax professional that has experience with tax collection laws.

You might want to consider making an "Offer in Compromise" to the IRS. You will be required to make a lump sum or a short-term payment plan with the IRS. The benefit is that you will get a reduced rate instead of what you currently owe. Granting an "Offer in Compromise" is at the complete discretion of the IRS. They will consider an "Offer in Compromise" if it is doubtful that they will be able to collect the full amount from the taxpayer. Meaning, beyond the taxpayer's financial means. They will also consider it if it is possible that the taxpayer is not liable for the tax debt. Usually, the "Offer in Compromise" is rejected and the IRS accepts only about 1/8 of the offers. However, you could be one of the approved applicants, so give it your best. The 656-1 form used for an "Offer in Compromise" is available online at: http://www.irs.gov/pub/irs-pdf/f656.pdf

If you are going through severe financial hardship you would be best served by asking a tax professional about the Not Currently Collectible IRS program. By using the 433-F form (available online at: http://www.irs.gov/pub/irs-pdf/f433f.pdf), if acceptable, the IRS will stop all collection activities including levies and garnishments. The statute of limitations on tax debt collection is ten years. While in the Not Currently Collectible status, the statute of limitations continues to run, and if the IRS is unable to collect within the ten-year period, the owed tax debt expires.

Overwhelming tax debt may sound like a problem that will never happen to you. You may be good at managing your finances and you get a refund every year. This used to be what my client Jack thought until his tax situation spiraled out of control. He made some poor decisions that resulted in large amounts of tax debt. As a musician and artist he always had a large amount of expenses associated with working a full-time job, and spending the rest of his time trying to succeed in music and film projects. He lived a lifestyle based on future success that he thought would alleviate his debt problems. He was leveraging his income against his artistic endeavors, with blind faith that hard work would prevail. He thought that he would catch up.

Along with some personal changes in his life, and a lapse in employment, he fell out of touch with the IRS. He stopped making payments on his debt and the IRS issued a tax lien against him. A tax lien is a devastating hit on a person's credit that takes a long time to remove. It can be stressful and create a negative momentum in a person's life, which at times can be crippling.

Jack turned his life in a new direction when he started implementing my techniques. Up to this point he had NOT been writing off expenses related to his personal business. Jack had been working full-time and also part-time creating music, writing screenplays, making films and editing video. With his professional pursuits untracked, and all the associated expenses, he had rolled himself into a growing IRS debt. What he didn't realize is that the IRS and U.S. government work intricately with individuals and businesses, helping to foster and nurture business creation and development. If you take a moment to think about it, this actually makes sense. The government wants people to succeed in business. New businesses create revenue and increase commerce. This eventually creates more revenue in the form of taxes that are going to the IRS. Which points to why the IRS also has some investment in the success of individuals. They understand that there are many expenses related to owning your own business. The IRS provides many deductions, knowing that a lot of overhead is usually required in order to succeed. So, why not take advantage of the deductions that are available to you? This is the area that so many people overlook and can cause them to overpay. Through letters and phone calls Jack explained to the IRS that he was an entrepreneur who was working hard to turn his life around, and that his tax debt to the IRS was a priority.

The techniques Jack learned provided resources and a new direction. As I advised him, he began tracking all expenses, travel and any cost associated with his artistic pursuits. He used the resources and gained inspiration to begin a dialogue with the IRS. Taking my advice, Jack learned that anyone, no matter how bad his/her situation, could manage their debts and turn an unfavorable situation around.

First, Jack wrote the IRS detailed letters explaining his personal situation, his strong desire to resolve the situation, and his commitment to paying his tax debt. He elaborated on how he had made the mistake of accumulating his tax debt, and beyond any consideration on their behalf, wanted to outline his work ethic and desire to resolve his debt.

A large tax debt and tax lien can be a crippling problem for anyone. The only answer is to face the problem, communicate with the IRS, and begin to utilize the resources that are available to any American who is trying to start their own business.

The IRS may want to help. Sometimes it will take some effort, and other times it could be easy. Tax debt mediators are able to prey upon people with tax problems because the individual, normally, would rather pay a lot more money than deal with a possible negative experience with the IRS. For Jack, this wasn't his experience. Tax consolidation services may not offer anything that individuals can't do themselves. The IRS offers the same debt resolution scenarios to anyone who contacts them for help, and who has the knowledge to ask the right questions. You must be persistent, honest and make a sincere effort to change areas of your life that have not worked in the past. If past tax debt is your problem, take the first step that Jack took. It will all get better from there.

My techniques, which outlined the rudiments of communication, organization, and the benefits of being an entrepreneur, were a big part of his turnaround. For the first time, he had communicated his problem. He contacted the IRS and outlined his income, his expenses, and they worked with him to create a monthly payment plan that he could manage. No matter what your situation, if you start paying something, it will open the doors to a different relationship with the IRS. In communicating with the IRS, have common courtesy that you would have with anyone else. If you contact the IRS and get someone that isn't very helpful, be polite and end the call. Call back again, and chances are you will find someone with compassion and knowledge, that can help you.

After he mediated a payment arrangement, he felt more at ease. The IRS was going to help him by only taking reasonable payments. He was no longer obsessed with the worry of what the IRS would do to him. This allowed him to focus on more sources of income, and created a synergy of good emotion and energy to achieve more.

Jack organized all of his debt. He used the Debt Eliminator Chart and Wealth Creation Chart to track all of his expenses. He restructured his tax debt and moved to filing tax returns on time, with no penalties. Jack was also able to claim a large series of deductions that are associated with his professional pursuits. His tax debt is now down by eight thousand dollars and it's all because of these simple techniques.

Jack realized that he had always been a sole proprietor. He had spent over ten years playing music, buying equipment, driving to practice, and making endless sacrifices, not realizing this was all a deduction. The equipment, the mileage, and the cost associated with his business. As he continued moving in this positive direction, he started seeking more work. All the anxiety and worry associated with his tax debt turned into energy when he didn't have to worry about the IRS anymore. He sought out other opportunities and worked a second part-time job. This additional job became another element of the sole proprietor qualification he had achieved. As a sole proprietor, Jack was able to deduct expenses associated with his travel, lodging, meals, and entertainment. These were all costs that he had been paying out of his own pocket for at least a decade.

If you are a real estate owner I have a great tip that can save you thousands, right now! This works for both residential and commercial real estate owners. Across the country, the market has been on a downward spiral. But don't panic, there may be a possible benefit from all of this. One of my clients was getting solicitation letters in the mail, offering to lower his residential property taxes. It was from a company that offered, on your behalf, to contact the tax assessor's office and get your property taxes lowered and/or a tax refund for overpayment. Being that this is usually an easy process, I advised my client to contact the tax assessor's office himself. You can write or call your tax assessor and ask to have your property reassessed. There is often a good chance you have overpaid your taxes. It is best if you have three comparable housing values in your area that are lower than the assessment value of your property. They may have been overcharging you for an assessed value that is too high. You could be due a refund for overpaying on your property taxes! You can also ask for a tax appeal that requires a reappraisal of the property. One of my clients who had a commercial real estate investment was able to apply this technique. She had decided to hire an attorney's office to handle her appeal, since her property was commercial, and would involve a bit more work. She received some news that brought her instant cash! The attorney's office argued that the property value had dropped significantly, due to loss of rent collected, and the drop in the economy. In just a short period of time, she received a refund of $55,000. The attorneys are now looking into past years to see if she is due more in refunds, for overpaying at a higher assessed value. With very little effort she received a large refund. You could be due some money for overpaying taxes. I suggest looking into it, right away!

Here is a quick tip with your taxes, which will allow you to get an instant pay raise without having to go in and ask your boss for one. Consider changing the number of withholdings on your Employee's Withholding Allowance Certificate. If you decide to increase the number of allowances you will see a raise in your paycheck.

In conclusion, whether you choose to tackle your taxes on your own or hire a qualified professional, do your due diligence to make sure you are getting all deductions and benefits available to you. If you would like more tax information visit my website.

Solution Summary

11: GET YOUR HEAD OUT OF THE SAND: TAX DEBT

- Keep current with your taxes.

- Organization and structure of your finances allows for identifying deductions.

- When hiring tax professionals interview them carefully, ask for rates, references and guarantees.

- Review the amount of dependants you are claiming. This simple change could result in an instant pay raise.

- Accuracy is crucial with your taxes.

- Review past tax returns and make sure you haven't overlooked deductions - learn to maximize your deductions.

- Compare basic standard deductions - with itemized deductions this could save you more money.

- Avoid penalties and fees.

- Communication with the IRS can resolve tax issues and create a payment plan or installment agreement.

- Do not default on your payment agreement with the IRS.

- If you have financial hardship, consider an offer in compromise. This is a lump sum payment option to the IRS, and if they accept this type of payment it releases you of your debt.

- The statute of limitations on tax debt is ten years. If the IRS is unable to collect within ten years, the tax debt expires.

- If you own real estate and the property value has decreased you can contact the tax assessor's office to request a property tax reassessment. This could lower your current tax bill and you can possibly apply for a refund of overpaid property taxes.

Good Bedside Manner

MEDICAL DEBT

Debt can be overwhelming at any time in a person's life. Medical illness can seem the worst of all and send you or your loved ones into a complete financial nightmare. This chapter is designed to help you find solutions to what may seem like a financial devastation. In so many cases medical debt can sneak up on you or it comes completely out of left field. You weren't counting on having the kind of medical bills that you have incurred, and at the same time you're also dealing with the emotional stress of illness, injury or healing. Please know you will get through this and there is help. You are not alone.

Most average Americans who have severe medical debt just happened to get sick one day. It was completely unexpected. The difficult part is that their insurance didn't cover a majority of their expenses and left them in devastation. The co-payments, the deductibles and huge bills for uncovered items; seems to be a list that just keeps piling up. The sad part of this is when you really need the insurance help and coverage, in many cases, it's just not there. For a good part of our life we pay for medical insurance. Later on, when catastrophe strikes, we don't have the protection we thought we had, or in some cases, no protection at all. An illness can lead to job loss, and subsequently, losing insurance coverage and income.

And this is when a person is most vulnerable.

A Harvard Medical School report shows, "illness often leads to financial catastrophe through loss of income as well as high medical bills." David U. Himmelstein, M.D., Professor of Medicine at Harvard Medical School states, "disability insurance and paid sick leave are crucial to survival of a serious illness." Studies have proven that approximately half of the debtors in bankruptcy courts are due to medical circumstances. The good news is that you now have the resources and information to help you avoid this type of hardship. When illness or hospitalization strikes you or your family, the first place to start is with your insurance company and making sure you have the coverage that you need. I know it is very tempting to ignore the medical bills when they start coming in. They can become so overwhelming, but please do not succumb to the behavior of ignoring your bills. Ignoring your bills is one of the worst things you can do, causing you more stress than necessary. Hospitals and providers, in most cases, will negotiate with you if you contact them immediately. I will explain more about this later in the chapter.

First, lets take a look at errors and how to find, correct, and avoid them. Often, there are many errors made with medical bills in regards to the insurance company covering a procedure or visit, or not covering the procedure or visit. This is where you need to get involved. Sometimes things can be overlooked, denied, or get tossed aside because of a simple code error. If a doctor codes the procedure or treatment incorrectly - if the number is off by only one number, or there is a code that is a similar procedure, it can make a huge difference between being covered or not covered. I suggest knowing your medical insurance coverage thoroughly before going to the doctor. Ask your doctor to do his best to work in the parameters of your insurance coverage. At the time of service make sure the doctor's office is coding your visit or procedure correctly. Remember, questions about your insurance coverage are just a phone call away. You can call your insurance company, or at the time of service at your doctor's office, ask them to verify what your insurance company covers for your visit or procedure. If you are savvy and know your coverage, you can do your best to make sure you are not hit with any surprise charges later. I suggest reviewing your medical bills very carefully and checking for any errors. Even if you are covered by insurance and have correspondence coming from the insurance company, there still may be errors coming from the insurance company or provider.

At the time of service your doctor should give you a receipt (if they do not, be sure to ask for one for your records). The doctor's office will usually follow up with a statement mailed to you at a later date. That statement will usually contain your service and what the insurance company has covered, or is not covering and why. When the insurance company pays the bill or portion of your bill that is covered by your insurance policy to the doctor, in most cases the insurance company will send you something that looks like a bill but it is not. It may be called an explanation of benefits and will contain an outline of the payment history. It will show you what the insurance company is paying for, what they are not paying for, and should give you an explanation of why or why they are not paying. Keep in mind that not all doctors send statements and not all insurance companies send an explanation of benefits. You may receive one or the other, or both.

As I mentioned, usually your doctor's office will send you a bill or statement. The statement will show you how much the doctor has billed your insurance company and for what services. If your insurance company has not paid yet, it is not necessary for you to make a payment until after the insurance company pays your doctor. Many people make the mistake of immediately paying this statement/bill in full, while the insurance company also pays the bill. It can end up being double or overpaid, and with all the confusion and paper work it could be overlooked and you never get a refund. This is why it's best to wait for the insurance company to pay first. You can always call them to find out the status of any payment. When the insurance company pays the bill, at that time you will be responsible for paying the remaining balance to the doctor.

There are some items you will want to look for and confirm to be sure they are correct on your statements and explanation of benefits. Be sure the dates and description of services match. If you find any discrepancies, contact your doctor's office first. If you find that your insurance company is not covering something or if you have a question about the balance due, contact your insurance company and ask them about your benefits. When contacting anyone with debt or billing, keep very extensive records, recording dates, names of people you have talked to, times of phone calls, results, etc. If a doctor's bill or statement comes with a 60 days past due and your insurance company has still not paid, contact your insurance company immediately.

If you do have an injury, hospitalization, or chronic illness, set up a file system either on the computer or via hand written paperwork. Back up all files by keeping organized records of all of your medical transactions, including service receipts, statements, and explanation of benefits. You will want to have an organized system in place where you have access to all of your paperwork, in case any questions should come up. This type of system can help alleviate stress in dealing with your paper work.

On your explanation of benefits the following are some categories that you are going to be looking for. The **member** is the person who has the health insurance. The **claim number** is a number that is usually assigned by the insurance company. This number is necessary and can be helpful if you are contacting the insurance company about questions. A **plan number** is a specific number relating to the **member's** specific plan. **Member ID** is usually the number that your insurance company assigns to the member for identification. **Date Paid** is the date that the insurance company made a payment to the provider. **Plan Sponsor** is usually the member's employer or an entity that helps pay for the insurance. **Patient ID** is the number that is assigned to identify the patient by the insurance company. The **Patient ID** could differ from the member ID, meaning, the member is the one having the insurance, and the **Patient ID** is the one covered under the member's plan. Keep in mind that it is not usual for the **Patient ID** and the member to be the same. **Patient** is usually the person's name who was provided with the healthcare service. **Relationship** is the patient to the member relationship (i.e. daughter, son, dependent, etc).

Now, let's go into more detail as to the specifics on the charges. You may see some categories listed, such as **provider name**. This is the healthcare company providing services to the patient. It may be a physician, a hospital, physical therapist, etc. A **Procedure Code** can be numbers with coding on a separate page with an explanation of those codes, or it may be spelled out in words such as office visit, physical therapy, etc. The negotiated savings column is where they state the savings that you are receiving through your insurance companies policy. They have negotiated discounted fees per their contract. **Remark Code** is a code that tells the reason why the insurance company has declined payment. Often times you may find an NA (not applicable) or another code, because they do cover the charge, **deductible, co-payment**, or **co-insurance**. This is where they list the amount that the patient owes in regards to their deductible, co-payment, or co-insurance. **Charges not covered** are self-explanatory. This is a column that may become the patient/member's responsibility. The total amount charged is the amount that the healthcare provider is charging the insurance company for the service. **Date of service** is just as stated – the date that the patient/member received services. **Total Amount Payable** is the amount that the insurance company has agreed to pay the healthcare provider. It usually is a reflection of the total, less negotiated savings, deductibles, co-payments and co-insurance amounts. The check amount is the amount of the check given to the health provider by the insurance company. Ultimately, this amount should be the same as the total amount payable. The **Member responsibility** is the amount that the member is responsible for paying to the healthcare provider.

The following will give you some ideas of how you can cross check your statements for errors. Every statement is different, however, they should list the date of service, the date of the statement, the patient's name, the description of the service, charge for the service, and any adjustment for the service and the payments made. The first place to start is to make sure that all information coincides between the two documents. One document should be coming from the service provider's office and the other coming from the insurance company. If you have been denied a service, try contacting your insurance company so you can get a more in depth explanation. Different insurance companies may have several codes and rules. By contacting your doctor, healthcare provider, or hospital, you can look more in depth into the coding. This can make all the difference in the world whether they will cover a service or you are denied coverage. This can possibly cost you thousands of dollars, so it is well worth spending the time making the contacts necessary to assure that everything is filed properly before ever paying any outstanding bills. It's worth the time and effort to make sure the coding is accurate in helping you receive the highest financial benefit.

After your insurance company pays your bills if you find you are in a state of financial hardship due to your illness, consider contacting the healthcare providers directly. You may be amazed at how they will work with you and rates can be negotiated. I will get more into this later. After you are sure all information is correct between your statements and explanation of benefits, you've spoken to your doctor and your insurance company, and you are positive that everything is paid, now you want to evaluate your entire debt and amounts owed to each and every health provider or hospital. Contact each one individually through their accounting department, having all your information at your fingertips. Also, befriend the healthcare professional office or billing department on the phone. I suggest always being endearing and personable. Sometimes you have to be vulnerable and give them your whole story and how this is a devastating hardship. Proceed without any anger or hostility and know this person could possibly help you. Ask if there is anything you can do to set up a payment plan and possibly reduce any of the debt. Mention that it is too overwhelming for you and you don't want to have to claim bankruptcy. Remember, if you claim bankruptcy there is a good chance they will collect nothing on the debt. If you are offering a payment plan they will at least collect something.

I can confidently report from personal experiences with my clients, reduction or payment plans happen quite often when getting to the right person and using the right communication techniques. So, if you do get a reduction or a payment plan, you will want to make your payments every month in a timely manner. If for some reason you can't make a payment, they may take the benefit away from you. However, I have found when you keep in communication with your healthcare provider on a regular basis, they will work with you as long as you pay them something every month. Sometimes this can be a bit time consuming and feel like it's taking a hit on your pride. However, the outcome can be extremely rewarding.

Remember the story I shared with you about my client, Dawn, in the "Plastic Jungle" chapter? Dawn had great success with extensively reducing her credit card debt by taking my suggestion of communication, communication, and even more communication. She would tell them her entire story about how she was a manicurist. She had an unexpected fall that had given her an injury on her thumb that put her into a stressful debt situation. She had to have surgery and her medical expenses were adding up, due to the loss of income during her down time from work. Remember how Dawn would befriend the person on the phone? She would tell her whole story. She ended up also having great success with using the same technique with her doctors.

Unfortunately, Dawn came to me and became a client after she had incurred her medical expenses. She had already put a majority of her expenses on her credit cards, and so we worked on getting her interest payments reduced. We did have much success. However, there are many reasons I don't advise putting your medical debts on credit cards. You will have interest attached to your credit card, which could raise the amount due by a substantial amount. Another reason is if you transfer your medical debt to a credit card this could possibly affect your eligibility for Medicaid. Some of your medical costs can be deducted from your gross income to determine your Medicaid eligibility. When your medical debt is on a credit card it may not qualify as a medical debt any longer, by putting your debt on a credit card you risk changing its medical status. You also may affect your eligibility for outside help. In her case, credit card debt may have been completely unnecessary. Nine times out of ten when you have unexpected illness, sometimes your doctors, hospitals, anesthesiologist, physical therapist, etc, will work out a no interest payment plan for you. Dawn actually did this. She had a bill for $2,500 with her anesthesiologist and she called and appealed her situation with them for help. She asked if they would work out a payment plan, and they were agreeable and willing to do it. She was able to make payments of $100 a month. Just call you doctor's office or hospital and talk to the billing department and inquire about payment plans. As in Dawn's case, if the hospital or doctor's office doesn't offer settling your debt or you can't afford to settle, they might let you make monthly payments. Just ask if you can make $25, $50 or $100 payments each month. Patients who lack adequate healthcare coverage will usually be able to work out some kind of arrangement.

There is another option. If after you have done everything to make a payment plan, check inaccuracies, etc, you feel it's still too much for you, I suggest looking into a claims assistant professional. Claims Assistance Professionals (CAP) help individuals and families dealing with medical claims. They will document, monitor and submit all elements of an insurance claim while teaching patients the best benefits and options.

People can get overwhelmed when dealing with health care provider hospital insurance companies. As you can see from the list above, with so many categories on it, it can send you into a tailspin not knowing which end is up. When you are dealing with a claims assistant professional the goal is to make sure that your stress is eliminated and that you don't overpay. In so many cases consumers end up doing just that. What happens is you may get a bill in the mail that states that the payment is due within 30 days or they're going to turn it over to collection. People get so nervous that they just pay the bill. Then what happens is the insurance company also pays the healthcare provider or hospital. So now you will have a credit sitting in some account, and good luck trying to get your credit back. This is why I say, even before you decide to use a CAP make sure that you understand your bill, and that you are charged correctly and do not overpay. My suggestion is to always try to negotiate for reduced rates. You may be able to handle this on your own. If it gets to be too much you do have the option of hiring a CAP, who is a trained professional that can negotiate your medical bills on your behalf. There are some cases of $500,000 in medical bills where a CAP, on behalf of the patient, has been able to get the charges down to less than ten dollars (according to J. MacDonald, Bankrate.com, in a segment on ABC 7 about managed medical bills). A CAP's fee usually varies and they typically charge by the hour. When considering the relief of stress and complete medical bill reduction, it's well worth the price of the ticket.

Many times insurance companies are such big companies that we just trust their billing procedures to be correct. After all, they are the big guys. Do not just take any bill/statement, medical or otherwise, at face value. There are often errors that randomly occur.

When medical bills become so overwhelming and pull people down to where they think they will never get out of that hole, many consider bankruptcy. Before you decide to go down that road there is another option. This can be a successful way in reducing your debt by thousands of dollars, and it doesn't require you to take out an outside loan. If you are in financial hardship over medical bills a debt settlement service may be the right choice for you. They can make arrangements with your creditors to lower the outstanding balances or the amounts owed. Debt settlement services can possibly reduce your debts by over half and more. The key is that medical institutions or the creditors would much rather accept a settlement with some type of payment than having you file for bankruptcy. If you file for bankruptcy they have the possibility of losing all the money or having to wait years to collect. There are some standards for debt settlement. Usually, if your debt is at least $10,000 or more you will get better results. You must also have some kind of income to be able to keep up with the payment or settlement plan.

Think outside the box for getting help from outside sources. There are many places where you can find help, whether it's family, charitable foundations, churches, community groups, and civic groups. All of these can often be of assistance.

There is a non-profit foundation called Patient Advocate Foundation (PAF) that can be a great resource for people with debts associated with medical conditions. On their website they state, "PAF seeks to empower patients to take control of their healthcare. Case managers work with patients to discover local, state, and federal programs that provide assistance for their individual needs. If you or someone you know needs assistance with their insurer, employer, and/or creditor regarding insurance, job retention and/or debt crisis matters relative to their diagnosis of a life threatening or debilitating diseases, please call at 1-800-532-5274." PAF have been around since 1996 and their website is www.patientadvocate.org.

A large number of hospitals have financial aid departments or charitable aid available through their billing and collections office. When discussing your bill with the billing department request any information they might have regarding financial aid and the requirements.

To qualify for financial aid a majority of hospitals have limits they place on your income. Typically this limit is based on your annual salary, which can't exceed 200% of the federal poverty level. Here is a guide to refer to:

Family Unit Size	100% of Poverty	110% of Poverty	125% of Poverty	150% of Poverty	175% of Poverty	185% of Poverty	200% of Poverty
1	$ 9,800	$10,780	$12,250	$14,700	$17,150	$18,130	$19,600
2	$13,200	$14,520	$16,500	$19,800	$23,100	$24,420	$26,400
3	$16,600	$18,260	$20,750	$24,900	$29,050	$30,710	$33,200
4	$20,000	$22,000	$25,000	$30,000	$35,000	$37,000	$40,000
5	$23,400	$25,740	$29,250	$35,100	$40,950	$43,290	$46,800
6	$26,800	$29,480	$33,500	$40,200	$46,900	$49,580	$53,600
7	$30,200	$33,220	$37,750	$45,300	$52,850	$55,870	$60,400
8	$33,600	$36,960	$42,000	$50,400	$58,800	$62,160	$67,200

For all states (except Alaska and Hawaii) and for the District of Columbia

For family units with more than 8 members, add $3,400 for each additional person at 100% of poverty, $3,740 at 110 %, $4,250 at 125%, $5,100 at 150%, $5,950 at 175%, $6,290 at 185% and $6,800 at 200% of poverty.

Note: For optional use in FFY 2006 and mandatory use in FFY 2007 some states may be using poverty levels published in the Federal Register January 2007, that are optional for FFY 2007.

If your income doesn't qualify you for financial aid, but a medical disaster is costing you a large percentage of your income, the financial aid department may be willing to cover some of your bills. The medical debt to income for most hospitals is 30%. If you are exceeding 30% of your income in medical debt most financial aid departments will pay for the portion of your bills over 30%. A stipulation with getting aid from a hospital's financial aid department is the exhaustion of all other available resources. The list starts with your insurance provider then you must apply for medical benefits, and finally, if bills still remain, the hospital's financial aid department will review your application.

To apply for medical financial aid, check with your hospital for information about their financial aid department. Start with their billing office to see what kind of financial aid they provide, and the contact information for that office. They will request proof of income for approximately one year preceding your medical services. This will be used to calculate your annual salary. They will also request a list of your assets; this includes your checking and savings account balances. They will also look to see if you have certificates of deposit (CDs), Individual Retirement Accounts (IRA), trust funds, and other investments in real estate besides your primary residence. The financial aid department will typically request a statement from your financial institution detailing your assets. Finally, if you don't have a job or assets, they will require you to sign an affidavit proving this.

The following story is about my client Diane who is 53 years old and lives in Albany, New York. Due to being sick numerous times throughout her employment, she is no longer able to work as a librarian. She was recently terminated from her job and cannot afford to pay her medical bills. Meanwhile, she is responsible for taking care of her six-year-old granddaughter. As you can imagine, this was creating enormous stress for her causing her to worry about how she was going to financially help her daughter and grandchild. During this process she continued to seek employment but was uncertain how long this would take. She had three potential jobs offers lined up but she was still worried about how she was going to cover all of her bills, and she was falling behind. She was concerned that even if she did find work, most employers don't start medical coverage until after a certain period of time of employment with the company. I tried to assure Diane that her situation was not hopeless and I was going to work with her to find a solution. I had informed her that she could try to apply for assistance in paying off her medical bills. There are organizations that will help people with medical debts, including various charitable organizations. I had reminded her that she could apply for her state's medical insurance program. With these programs people can find help to mediate their medical debts. If you have notes and have informed your company of your illness you may be able to utilize your state's legal assistance program. In our search we found a local charitable organization that gave her aid with her medical bills. I am happy to report that Diane now has a job and she had her medical bills reduced with the aid of local assistance.

Whatever your situation, always remember there are options and resources available to help you that you may not have considered. Sometimes it's as simple as a phone call away.

Solution Summary

12: GOOD BEDSIDE MANNER: MEDICAL DEBT

- If illness strikes, start with your insurance company for help.
- Know your medical insurance coverage thoroughly before going to the doctor.
- Do not ignore your bills.
- Negotiate with hospitals and service providers immediately for lower rates.
- Simple code errors by doctors create billing errors and higher fees that can be passed on to the patient.
- Request that your doctor works within your insurance parameters.
- Review your medical bills.
- Make sure you receive a receipt at the time of your visit.
- If a statement is mailed, review it immediately for accuracy.
- Immediately review the explanation of benefits from your insurance provider, do not overpay and be clear on who will be paying your doctor's office bill.
- If there are discrepancies contact your insurance company immediately.
- Document names, dates, and the time of the people you talk to.
- If you receive a bill from your doctor that is 60 days past due and your insurance was billed, contact your insurance company immediately.
- Create a filing system and backup all your documentation on computer or handwritten paperwork. An organized system is crucial to resolve discrepancies.
- If you have difficulty making payments on a payment plan, communicate immediately with your service provider for options.
- Sometimes your provider will work out a no interest payment plan if you are experiencing financial hardship.

- Avoid putting medical debt on a credit card, as your debt can spiral out of control and it can alter your chances to qualify for Medicaid.

- After you have exhausted all other measures, consider hiring a claims assistant professional (CAP). They will document, monitor and submit all elements of an insurance claims and have specialized knowledge. Also, they can sometimes reduce bills significantly.

- Before you file bankruptcy for medical debt, first consider working with debt consolidation company.

- Check with hospitals to see if they have financial aid available through their billing and collections offices.

- If you are exceeding 30% of your income in medical debt, most financial aid departments will pay a portion of your bills over 30%.

XIII
Chapter

The Young and the Reckless

STUDENT LOANS

This chapter is lovingly titled, "The Young and the Reckless," because all too often young people do not have the knowledge or experience in dealing with finances. After graduating high school they are suddenly expected to know how to handle finances, and living on their own for the first time. Most are coming from homes where their parents paid for everything. Now they have to work with budgets and develop their own credit, as well as handle bills and make decisions on getting loans. Usually we are not taught in school how to handle our finances, ever! Parents are usually busy dealing with their own issues and all the work that goes into raising a family, and so finances are usually not taught at home, either. Where do we learn how to make good financial decisions? Where do we learn one of the most important things in life that will affect us everyday? In most cases, we learn about personal finances from trial and error. Some people have good instincts, some do not, some are lucky, and some are not so lucky. Some will imitate how their parents handle their finances, which can be a good thing, or a very bad idea. It can be very overwhelming if young people have not had some preparation, knowledge, and tools to make the best, in many cases, life-altering decisions.

We hear unfortunate stories all the time about young people getting in over their heads with debt. It can be from credit cards, student loans or personal loans. The resource does not matter, what does matter is the feeling of being overwhelmed to the point in some cases of taking their own lives. This is so unnecessary and infuriating to me. My goal is to educate as many young people as possible and to have parents be proactive with their kids, and teach good financial habits so we never hear those stories. I am going to give you information to help you make good decisions with student loans. After reading "Debt a Good Thing?" you should have more insight into student loans and education. Reading the "Alter Ego" chapter will help you with creating your credit identity.

The following story about one of my clients may sound all too familiar. The good news is there is a solution. Robert is a sophomore in college, majoring in information technology at the University of Phoenix. He had money that he had saved from a job in high school and also gifts from graduation. His freshman year he lived on campus and didn't plan to move off campus until he graduated. He ran into some financial difficulty and felt he was no longer able to pay for his education. He didn't have anyone that could help him pay his tuition. His parents had a lot of debt of their own and weren't able to help him. In order to continue going to school he had to take out two student loans for about $5,000 to pay for books, tuition, a laptop, and other school supplies. He had a part-time job as a web designer, but the amount he made barely covered his bills and left very little to pay his student loans. Along with his heavy school load, he was in the beginning stages of starting a web design company, and getting business referrals from friends and family. He anticipated bringing in about five new clients a month, but he didn't want to take out more in loans to fund his business. First, I applauded Robert for the amazing character and ambition it took to finance his education on his own. I reminded him that it might seem impossible at first, but what was important was to just keep working hard. I suggested that he seek financial aid, and apply for a grant instead of Stafford loans. I also suggested he check into his university's work-study program. Many universities offer programs that will allow the student to work in their field while sometimes still getting credit for working. Earning the extra money and credit at the same time really helps with the finances. This would allow Robert the opportunity to work and earn a steady income, while learning and gaining experience within his major.

This next story may be more familiar to some of you who are closer to graduating. Laura is a 32-year old married mother of twins. She contacted me three months before she was planning to graduate from college. She was worried about managing her student loan payments. She had spoken to several other students that had graduated with student loan debts, and what she was hearing wasn't good. So, needless to say, Laura was in a bit of a panic. Many of them were having problems making the payments and she was concerned about just finishing college and already having negative items appearing on her credit report. Some of her friends had payments as high as $400 - $500 a month! Her husband was very supportive, but she was still worried. According to the U.S. Department of Education, if a student takes out a direct Stafford Loan, their first payment is due six months after graduation. If you take out a Federal Perkins Loan the repayment for the loan starts nine months after you graduate. The U.S. Department of Education granted the delay for loan repayment to start because once a student graduates, it sometimes takes a while for his/her first offer of employment. I informed her that if for some reason she isn't able to find employment, the U.S. Department of Education would work with her to come up with a payment plan. Once you graduate, after the six or nine month grace period, you will have to fill out a payment form. Every month, your options of repayment will be based on your current financial situation. You can imagine, knowing this information put her more at ease. In many cases, you just need to know your rights and exercise them.

Another client of mine, Susan, is from Jacksonville, North Carolina. She seemed to have it all, so many great joys in life happening all at once. To top off everything, she was in the process of transferring to another school. She works full-time as a retail sales clerk and in six months was planning on marrying her fiancé. She had recently given birth to her first child and was trying to save as much money as possible. On a very tight budget, she was trying to save enough money for a private wedding. It wasn't going to be a huge wedding, however, nothing too small either. Yes, you guessed it; Susan is quite the ambitious one. She wanted to have the wedding she had always dreamed of, or at least close to it. Because of her tight budget, she was even considering looking for a second part-time or another full-time job to supplement her income. Her fiancé already had a full-time and a part-time job, and they still weren't able to keep up with their bills, even with all three incomes coming in every month. Before she had met her fiancé, she had managed to get herself $10,384 in debt from overspending. And this was on top of her student loans, which required that she start making payments within a few months. Susan felt in over her head. In the midst of all her joy with her upcoming wedding, baby, and new career, she really did not know what to do. She wasn't sure how she would be able to afford to make payments while she was still in school, and wasn't going to graduate for a couple more years. First we had her work on her "Debt Elimination Chart" and created a plan for her. She had to scale the wedding down a bit, but she was still going to have an amazing day and was very excited about it. Susan was learning how to prioritize her financial goals so it would become more manageable for her. I also told her to contact the U.S. Department of Education and explain her situation. I advised her to check with her school's financial aid office for a deferment form. Usually a financial aid officer at your school will provide evidence that you are still attending college, and they will be able to mediate with the U.S. Department of Education on your behalf. I am happy to report that Susan is on her way to creating her new life with her family while having peace of mind.

Choosing the right loan and debt management program can be critical to your future. There are many options for you to choose from. Read on as you are given information on some of the various loans available to you, and make the best decision for your specific future. Also know, that if handled properly, education can be good debt. Look at the ROI for your education, this can help you make a good decision.

FEDERAL AND PRIVATE LOANS

Federal student loans are the largest loans provided for education. Anyone can get these loans and their terms are better than private loans. Prioritize the process of seeking student loans and apply for all the federal funding you can before applying for private loans.

Just about every student is eligible to receive funds through federal student loans. Best of all, they don't base the loans on your financial records or your credit score. The interest rates are lower because the government sets them. There is also some payment flexibility, including the possibility of delaying making payments, as well as extended repayment schedules. After school completion they provide a grace period before payments are due to allow you to secure employment and to get on your feet.

VARIOUS TYPES OF FEDERAL STUDENT AID

Pell Grant:

The first place to seek financial aid should always be grants, since grants do not have to be repaid. They are typically awarded to undergraduate students who have not attained their bachelors or professional degrees. Pell grants can be added to federal financial aid from other sources, and private sources, as well.

It is capped at $4,731 for the 2008 – 2009 award year. The maximum award can change each year, depending on funding. The amount of your award is based on your financial needs, the cost to attend school, whether you are a full-time or part-time student, and if you are going to be attending a university for a full academic year.

Distribution of Pell grant funds is done by your school either paid directly to you by check, applied to your school costs, or a combination of the two. Your school will notify you in writing to inform you of the amount of your award, and then you will be paid. Universities are required to disburse funds at least once per term.

PLUS Loans:

The Federal Family Education Loan (FFEL) Program and the William D. Ford Federal Direct Loan offer parents the ability to help their children if the child is a dependent and an undergraduate student. To apply, parents must complete a Direct PLUS Loan application and promissory note available from your school. Once the application is submitted the school will review it and complete its portion of the application. They will then send it to a lender for evaluation. Unlike Stafford Loans, a credit check is required to receive PLUS loans. If credit scores and general credit standing are in question, you may be able to ask a relative or friend to be an endorser on the loan. Like a co-signer, an endorser of a PLUS loan guarantees the loan if you are not able to repay the debt.

Federal Stafford Loan:

Federal Stafford Loans are student loans available to enrolled students in accredited American Universities. As part of the Higher Education Act of 1965, the Stafford Loans were created to help students. The U.S. Government guarantees the loans, in the event that the student defaults. This means the loans have more lenient requirements, better interest rates, and don't require a credit report. Stafford loans are named after United States Senator, Robert Stafford. His work in higher education was renowned and eventually spawned the renaming of the Federal Guaranteed Student Loan program in 1988.

Based on the student's financial situation, Stafford loans come as either subsidized or unsubsidized. To qualify for a subsidized Stafford loan you need to meet the financial requirements.

STAFFORD LOAN LIMITS

Dependent Students	Annual Loan Limits
First Year	$5,500 ($3,500 subsidized/$2,000 unsubscribed)
Second Year	$6,500 ($4,500 subsidized/$2,000 unsubsidized)
Third Year and Beyond	$7,500 ($5,500 subsidized/$2,000 unsubsidized)
Independent Students	**Annual Loan Limits**
First Year	$9,500 ($3,500 subsidized/$6,000 unsubsidized)
Second Year	$10,500 ($4,500 subsidized/$6,000 unsubsidized)
Third Year Through Degree	$12,500 ($5,500 subsidized/$7,000 unsubsidized)
Graduate or Professional	$20,500 ($8,500 subsidized/$12,000 unsubsidized)
Lifetime Limits	
Undergraduate Dependent	$31,000 (Up to $23,000 may be subsidized)
Undergraduate Independent	$57,500
Graduate or Professional	$138,500 (Up to $65,00 may be subsidized) or $224,000 (for Health Professionals)

STAFFORD LOAN RATES CALCULATIONS TABLE

Stafford Loan Date of Distribution	Rate Classification	Interest Rate (Subsidized)	Interest Rate (Unsubscribed)	Current Rate
Before July 1, 1998	Variable	91-Day T-Bill + 3.1%	91-Day T-Bill + 3.1%	8.02%
July 1, 1998 to June 30, 2006	Variable	91-Day T-Bill + 2.3%	91-Day T-Bill + 2.3%	7.22%
July 1, 2006 to June 30, 2008	Fixed	6.8%	6.8%	6.8%
July 1, 2008 to June 30, 2009	Fixed	6.0%	6.8%	6.8%
July 1, 2009 to June 30, 2010	Fixed	5.6%	6.8%	6.8%
July 1, 2010 to June 30, 2011	Fixed	4.5%	6.8%	6.8%
July 1, 2011 to June 30, 2012	Fixed	3.4%	6.8%	6.8%
July 1, 2012 to June 30, 2013	Fixed	6.8%	6.8%	6.8%

Source Stafford Loan

QUALIFYING FOR A STAFFORD LOAN

The FAFSA:

The FAFSA, or the Free Application for Federal Student Aid is a form used by students, and occasionally their parents to see if they qualify for federal student financial aid. The FAFSA is also the basis in many states for non-federal aid, as well. Based on a series of questions, the FAFSA calculates a student's eligibility by determining their EFC, or Expected Family Contribution. The EFC is calculated by ascertaining the size of the student's family, their income, assets, and number of their children in higher education, at the time. This doesn't include the parent's retirement or 401(k) plans, which for purposes of federal student loan applications are exempt. Even though most students are over eighteen when they begin attending college and are considered legal adults, the FAFSA does estimate some parent support and includes their assets in the application. There is an ongoing discussion as to why parent's assets are brought into play at all, considering they do not have an obligation to support their child's education. I'll leave that topic to the masses. At this point it is a part of the FAFSA.

Once the FAFSA is completed and submitted a SAR or Student Aid Report is generated, which summarizes the FAFSA responses. Reviewing the Student Aid Report is very important. Be sure that when you receive the report you review it thoroughly to ensure there aren't any errors. Also, as incorrect information on your credit report can adversely affect your ability to apply for and receive credit, errors on your FAFSA can result in processing delays or rejections of your application for financial aid.

It can take as little as a week to four weeks to receive your Student Aid Report. How quickly it is processed depends on whether you submitted the paper SAR forms by mail or if you submitted it online. As I stated above, review your SAR very carefully. Have a copy of your FAFSA handy so you can check it against the SAR to make sure all the information was processed correctly. Make sure all the financial information about your parents (if applicable) is correct, since this is used to calculate your Estimated Family Contribution.

If you haven't filed yet and notice errors in the saved version of your electronic submission, you can make changes using the Department of Education website where you can log on at www.fafsa.ed.gov. Once you have logged in there is an option to access your saved application where you can make changes. If you have submitted your FAFSA electronically and you realize you've made a mistake, you will have to wait until your Student Aid Report is sent to you to make any of the necessary corrections. Your options for making corrections to your SAR will relate directly to how you filed. If you filed electronically you will receive an e-mail notice with a secure link, allowing you to access you SAR online. If you are filing online, make sure to leave an e-mail address for correspondence. If you submitted your FAFSA via the paper form, you will have to wait for the SAR to be returned before you will be able to review it and discover any possible errors.

If you do discover errors on your SAR you can go to page four of your SAR and follow the instructions for correcting errors. Once you have made the corrections, contact your financial aid office. See if your school can submit the corrections electronically, or mail the corrections you have made to the address you will find on page four of the SAR.

If you filed electronically and need to make corrections you can do this on the U.S. Department of Education FAFSA website www. fafsa.ed.gov. You will need to have your Federal Aid Personal Identification Number (PIN). You cannot make any changes online to your FAFSA without a PIN. If you need a PIN you can get one by going to www.pin.ed.gov. When you log on the system it will also request that you create a password for later access. Requesting a PIN will take a few days to process. You should receive your PIN via email within three days. As a general rule with websites sending you critical information, make sure you check your junk folder and/ or spam folder for messages. If you don't typically do this you may want to check it before you process your PIN request. Be sure to delete all of the existing spam so you won't have to go through pages of it looking for the Department of Education letter that may have accidentally been placed there.

When your PIN arrives log back onto www.fafsa.ed.gov and you can proceed to make changes to your FAFSA. Look for the menu entitled, "Make Corrections to a Processed FAFSA." From there the process is self-explanatory. Follow the series of windows, making changes to whatever erroneous information exists in your FAFSA. Once you have made all the necessary changes don't leave the website until you receive a confirmation. You may be prompted to have a parent sign the electronic confirmation if you are a dependent. Your parent has the option to sign the form electronically or print the signature page and send via mail. Remember, always follow procedures very closely. Follow-up is crucial. Pay close attention to all instructions, document the name, time and date of any verbal conversation you have, print out PDF copies of all website confirmation pages, and don't assume anything. Everyone makes mistakes, even computers. It is in your best interest to follow up and keep as much detailed information as possible.

Some FAFSA applications will be selected for verification. If the first page of your SAR has the message, "you will be asked by your school(s) to provide copies of certain financial documents," your application has been selected for verification.

FAFSA verification is another reason you want to make sure that your FAFSA is filed accurately and completely. Verification is determined by the U.S. Department of Education. It is based on the criteria of: random selection, your estimated financial information, if some portion of the FAFSA was incomplete, and if inconsistencies were discovered in your FAFSA. If you are selected for verification you will need to complete the Federal Student Aid Programs Verification Worksheet. The quicker you respond and submit the verification form the quicker you will be able to get funding.

For Assistance with FAFSA Corrections contact: The Federal Student Aid Information Center at 1-800-433-3243. You can also contact them to check your application status, request a four-page paper SAR (if you filed electronically and didn't receive one), or to change an address or add and/or delete a school via phone.

PRIVATE STUDENT LOANS

Career Training Loan:

Once again, unlike federal student loans, private student loans do require credit checks and have interest rates that fluctuate based on how good the applicant's credit score is. The Career Training Loan not only rewards good credit with better interest rates, but also allows the borrower to use the funds for both tuition and education based expenses. Other benefits of this loan include access through online account management on the web, available 24 hours a day and 7 days a week. Another noteworthy benefit is the feature that allows the request to release a co-signer after 24 consecutive on-time monthly payments, meaning, the Career Training Loan also rewards the borrower for maintaining a strong payment record. This loan has no aggregate loan limit. Loan fees are typically 0-8%.

Repayment options for this loan include the standard repayment, which allows you to make balanced monthly payments of principal and interest and a minimum monthly payment of $30 per month.

The second option, the interest-only repayment allows you to make payments towards only the interest during your attendance in school, and then changing to the standard repayment of principal and interest after you have completed your education.

The $10 deferred repayment option allows the borrower the ability to defer payments for up to 12 months, stipulating that the borrower cannot exceed the estimated graduation date on the application. During the deferment you are required to make a $10 monthly payment, which will be applied to the interest on your account that accrues during the deferment. Once the deferment ends you will start the basic repayment of principal and interest.

Continuing Education Loan:

The Continuing Education Loan is a loan offered to students that has prerequisites that are similar to the Career Training Loan. The borrower must be a permanent resident or United States citizen and have established credit. The college or university must be accredited or licensed by the department of education in their corresponding state. The features also include more beneficial fees and rates for better credit ratings. There is also an option if your credit is somewhat challenged to be able to have a co-signer on the loan with you. If the co-signer has good to excellent credit this can offset your credit issues in the loan application. Also identical to the Career Training Loan you can release the co-signer for excellent payment history. Twenty-four consecutive, on-time payments of principal and interest allows the borrower to request that the co-signer be removed from the loan. Funds can be applied to tuition and education-related expenses. Combined billing through Sallie Mae means that any other loans you apply for and receive through Sallie Mae will all be managed from the same billing statement. This is a great asset in simplifying the billing and tracking process so you don't accidentally miss a payment by forgetting about one of your loans. Additionally, they offer no prepayment penalties and online management 24/7, including the life of loan servicing from Sallie Mae.

The Continuing Education Loan has no aggregate loan limit, it rewards properly managed credit, and generally, good credit worthiness. Loan fees are typically 0 - 8% and a borrower can take up to 15 years to repay the loan. Repayment options for this loan include the standard repayment, which allows you to make balanced monthly payments of principal and interest, and a minimum monthly payment of $30 per month.

The second option, the interest-only repayment allows you to make payments towards the interest during your attendance in school, and then changing to the standard repayment of principal and interest after you have completed your education.

The $10 deferred repayment option allows the borrower the ability to defer payments for up to 12 months, stipulating that the borrower cannot exceed the estimated graduation date on the application. During the deferment you are required to make a $10 monthly payment, which will be applied to the interest on your account that accrues during the deferment. Once the deferment ends you will start the basic repayment of principal and interest.

Dentaloan Graduate Private Loan:

To be eligible for the Dentaloan Graduate Private Loan you must be a U.S. Citizen or permanent resident. You can also be a foreign borrower but you must have a creditworthy U.S. citizen or permanent resident as a co-signer. This is a key point. You must not have any student loans that are delinquent or in default. The features also include more beneficial fees and rates for better credit ratings. There is also an option if your credit is somewhat challenged to be able to have a co-signer on the loan with you. If the co-signer has good credit, this can offset your credit issues in the loan application. Also, if you have good credit history a co-signer may help you qualify for even lower interest rates. You can release the co-signer for excellent payment history. Twenty-four consecutive, on-time payments of principal and interest allows the borrower to request that the co-signer be removed from the loan. The funds can then be applied to tuition and education-related expenses. This loan offers combined billing through Sallie Mae, no prepayment penalties, 24/7 online management, including life of the loan servicing from Sallie Mae.

Signature Student Loan:

If you are attending a community college or are enrolled part-time in a four or five-year college program working towards your degree, the Signature Student Loan might be a good loan for you. Beneficial elements of this loan include an online application process, easy to follow instructions, and an electronic signature feature that allows the process to be completed online. Available to students both domestically and in programs overseas, the Signature Student Loan offers no minimum income required for borrowers and a six-month grace period. This loan is also available to international students with a qualifying co-signer. The qualification requirements for the co-signer include, being a U.S. citizen or permanent resident, and the appropriate CIS documents. Account management is available online, 24 hours a day, 7 days a week, and there is combined billing with other Sallie Mae loans.

The aggregate loan limit allows the borrower to apply for as much funding as needed to cover costs of attendance, minus other financial assistance already received. Depending on your credit history a fee may be assessed. Repayment options include, standard repayment, which is the most economical repayment plan. It allows the borrowers to make level monthly payments that cover a portion of the principal and accruing interest. Through Sallie Mae funding you have the ability to change your repayment plan if your situation and goals change. Also available as a repayment option is the graduated repayment. This allows the borrower to pay in lowered payments. Some of them are as low as the interest for the length of the loan up to four years, with the repayment plan changing to standard for the remainder of the loan. Like any loan, if you choose to lower your payments you will be paying the loan for a longer period of time, which will add to the total cost of the loan. Finally, the extended repayments are available that allows the borrower to make payments as interest-only during the first few years, or monthly payments of interest and principal. With this repayment program the borrower can "extend" their repayment of student loans up to 25 years.

Tuition Answer Loan:

This loan provides coverage in your higher education funding. Generally, after you have pursued most of the other funding opportunities, if you still find you need funding to pick up the remaining costs, this loan can help.

Requirements for this loan include the standard United States citizenship, a good credit standing, and a social security number. The borrower can request anywhere from $1,500 to $40,000 per year to cover various qualified education-related expenses that includes, room and board, textbooks, laptops or desktop computers, study abroad, and tuition. Rather than payment going directly to the university, the check is sent directly to the borrower. The loan is offered with no consideration of income and there are no application deadlines.

Other Benefits:

- Various repayment options, including deferment
- 24/7 online account management
- Combined billing of Sallie Mae service loans
- Competitive interest rates with strong credit
- Ability to add a co-signer to help qualify for the loan
- Reduction of interest rate by 50 percent, if payments are made on time for 24 consecutive months

Fees for this loan include a one-time fee at the time the loan is disbursed. Repayment options include paying immediately (when the loan is disbursed), both the interest and principal, paying interest during enrollment in school, and deferring all student payments while the student is enrolled in school at least half-time.

Other Private Student Loans include:

- K-12 Family Education Loan
- Lawloan Private Loan
- Lawloans Bar Study Loan
- MBA Loans Private Loan
- Medical School Loans Private Student Loan
- Medical School Loans Residency and Relocation Loan
- Signature Student Loan for Community Colleges
- Tutorial Financing Program

My goal with this chapter is to outline some of the many resources and options available to you. This should aid you in your research for financial assistance if you are seeking education for yourself or your children. I am a huge advocate of education. Education is a great tool, leading to a financially successful life.

Solution Summary

13: THE YOUNG AND THE RECKLESS: STUDENT LOANS

- Young people typically do not have experience dealing with finances, and after graduating high school they are often expected to handle their own money.

- Research information about finances, how to build credit, and also about managing a budget.

- Education loans can be a good debt if you will have a good ROI. Do your research.

- First, seek financial aid with grants - government grants do not have to be repaid.

- Avoid the common story of getting in over your head with debt from credit cards, student loans, and personal loans.

- Choosing the right loan and debt management program is critical.

- Do your research on any loan. This is your future so be proactive.

- Students running into financial problems should seek assistance.

- Create a plan for your credit identity and credit future.

- Apply for federal loans first before private loans.

- Federal loans are not based on your credit score and can offer lower interest rates, payment flexibility, and extended payment schedules.

- Grants can be given to undergraduates.

1, 2, 3 Qualify Me

GRANTS

Have you ever dreamed of money falling from the sky? Grant's are in a sense, free money that can seem like it fell from the sky. You may be asking yourself, "Free money? How can that be? If there's free money, why wouldn't everyone be getting this???" This chapter will teach you how to apply for grants. Essentially, grants are free money because usually you do not have to pay them back! A grant does not put you into debt, and all you have to do is qualify for a grant to get one. Many people don't even know about grants, or that they could possibly qualify for them. That is why many people do not even try to get one. Typically, most people think of grants as only for college students, getting them for education. Or they think they only qualify for a grant if they have the most horrific life situation, and that is not necessarily true. There are numerous types of grants and many ways to qualify. In the following pages I will give you a jump-start on qualifying for a grant. This will save you countless hours and days of work you would have to do on your own to qualify. I call it 1, 2, 3 qualify me.

This is an example of a client who wanted something a bit different from a typical educational grant. Sarah contacted me when she was in a lot of debt. She was 25 years old and living in Miami, Florida. Her budget and income were not looking so great. She had many bills and other expenses she had to pay every month. She was bringing home about $2,500 a month and had a savings account with about $560 saved for emergencies. She wasn't able to sustain much of a balance in her savings because there were several occasions when she had no choice but to borrow money from her savings account in order to pay a bill. She was feeling very lost but was determined to find a way to attend college without jeopardizing her job and small savings. She was a single parent and even though she was passionate about attending college she had the demands and expenses of parenthood preventing her from doing so. She knew there must be a way to balance her budget, support her child, and still pursue her education. She was the only person able to support her son and wasn't receiving any financial assistance. She had looked through several websites searching for resources for college bound students. After a fairly exhaustive search she was a little frustrated at not being able to find any suitable answers or support. She wanted to support her son while going to school, and knew with a child she wouldn't be able to work two jobs. Because of her situation she told me that she would rather attend a community college. Their program was two years instead of the four to five years she would need to spend at a conventional university. She wanted to earn a bachelors degree, but what she really needed was to earn a degree as soon as possible. She was looking for funds that would cover her expenses, since this was only for a short time and would be more beneficial to her situation. The additional funding would ensure that she would be capable of completing her degree within the two or four year time frame.

The first suggestion I gave her was to check her eligibility for various grants, knowing that she met the criteria for various educational grants based on her status as a single parent. Single income households qualify for many different educational grants. There are some grants that will send funding to your school and then when the school takes the necessary funds out of your college education, including course fees and other expenses, a refund check will be issued to you that you can place in a savings account. Another option with some grant funding is to work a part-time job while you attend your school, using the grant funding to supplement your income. Many single parents use this method as a great way to pursue their education while still having time to spend with their children.

GOVERNMENT GRANTS

The United States government gives away billions of dollars every single year to businesses and individuals. Funding for school supplies, personal improvement (music lessons, painting or art lessons), to purchase a home, to purchase equipment, to help get out of debt, to cover salaries, to purchase a wardrobe, and many other things. Government grants are available to everyone, and the good news is you don't have to pay government grants back. They are not considered loans. To qualify, you just need to be a U.S. citizen or a resident. Filling out the application only takes a few minutes! If you would like to apply for a government grant, go to: www.grants.gov.

What they do is they post federal government agency grant listings. It's a great resource for electronic applications, gathering general information about government grants, and accessing the Federal Register, which is the listing of all government grants. There are three ways to apply for a government grant. Fill out an application by phone, electronically, or have a certified application assistant process one for you. For assistance on grants you can contact the Grants Program Management office via email at support@ grants.gov or by phone at 800-518-4726. You can also go to www. gpoaccess.gov and search grant notices for the most recent listing of announcements and for application notices.

If you are applying electronically with an electronic application, information about the submission process and the specific forms are available through the grant funding source. For example, information about electronic submission to the NIH is available at http://era.nih.gov/electronicreceipt.

Together, let's go through the process of what you need to do to search for a grant in your area. Let's say, for example, you live in Michigan and you want to gain help for starting your small business. You would go to the Michigan government website and do a key search for business assistance, government aid for businesses, or corresponding words or phrases. I suggest also doing state or city searches for any organizations relating to the type of business or type of grant you are looking for.

You can do local research of your county, community or city to find what local grants may be available to you. Local information is not as accessible and it may be a little tougher to gain the information straight from the website. I suggest making phone calls to your city or county. In some cases, make phone calls to community government offices to find more specific information on grant offerings. Just like anything else that I have recommended in this book, this is based on your communication skills and relationships. Remember, when you are calling anyone at any given time, you will want to use your best people skills. Use charm, communication, humor, relatability, and whatever it is that will work for you to get as much information and to be able to get to the right people. Remember, if you try once and do not get to the right person, do not give up. Sometimes, making the second phone call can make all the difference. You might get to the person that gives you valuable information that can possibly get you a grant worth tens of thousands of dollars or more.

WRITING A WINNING PROPOSAL

Writing a winning proposal is essential when applying for a grant. Even though each year brings many changes that will influence grant writing, considering the sheer volume of grant proposals written, writing a successful grant proposal is key. In successful proposals there are common recurring elements that exist in all of them...

When writing your proposal, consider that you want it to be memorable and compelling to encourage them to read further and they will have the desire to grant you the money. Keep it specific and focused with the intent of not wasting anyone's time while they read it. You will want to include an introduction letter, an outline or summary, your personal project outline or description, an outline or personal statement of your need, a description of the project, detailed information about the budget and exactly what you need the funding for, specific information on how you have organized your project and how the funds will be used to achieve the goal of your proposal, and finally, a conclusion or summary. Here you want to concisely summarize your submission while restating the major points. You don't want to add any new information in the conclusion, just the vital information necessary for the reviewer to get a clear understanding of your proposal.

If you are submitting your grant online using the www.grants.gov website you can follow these procedures for submission to help ensure your application is received promptly.

There is software available from the grants.com website that aids the applicant in viewing and modifying their application. On the grants. gov website go to the link "For Applicants" on the left side of the webpage and select applicant resources. Under the list of applicant resources click on the "Download Software" link. You can also go to http://www.grants.gov/PEViewer/ICSViewer602_grants.exe. You will need a PC to access the software. Once you have installed the software you will need some information in order to proceed with the application process. You will need either the Catalog of Federal Domestic Assistance (CFDA) number or the program announcement number for the grant you are applying. This will ensure that you are routed to the proper grant. You can check the Request for Proposal or the listing on the Federal Register for the correct CFDA number. After you insert the proper CFDA number, grants.gov will go through its database and retrieve the grant application. Here you will be able to provide your email address, allowing grants.gov to send you an email if there are any changes to the application kit and/or application guidelines. Sometimes there are addendums or deadline extensions to the original Request for Proposal, and this contact information is crucial for you to receive information in a timely manner. At this point you download the application kit. Assuming at this point you have the Request for Proposal or application guidelines you can proceed with filing your online application.

There are many organizations and programs that will help you find government grants.

INFORMATION ON HEALTHCARE FOR FAMILIES

Each state offers assistance for healthcare for families. The US government provides websites that provide direct resources where all you need to do is apply by going to: www.healthyfamilies.ca.gov. This program is for children 18 years and younger who live in California. Qualifying is based on income limitations and various immigration rules.

www.healthyfamiilies.ca.gov This program is for children 18 years and younger who live in California. Qualifying is based on income limitations and various immigration rules.

Insure Kids Now is a great resource for insurance for children. Check out the website: www.insurekidsnow.org or call 1-877-KIDS-NOW for assistance to qualify for free kids insurance.

SCHOOL FUNDING GRANTS

If you work in a PK through 12 school and are seeking funding for your school, this website www.schoolgrants.org is a great resource that lists various grants that are offerdirect funding for schools.

SINGLE PARENT GRANTS

Grants for single parents are available but they are not easy to find. There has been a steady rise in the amount of single parents in America and around the world. Like my story about Sarah, being a single parent is not easy, and seeking out grants for assistance can help. The qualities that are associated with being a single parent such as being courageous and determined are also essential if you are going to seek out assistance to improve your child's life. One must have the courage to ask for assistance and seek out all the assistance possible.

The government will provide financial assistance to most parents who can prove they need the assistance to raise their child. Government grants for sole guardians were created because the U.S. government recognized that raising a child as a single parent on one income can be a very difficult task. Assistance grants are occasionally awarded to ease the pressures a single parent faces on a daily basis. To obtain government funding as a single parent you need to check with the city hall in the city where you live. Be sure to fill out the forms accurately and honestly as they will be reviewed and validated in the process of reviewing and deciding whether or not to approve your request. Specific attention to detail may make the difference of approval or denial of your request. Keep in mind that financial assistance will not be awarded if your salary is large enough to provide for your children comfortably or even luxuriously. The government will determine using their own criteria what constitutes "need."

EDUCATIONAL GRANTS

Grants for education are available through corporations, foundations, trusts, and sometimes the U.S. Government. Navigating the enormous volume of grants available requires some patience and discipline, as you will need to do some serious research to find the grants specific to your situation. In applying for a grant you need to become versed in some basic elements of grant writing and how grants are awarded. The process of grant writing involves creating a submission based on specific outlined criteria, most notably, a request for a proposal from the funding corporation, foundation, trust or governmental agency. Grant seekers may also take it upon themselves or hire a professional to draft a proposal for a grant. Whether you pursue a grant individually or with the assistance of a professional it is entirely based on how focused and how much work you are willing to apply to the process. It is completely possible to write a proposal for a grant without hiring a professional grant writer but you need to commit yourself to a very intensive and demanding process. It will involve very methodical research and study that will be critical in separating your grant submission from tens of thousands of others.

RESOURCES

As an individual there are resources available to help you seek out the various funding sources. Because there may be such an intensive and detailed process to seeking funding through grants, you may want to pursue resources that have some applicable fees for their services. The website www.foundationcenter.org offers an up-to-date online database that has more than 6,500 foundation and public charity programs that fund researchers, individual grant seekers, students and artists for various monthly, quarterly or yearly fees. The depth of the grant programs and processes are so expansive that you would be spending endless hours reading through lengthy grant lists and reviewing technical, multi-page descriptions for opportunities that might apply to you. Whereas, resources like Foundation Grants to Individuals Online have already done a huge amount of the work for you.

OTHER VARIOUS GRANTS

There are grants that exist for all kinds of different situations. Below are just some of the grants and their resources available to you.

GRANTS FOR EMERGENCIES

Grants for emergencies are available through the Clara Abbott Foundation. This is a resource for individuals unable to cover basic expenses such as rent, utilities or food. Go to http://clara.abbott.com/us/financialhardship/ if you think you might qualify, check out the eligibility section to review the qualification criteria. If you do qualify you can fill out the financial assistant application and then print or fax it to the foundation for processing. If you have any questions or need assistance you can call them toll free at: 1-800-972-3859.

If you are going to mail your application send it to:
> The Clara Abbott Foundation
> 1505 White Oak Drive
> Waukegan, IL 60085
> Or fax to: 1-847-938-6511

A financial consultant can help you go through your application and also assist you with a financial plan. After the foundation has received your application they will make a complete review of your application and let you know your status. Included in their review will be your personal resources. The resources available through community and government agencies, friends and family will all be used as part of the evaluation process to determine what kind of support they may be able to provide you. After they have concluded their evaluation process they will respond with assistance that can include a referral to outside resources or agencies, budget counseling and grants.

RAISE THE NATION

If you are a single mother Raise the Nation is a great organization that can help. They provide economic support to single mothers for education or aid in repaying student loans. Raise the Nation offers both grants and scholarships. With 45.5% of single mothers having two jobs just to survive, and costs for childcare composing 1/3 of a woman's weekly income, the need for single mothers is clear. The national average of people living at the poverty level is 13%. Single mothers living at or below the poverty level is 38%. Even with these staggering statistics women working full-time still return to school. The costs of tuition, books and childcare compound a single mother's situation and make it near impossible to succeed without some kind of support. There is a profound reality that education is the cornerstone of success and having education helps to provide an adequate and beneficial home environment for their children.

To apply for grants or scholarships you can go to their website at www.raisethenation.com. Click on the link to grants and scholarships for more information.

If you are concerned about your academic standing, Raise the Nation does not request it, so there is no need to be worried. They base their awards on a scoring system created by their Board of Directors. They evaluate candidates on a set of criteria focusing on personal development, community leadership, and academic achievement.

If you are seeking help with a student loan, Raise the Nation has a Student Loan Repayment Grant which assists in repaying these loans. It also seeks woman who are devoted to community service and have been volunteers in their communities.

Federal Resources for Home Improvement and Housing Assistance

DISABLED RENTERS

The U.S. Department of Housing and Urban Development (HUD) provides grants for various housing support. In 2007 HUD awarded grants for over 39 million dollars in 21 states to help non-elderly individuals and families with disabilities in renting private housing. Many disabled individuals and families have problems finding accessible housing that is affordable, and HUD awarded grants will help.

Depending on the state you live in there is various support you can receive if you are disabled. For more information about these programs and how to apply for vouchers for assistance with rent, you can go to: www.hud.gov/proddesc/mixpop.cfm

FREE MONEY FROM FOUNDATIONS
AND LARGE CORPORATIONS

Another great resource for free money is through funds made available through the philanthropic offerings done by various foundations and large corporations. Many private organizations set aside various portions of their annual budgets to be disbursed, which help individuals with different types of assistance.

To search out foundations go to www.foundations.org where they have a listing of all the corporate and charitable foundations nationwide.

I suggest that you research the organizations and companies that have a common interest with you or the business you are starting. For instance, if you are a fashion designer you may want to find a company who does fashion and has a passion for new designers. Also, look for common interests or things that could reflect you in a good light. Say, if in your research you find a company that has an interest in saving greyhound dogs and this is a passion of yours that you do volunteer work for, you can now add that in your proposal. Another approach you can use is if you find a particular philanthropic work that a corporation focuses on, you may offer to donate a portion of your profits to the cause they are passionate about. If you get the grant you can give them your future plans of how it can relate to them. This could help you get a grant.

Below is the Fortune 500 list, as of the first quarter 2008. Many of these companies provide some form of philanthropy through charities and funding. So, this is another great place to do some research to seek funding:

3M Company	St. Paul, MN
Abbott Laboratories	Abbott Park, IL
ADM	Decatur, IL
Advance Auto Parts, Inc.	Roanoke, VA
Advanced Micro Devices, Inc.	Sunnyvale, CA
Aetna Inc.	Hartford, CT
Affiliated Computer Services, Inc.	Dallas, TX
Aflac Incorporated	Columbus, GA
AGCO Corporation	Duluth, GA
Agilent Technologies, Inc.	Palo Alto, CA

Air Products and Chemicals, Inc.	Allentown, PA
AK Steel Holding Corporation	Middletown, OH
Albertson's, Inc.	Boise, ID
Alcoa Inc.	New York, NY
Allied Waste Industries, Inc.	Scottsdale, AZ
ALLTEL Corporation	Little Rock, AR
Altria Group, Inc.	New York, NY
Amazon.com, Inc.	Seattle, WA
Ameren Corporation	St. Louis, MO
American Electric Power Company, Inc.	Columbus, OH
American Express Company	New York, NY
American Family Insurance Group	Madison, WI
American Financial Group, Inc.	Cincinnati, OH
American International Group, Inc.	New York, NY
American Standard Companies Inc.	Piscataway, NJ
AmerisourceBergen Corporation	Chesterbrook, PA
Amgen Inc.	Thousand Oaks, CA
AMR Corporation	Fort Worth, TX
Anadarko Petroleum Corporation	The Woodlands, TX
Anheuser-Busch Companies, Inc.	St. Louis, MO
Aon Corporation	Chicago, IL
Apache Corporation	Houston, TX
Apple Computer, Inc.	Cupertino, CA
Applied Materials, Inc.	Santa Clara, CA
ARAMARK Corporation	Philadelphia, PA
Arrow Electronics, Inc.	Melville, NY
ArvinMeritor, Inc.	Troy, MI
Asbury Automotive Group, Inc.	New York, NY
Ashland Inc.	Covington, KY
Assurant, Inc.	New York, NY
AT&T Inc.	San Antonio, TX
Atmos Energy Corporation	Dallas, TX
Autoliv, Inc.	Stockholm, Sweden
Automatic Data Processing, Inc.	Roseland, NJ
AutoNation, Inc.	Fort Lauderdale, FL
Auto-Owners Insurance Group	Lansing, MI
AutoZone, Inc.	Memphis, TN
Avaya Inc.	Basking Ridge, NJ
Avery Dennison Corporation	Pasadena, CA
Avnet, Inc.	Phoenix, AZ
Avon Products, Inc.	New York, NY

Baker Hughes Incorporated	Houston, TX
Ball Corporation	Broomfield, CO
Bank of America Corporation	Charlotte, NC
Barnes & Noble, Inc.	New York, NY
Baxter International Inc.	Deerfield, IL
BB&T Corporation	Winston-Salem, NC
Beazer Homes USA, Inc.	Atlanta, GA
Becton, Dickinson and Company	Franklin Lakes, NJ
Bed Bath & Beyond Inc.	Union, NJ
BellSouth Corporation	Atlanta, GA
Berkshire Hathaway Inc.	Omaha, NE
Best Buy Co., Inc.	Richfield, MN
Big Lots, Inc.	Columbus, OH
BJ's Wholesale Club, Inc.	Natick, MA
Blockbuster Inc.	Dallas, TX
BlueLinx Holdings Inc.	Atlanta, GA
Borders Group, Inc.	Ann Arbor, MI
BorgWarner Inc.	Auburn Hills, MI
Boston Scientific Corporation	Natick, MA
Bristol-Myers Squibb Company	New York, NY
Brunswick Corporation	Lake Forest, IL
Burlington Northern Santa Fe Corporation	Fort Worth, TX
C.H. Robinson Worldwide, Inc.	Eden Prairie, MN
Cablevision Systems Corporation	Bethpage, NY
Calpine Corporation	San Jose, CA
Campbell Soup Company	Camden, NJ
Capital One Financial Corporation	McLean, VA
Cardinal Health, Inc.	Dublin, OH
Caremark Rx, Inc.	Nashville, TN
CarMax, Inc.	Richmond, VA
Caterpillar Inc.	Peoria, IL
CBS Corporation	New York, NY
CDW Corporation	Vernon Hills, IL
Celanese Corporation	Dallas, TX
Cendant Corporation	New York, NY
CenterPoint Energy, Inc.	Houston, TX
Centex Corporation	Dallas, TX
Charter Communications, Inc.	St. Louis, MO
Chesapeake Energy Corporation	Oklahoma City, OK
Chevron Corporation	San Ramon, CA
CHS Inc.	Inver Grove Heights, MN

CIGNA Corporation	Philadelphia, PA
Circuit City Stores, Inc.	Richmond, VA
Cisco Systems, Inc.	San Jose, CA
CIT Group Inc.	New York, NY
Citigroup Inc.	New York, NY
Clear Channel Communications, Inc.	San Antonio, TX
CMS Energy Corporation	Jackson, MI
Coca-Cola Enterprises Inc.	Atlanta, GA
Colgate-Palmolive Company	New York, NY
Comcast Corporation	Philadelphia, PA
Commercial Metals Company	Irving, TX
Computer Sciences Corporation	El Segundo, CA
ConAgra Foods, Inc.	Omaha, NE
ConocoPhillips	Houston, TX
Conseco, Inc.	Carmel, IN
Consolidated Edison, Inc.	New York, NY
Constellation Brands, Inc.	Fairport, NY
Constellation Energy Group, Inc.	Baltimore, MD
Continental Airlines, Inc.	Houston, TX
Con-way Inc.	San Mateo, CA
Corning Incorporated	Corning, NY
Costco Wholesale Corporation	Issaquah, WA
Countrywide Financial Corporation	Calabasas, CA
Coventry Health Care, Inc.	Bethesda, MD
Cox Communications, Inc.	Atlanta, GA
Crown Holdings, Inc.	Philadelphia, PA
CSX Corporation	Jacksonville, FL
Cummins, Inc.	Columbus, IN
CVS Corporation	Woonsocket, RI
D.R. Horton, Inc.	Fort Worth, TX
Dana Corporation	Toledo, OH
Danaher Corporation	Washington, DC
Darden Restaurants, Inc.	Orlando, FL
Dean Foods Company	Dallas, TX
Deere & Company	Moline, IL
Dell Inc.	Round Rock, TX
Delphi Corporation	Troy, MI
Delta Air Lines, Inc.	Atlanta, GA
Devon Energy Corporation	Oklahoma City, OK
Dillard's, Inc.	Little Rock, AR
Dole Food Company, Inc.	Westlake Village, CA

Dollar General Corporation	Goodlettsville, TN
Dominion Resources, Inc.	Richmond, VA
Dover Corporation	New York, NY
DTE Energy Company	Detroit, MI
Duke Energy Corporation	Charlotte, NC
Dynegy Inc.	Houston, TX
E. I. du Pont de Nemours and Company	Wilmington, DE
Eastman Chemical Company	Kingsport, TN
Eastman Kodak Company	Rochester, NY
Eaton Corporation	Cleveland, OH
eBay Inc.	San Jose, CA
EchoStar Communications Corporation	Englewood, CO
Ecolab Inc.	St. Paul, MN
Edison International	Rosemead, CA
El Paso Corporation	Houston, TX
Electronic Data Systems Corporation	Plano, TX
Eli Lilly and Company	Indianapolis, IN
EMC Corporation	Hopkinton, MA
EMCOR Group, Inc.	Norwalk, CT
Emerson Electric Co.	St. Louis, MO
Enbridge Energy Partners, L.P.	Houston, TX
Energy East Corporation	Albany, NY
Energy Transfer Partners, L.P.	Dallas, TX
Engelhard Corporation	Iselin, NJ
Entergy Corporation	New Orleans, LA
Enterprise Products Partners L.P.	Houston, TX
Erie Insurance Group	Erie, PA
Exelon Corporation	Chicago, IL
Express Scripts, Inc.	Maryland Heights, MO
Exxon Mobil Corporation	Irving, TX
Family Dollar Stores, Inc.	Matthews, NC
Federal-Mogul Corporation	Southfield, MI
Federated Department Stores, Inc.	Cincinnati, OH
FedEx Corporation	Memphis, TN
Fidelity National Financial, Inc.	Jacksonville, FL
Fifth Third Bancorp	Cincinnati, OH
First Data Corporation	Greenwood Village, CO
FirstEnergy Corp.	Akron, OH
Fiserv, Inc.	Brookfield, WI
Fisher Scientific International Inc.	Hampton, NH
Fluor Corporation	Aliso Viejo, CA

Foot Locker, Inc.	New York, NY
Ford Motor Company	Dearborn, MI
Fortune Brands, Inc.	Deerfield, IL
FPL Group, Inc.	Juno Beach, FL
Franklin Resources, Inc.	San Mateo, CA
Freeport-McMoRan Copper & Gold Inc.	New Orleans, LA
Freescale Semiconductor, Inc.	Austin, TX
Frontier Oil Corporation	Houston, TX
Gannett Co., Inc.	McLean, VA
Gap Inc.	San Francisco, CA
General Dynamics Corporation	Falls Church, VA
General Electric Company	Fairfield, CT
General Mills, Inc.	Minneapolis, MN
General Motors Corporation	Detroit, MI
Genuine Parts Company	Atlanta, GA
Genworth Financial, Inc.	Richmond, VA
Golden West Financial Corporation	Oakland, CA
Goodrich Corporation	Charlotte, NC
Google Inc.	Mountain View, CA
Graybar Electric Company, Inc.	St. Louis, MO
Group 1 Automotive, Inc.	Houston, TX
H&R Block, Inc.	Kansas City, MO
H. J. Heinz Company	Pittsburgh, PA
Halliburton Company	Houston, TX
Harley-Davidson, Inc.	Milwaukee, WI
Harrah's Entertainment, Inc.	Las Vegas, NV
HCA Inc.	Nashville, TN
Health Net, Inc.	Woodland Hills, CA
Henry Schein, Inc.	Melville, NY
Hess Corporation	New York, NY
Hewlett-Packard Company	Palo Alto, CA
Hexion Specialty Chemicals, Inc.	Columbus, OH
Hilton Hotels Corporation	Beverly Hills, CA
Honeywell International Inc.	Morristown, NJ
Hormel Foods Corporation	Austin, MN
Hovnanian Enterprises, Inc.	Red Bank, NJ
Hughes Supply, Inc.	Orlando, FL
Humana Inc.	Louisville, KY
Huntsman Corporation	Salt Lake City, UT
IAC/InterActiveCorp	New York, NY
IKON Office Solutions, Inc.	Malvern, PA

Illinois Tool Works Inc.	Glenview, IL
Ingram Micro Inc.	Santa Ana, CA
Intel Corporation	Santa Clara, CA
International Business Machines Corporation	Armonk, NY
International Paper Company	Stamford, CT
ITT Industries, Inc.	White Plains, NY
J. C. Penney Company, Inc.	Plano, TX
Jabil Circuit, Inc.	St. Petersburg, FL
Jacobs Engineering Group Inc.	Pasadena, CA
Johnson & Johnson	New Brunswick, NJ
Johnson Controls, Inc.	Milwaukee, WI
Jones Apparel Group, Inc.	Bristol, PA
JPMorgan Chase & Co.	New York, NY
KB Home	Los Angeles, CA
Kellogg Company	Battle Creek, MI
Kelly Services, Inc.	Troy, MI
Kerr-McGee Corporation	Oklahoma City, OK
KeyCorp	Cleveland, OH
KeySpan Corporation	Brooklyn, NY
Kimberly-Clark Corporation	Irving, TX
Kinder Morgan Energy Partners, L.P.	Houston, TX
Kindred Healthcare, Inc.	Louisville, KY
Kohl's Corporation	Menomonee Falls, WI
L-3 Communications Holdings, Inc.	New York, NY
Land O'Lakes, Inc.	Arden Hills, MN
LandAmerica Financial Group, Inc.	Richmond, VA
Lear Corporation	Southfield, MI
Leggett & Platt, Incorporated	Carthage, MO
Lehman Brothers Holdings Inc.	New York, NY
Lennar Corporation	Miami, FL
Levi Strauss & Co.	San Francisco, CA
Lexmark International, Inc.	Lexington, KY
Liberty Global, Inc.	Englewood, CO
Liberty Media Holding Corporation	Englewood, CO
Liberty Mutual Holding Company Inc.	Boston, MA
Limited Brands, Inc.	Columbus, OH
Lincoln National Corporation	Philadelphia, PA
Liz Claiborne, Inc.	New York, NY
Lockheed Martin Corporation	Bethesda, MD
Loews Corporation	New York, NY
Longs Drug Stores Corporation	Walnut Creek, CA

Lowe's Companies, Inc.	Mooresville, NC
Lucent Technologies Inc.	Murray Hill, NJ
Lyondell Chemical Company	Houston, TX
M.D.C. Holdings, Inc.	Denver, CO
Manpower Inc.	Milwaukee, WI
Marathon Oil Corporation	Houston, TX
Marriott International, Inc.	Washington, DC
Marsh & McLennan Companies, Inc.	New York, NY
Marshall & Ilsley Corporation	Milwaukee, WI
Masco Corporation	Taylor, MI
Massachusetts Mutual Life Insurance Company	Springfield, MA
Mattel, Inc.	El Segundo, CA
McDonald's Corporation	Oak Brook, IL
McKesson Corporation	San Francisco, CA
MeadWestvaco Corporation	Stamford, CT
Medco Health Solutions, Inc.	Franklin Lakes, NJ
Medtronic, Inc.	Minneapolis, MN
Mellon Financial Corporation	Pittsburgh, PA
Merck & Co., Inc.	Whitehouse Station, NJ
Merrill Lynch & Co., Inc.	New York, NY
MetLife, Inc.	New York, NY
MGM MIRAGE	Las Vegas, NV
Micron Technology, Inc.	Boise, ID
Microsoft Corporation	Redmond, WA
Mirant Corporation	Atlanta, GA
Mohawk Industries, Inc.	Calhoun, GA
Molson Coors Brewing Company	Golden, CO
Monsanto Company	St. Louis, MO
Morgan Stanley	New York, NY
Motorola, Inc.	Schaumburg, IL
Murphy Oil Corporation	El Dorado, AR
Nash-Finch Company	Minneapolis, MN
National City Corporation	Cleveland, OH
National Oilwell Varco, Inc.	Houston, TX
Nationwide Mutual Insurance Company	Columbus, OH
Navistar International Corporation	Warrenville, IL
NCR Corporation	Dayton, OH
New York Life Insurance Company	New York, NY
Newell Rubbermaid Inc.	Atlanta, GA
Newmont Mining Corporation	Denver, CO
News Corporation	New York, NY

NIKE, Inc.	Beaverton, OR
NiSource Inc.	Merrillville, IN
Nordstrom, Inc.	Seattle, WA
Norfolk Southern Corporation	Norfolk, VA
Northeast Utilities	Berlin, CT
Northrop Grumman Corporation	Los Angeles, CA
Northwest Airlines Corporation	Eagan, MN
Nucor Corporation	Charlotte, NC
NVR, Inc.	Reston, VA
Occidental Petroleum Corporation	Los Angeles, CA
Office Depot, Inc.	Delray Beach, FL
OfficeMax Incorporated	Itasca, IL
OGE Energy Corp.	Oklahoma City, OK
Omnicare, Inc.	Covington, KY
Omnicom Group Inc.	New York, NY
ONEOK, Inc.	Tulsa, OK
Oracle Corporation	Redwood City, CA
Owens & Minor, Inc.	Mechanicsville, VA
Owens Corning	Toledo, OH
Owens-Illinois, Inc.	Toledo, OH
PACCAR Inc	Bellevue, WA
Pacific Mutual Holding Company	Newport Beach, CA
Parker Hannifin Corporation	Cleveland, OH
Pathmark Stores, Inc.	Carteret, NJ
Peabody Energy Corporation	St. Louis, MO
Pepco Holdings, Inc.	Washington, DC
PepsiCo, Inc.	Purchase, NY
Performance Food Group Company	Richmond, VA
Peter Kiewit Sons', Inc.	Omaha, NE
Pfizer Inc.	New York, NY
PG&E Corporation	San Francisco, CA
Phelps Dodge Corporation	Phoenix, AZ
Pilgrim's Pride Corporation	Pittsburg, TX
Pitney Bowes Inc.	Stamford, CT
Plains All American Pipeline, L.P.	Houston, TX
PPG Industries, Inc.	Pittsburgh, PA
PPL Corporation	Allentown, PA
Praxair, Inc.	Danbury, CT
Principal Financial Group, Inc.	Des Moines, IA
Progress Energy, Inc.	Raleigh, NC
Prudential Financial, Inc.	Newark, NJ

Public Service Enterprise Group Incorporated	Newark, NJ
Publix Super Markets, Inc.	Lakeland, FL
Pulte Homes, Inc.	Bloomfield Hills, MI
QUALCOMM Incorporated	San Diego, CA
Quest Diagnostics Incorporated	Lyndhurst, NJ
Qwest Communications International Inc.	Denver, CO
R.R. Donnelley & Sons Company	Chicago, IL
RadioShack Corporation	Fort Worth, TX
Raytheon Company	Waltham, MA
Regions Financial Corporation	Birmingham, AL
Reliant Energy, Inc.	Houston, TX
Reynolds American Inc.	Winston-Salem, NC
Rite Aid Corporation	Camp Hill, PA
Rockwell Automation, Inc.	Milwaukee, WI
Rohm and Haas Company	Philadelphia, PA
Ross Stores, Inc.	Pleasanton, CA
Ryder System, Inc.	Miami, FL
Ryerson, Inc.	Chicago, IL
Ryland Group Ltd.	Birmingham, England
Safeco Corporation	Seattle, WA
Safeway Inc.	Pleasanton, CA
Saks Incorporated	Birmingham, AL
Sanmina-SCI Corporation	San Jose, CA
Sara Lee Corporation	Chicago, IL
SCANA Corporation	Columbia, SC
Schering-Plough Corporation	Kenilworth, NJ
Science Applications International Corporation	San Diego, CA
Sealed Air Corporation	Saddle Brook, NJ
Sears Holdings Corporation	Hoffman Estates, IL
Sempra Energy	San Diego, CA
SLM Corporation	Reston, VA
Smith International, Inc.	Houston, TX
Smithfield Foods, Inc.	Smithfield, VA
Smurfit-Stone Container Corporation	Chicago, IL
Solectron Corporation	Milpitas, CA
Sonic Automotive, Inc.	Charlotte, NC
Southern Company	Atlanta, GA
Southwest Airlines Co.	Dallas, TX
Sprint Nextel Corporation	Reston, VA
SPX Corporation	Charlotte, NC
Standard Pacific Corp.	Irvine, CA

Staples, Inc.	Framingham, MA
Starbucks Corporation	Seattle, WA
Starwood Hotels & Resorts Worldwide, Inc.	White Plains, NY
State Farm Mutual Automobile Insurance Company	Bloomington, IL
State Street Corporation	Boston, MA
Stryker Corporation	Kalamazoo, MI
Sun Microsystems, Inc.	Santa Clara, CA
SunGard Data Systems Inc.	Wayne, PA
Sunoco, Inc.	Philadelphia, PA
SunTrust Banks, Inc.	Atlanta, GA
SUPERVALU INC.	Eden Prairie, MN
SYSCO Corporation	Houston, TX
Target Corporation	Minneapolis, MN
Teachers Insurance and Annuity Association - College Retirement Equities Fund	New York, NY
Tech Data Corporation	Clearwater, FL
Temple-Inland Inc.	Austin, TX
Tenet Healthcare Corporation	Dallas, TX
Tenneco Inc.	Lake Forest, IL
TEPPCO Partners, L.P.	Houston, TX
Terex Corporation	Westport, CT
Tesoro Corporation	San Antonio, TX
Texas Instruments Incorporated	Dallas, TX
Textron Inc.	Providence, RI
The AES Corporation	Arlington, VA
The Allstate Corporation	Northbrook, IL
The Bank of New York Company, Inc.	New York, NY
The Bear Stearns Companies Inc.	New York, NY
The Black & Decker Corporation	Towson, MD
The Boeing Company	Chicago, IL
The Brink's Company	Richmond, VA
The Charles Schwab Corporation	San Francisco, CA
The Chubb Corporation	Warren, NJ
The Clorox Company	Oakland, CA
The Coca-Cola Company	Atlanta, GA
The DIRECTV Group, Inc.	El Segundo, CA
The Dow Chemical Company	Midland, MI
The Estée Lauder Companies Inc.	New York, NY
The First American Corporation	Santa Ana, CA
The Goldman Sachs Group, Inc.	New York, NY
The Goodyear Tire & Rubber Company	Akron, OH

The Guardian Life Insurance Company of America	New York, NY
The Hartford Financial Services Group, Inc.	Hartford, CT
The Hershey Company	Hershey, PA
The Home Depot, Inc.	Atlanta, GA
The Interpublic Group of Companies, Inc.	New York, NY
The Kroger Co.	Cincinnati, OH
The Lubrizol Corporation	Wickliffe, OH
The McGraw-Hill Companies, Inc.	New York, NY
The Mosaic Company	Plymouth, MN
The Mutual of Omaha Companies	Omaha, NE
The Northwestern Mutual Life Insurance Company	Milwaukee, WI
The Pepsi Bottling Group, Inc.	Somers, NY
The PNC Financial Services Group, Inc.	Pittsburgh, PA
The Procter & Gamble Company	Cincinnati, OH
The Progressive Corporation	Mayfield Village, OH
The ServiceMaster Company	Downers Grove, IL
The Sherwin-Williams Company	Cleveland, OH
The St. Paul Travelers Companies, Inc.	St. Paul, MN
The Timken Company	Canton, OH
The TJX Companies, Inc.	Framingham, MA
The Walt Disney Company	Burbank, CA
The Williams Companies, Inc.	Tulsa, OK
Thrivent Financial for Lutherans	Minneapolis, MN
Time Warner Inc.	New York, NY
Toll Brothers, Inc.	Horsham, PA
Toys "R" Us, Inc.	Wayne, NJ
TransMontaigne Inc.	Denver, CO
Triad Hospitals, Inc.	Plano, TX
Tribune Company	Chicago, IL
TRW Automotive Holdings Corp.	Livonia, MI
TXU Corp.	Dallas, TX
Tyson Foods, Inc.	Springdale, AR
U.S. Bancorp	Minneapolis, MN
UAL Corporation	Elk Grove Township, IL
UGI Corporation	King of Prussia, PA
Union Pacific Corporation	Omaha, NE
Unisys Corporation	Blue Bell, PA

United Auto Group, Inc.	Bloomfield Hills, MI
United Parcel Service, Inc.	Atlanta, GA
United States Steel Corporation	Pittsburgh, PA
United Stationers Inc.	Des Plaines, IL
United Technologies Corporation	Hartford, CT
UnitedHealth Group Incorporated	Minnetonka, MN
Universal Health Services, Inc.	King of Prussia, PA
UnumProvident Corporation	Chattanooga, TN
US Airways Group, Inc.	Tempe, AZ
USAA	San Antonio, TX
USG Corporation	Chicago, IL
Valero Energy Corporation	San Antonio, TX
Verizon Communications Inc.	New York, NY
VF Corporation	Greensboro, NC
Viacom Inc.	New York, NY
Visteon Corporation	Van Buren Township, MI
W. R. Berkley Corporation	Greenwich, CT
W.W. Grainger, Inc.	Lake Forest, IL
Wachovia Corporation	Charlotte, NC
Walgreen Co.	Deerfield, IL
Wal-Mart Stores, Inc.	Bentonville, AR
Washington Mutual, Inc.	Seattle, WA
Waste Management, Inc.	Houston, TX
WellPoint, Inc.	Indianapolis, IN
Wells Fargo & Company	San Francisco, CA
WESCO International, Inc.	Pittsburgh, PA
Western & Southern Financial Group	Cincinnati, OH
Weyerhaeuser Company	Federal Way, WA
Whirlpool Corporation	Benton Harbor, MI
Whole Foods Market, Inc.	Austin, TX
Winn-Dixie Stores, Inc.	Jacksonville, FL
Wm. Wrigley Jr. Company	Chicago, IL
World Fuel Services Corporation	Miami, FL
WPS Resources Corporation	Green Bay, WI
Wyeth	Madison, NJ
Xcel Energy Inc.	Minneapolis, MN
Xerox Corporation	Stamford, CT
Yahoo! Inc.	Sunnyvale, CA
YRC Worldwide Inc.	Overland Park, KS
YUM! Brands, Inc.	Louisville, KY

According to CNNMoney.com the following is the list for Fortune 1000 companies after the first quarter 2008.

Rank	Company	Revenues ($ millions)	Profits ($ millions)
1	Wal-Mart Stores	378,799.0	12,731.0
2	Exxon Mobil	372,824.0	40,610.0
3	Chevron	210,783.0	18,688.0
4	General Motors	182,347.0	-38,732.0
5	ConocoPhillips	178,558.0	11,891.0
6	General Electric	176,656.0	22,208.0
7	Ford Motor	172,468.0	-2,723.0
8	Citigroup	159,229.0	3,617.0
9	Bank of America Corp.	119,190.0	14,982.0
10	AT&T	118,928.0	11,951.0
11	Berkshire Hathaway	118,245.0	13,213.0
12	J.P. Morgan Chase & Co.	116,353.0	15,365.0
13	American International Group	110,064.0	6,200.0
14	Hewlett-Packard	104,286.0	7,264.0
15	International Business Machines	98,786.0	10,418.0
16	Valero Energy	96,758.0	5,234.0
17	Verizon Communications	93,775.0	5,521.0
18	McKesson	93,574.0	913.0
19	Cardinal Health	88,363.9	1,931.1
20	Goldman Sachs Group	87,968.0	11,599.0
21	Morgan Stanley	87,879.0	3,209.0
22	Home Depot	84,740.0	4,395.0
23	Procter & Gamble	76,476.0	10,340.0
24	CVS Caremark	76,329.5	2,637.0
25	UnitedHealth Group	75,431.0	4,654.0
26	Kroger	70,234.7	1,180.5
27	Boeing	66,387.0	4,074.0
28	AmerisourceBergen	66,074.3	469.2
29	Costco Wholesale	64,400.2	1,082.8
30	Merrill Lynch	64,217.0	-7,777.0
31	Target	63,367.0	2,849.0
32	State Farm Insurance Cos.	1,611.6	5,463.7
33	WellPoint	61,134.3	3,345.4
34	Dell	61,133.0	2,947.0
35	Johnson & Johnson	61,095.0	10,576.0
36	Marathon Oil	60,044.0	3,956.0

Rank	Company	Revenues ($ millions)	Profits ($ millions)
37	Lehman Brothers Holdings	59,003.0	4,192.0
38	Wachovia Corp.	55,528.0	6,312.0
39	United Technologies	54,759.0	4,224.0
40	Walgreen	53,762.0	2,041.3
41	Wells Fargo	53,593.0	8,057.0
42	Dow Chemical	53,513.0	2,887.0
43	MetLife	53,150.0	4,317.0
44	Microsoft	51,122.0	14,065.0
45	Sears Holdings	50,703.0	826.0
46	United Parcel Service	49,692.0	382.0
47	Pfizer	48,418.0	8,144.0
48	Lowe's	48,283.0	2,809.0
49	Time Warner	46,615.0	4,387.0
50	Caterpillar	44,958.0	3,541.0
51	Medco Health Solutions	44,506.2	912.0
52	Archer Daniels Midland	44,018.0	2,162.0
53	Fannie Mae	43,355.0	-2,050.0
54	Freddie Mac	43,104.0	-3,094.0
55	Safeway	42,286.0	888.4
56	Sunoco	42,101.0	891.0
57	Lockheed Martin	41,862.0	3,033.0
58	Sprint Nextel	40,146.0	-29,580.0
59	PepsiCo	39,474.0	5,658.0
60	Intel	38,334.0	6,976.0
61	Altria Group	38,051.0	9,786.0
62	Supervalu	37,406.0	452.0
63	Kraft Foods	37,241.0	2,590.0
64	Allstate	36,769.0	4,636.0
65	Motorola	36,622.0	-49.0
66	Best Buy	35,934.0	1,377.0
67	Walt Disney	5,882.0	4,687.0
68	FedEx	35,214.0	2,016.0
69	Ingram Micro	35,047.1	275.9
70	Sysco	35,042.1	1,001.1
71	Cisco Systems	34,922.0	7,333.0
72	Johnson Controls	34,678.0	1,252.0
73	Honeywell International	34,589.0	2,444.0
74	Prudential Financial	34,401.0	3,704.0
75	American Express	32,316.0	4,012.0

Rank	Company	Revenues ($ millions)	Profits ($ millions)
76	Northrop Grumman	32,032.0	1,790.0
77	Hess	31,924.0	1,832.0
78	GMAC	31,490.0	-2,332.0
79	Comcast	30,895.0	2,587.0
80	Alcoa	30,748.0	2,564.0
81	DuPont	30,653.0	2,988.0
82	New York Life Insurance	29,279.6	1,141.8
83	Coca-Cola	28,857.0	5,981.0
84	News Corp.	28,655.0	3,426.0
85	Aetna	27,599.6	1,831.0
86	TIAA-CREF	27,526.0	1,438.8
87	General Dynamics	27,294.0	2,072.0
88	Tyson Foods	26,900.0	268.0
89	HCA	26,858.0	874.0
90	Enterprise GP Holdings	26,713.8	109.0
91	Macy's	26,340.0	893.0
92	Delphi	26,160.0	-3,065.0
93	Travelers Cos.	26,017.0	4,601.0
94	Liberty Mutual Insurance Group	25,961.0	1,518.0
95	Hartford Financial Services	25,916.0	2,949.0
96	Abbott Laboratories	25,914.2	3,606.3
97	Washington Mutual	25,531.0	-67.0
98	Humana	25,290.0	833.7
99	Massachusetts Mutual Life Insurance	25,268.2	722.0
100	3M	24,462.0	4096.0
101	Merck	24,197.7	3,275.4
102	Deere	24,082.2	1,821.7
103	Apple	24,006.0	3,496.0
104	Countrywide Financial	23,442.1	-703.5
105	Tech Data	23,423.1	108.3
106	McDonald's	23,230.7	2,395.1
107	Publix Super Markets	23,193.6	1,183.9
108	Nationwide	22,962.0	1,994.0
109	AMR	22,935.0	504.0
110	Northwestern Mutual	22,596.6	1,000.0
111	Emerson Electric	2,572.0	2,136.0
112	Raytheon	22,426.0	2,578.0
113	Wyeth	22,399.8	4,616.0
114	International Paper	22,284.0	1,168.0

Rank	Company	Revenues ($ millions)	Profits ($ millions)
115	Electronic Data Systems	22,135.0	716.0
116	Tesoro	21,675.0	566.0
117	Constellation Energy	21,193.2	821.5
118	Coca-Cola Enterprises	20,936.0	711.0
119	Goodyear Tire & Rubber	20,538.0	602.0
120	Manpower	20,500.3	484.7
121	Plains All American Pipeline	20,394.0	365.0
122	U.S. Bancorp	20,308.0	4,324.0
123	Occidental Petroleum	20,206.0	5,400.0
124	UAL	20,143.0	403.0
125	Bristol-Myers Squibb	19,977.0	2,165.0
126	J.C. Penney	19,860.0	1,111.0
127	Whirlpool	19,451.0	640.0
128	Staples	19,372.7	995.7
129	Delta Air Lines	19,154.0	1,612.0
130	Capital One Financial	18,965.5	1,570.3
131	Exelon	18,925.0	2,736.0
132	TJX	18,647.1	771.8
133	Eli Lilly	18,633.5	2,953.0
134	Murphy Oil	18,439.1	766.5
135	Express Scripts	18,377.8	567.8
136	Kimberly-Clark	18,266.0	1,822.9
137	Oracle	17,996.0	4,274.0
138	AutoNation	17,950.6	278.7
139	Loews	17,920.0	2,489.0
140	Freeport-McMoRan Copper & Gold	17,876.0	2,977.0
141	Cigna	17,623.0	1,115.0
142	Rite Aid	17,507.7	26.8
143	DirecTV Group	17,246.0	1,451.0
144	Xerox	17,228.0	1,135.0
145	CHS	17,216.0	750.3
146	United States Steel	16,873.0	879.0
147	Weyerhaeuser	16,871.0	790.0
148	Fluor	16,691.0	533.3
149	Anheuser-Busch	16,685.7	2,115.3
150	Google	16,594.0	4,203.7
151	Nucor	16,593.0	1,471.9
152	Kohl's	16,473.7	1,083.9
153	Nike	16,325.9	1,491.5

Rank	Company	Revenues ($ millions)	Profits ($ millions)
154	Union Pacific	16,283.0	1,855.0
155	Illinois Tool Works	16,278.9	1,869.9
156	Bear Stearns	16,151.0	233.0
157	Lear	15,995.0	241.5
158	Arrow Electronics	15,985.0	407.8
159	Anadarko Petroleum	15,916.0	3,781.0
160	Burlington Northern Santa Fe	15,802.0	1,829.0
161	Dominion Resources	15,790.0	2,539.0
162	Gap	15,779.0	833.0
163	Avnet	15,681.1	393.1
164	Office Depot	15,527.5	395.6
165	AFLAC	15,393.0	1,634.0
166	Southern	15,353.0	1,734.0
167	Halliburton	15,264.0	3,499.0
168	FPL Group	15,263.0	1,312.0
169	Paccar	15,221.7	1,227.3
170	Computer Sciences	14,856.6	388.8
171	Amazon.com	14,835.0	476.0
172	Bank of New York Mellon Corp.	14,798.0	2,039.0
173	Amgen	14,771.0	3,166.0
174	TRW Automotive Holdings	14,702.0	90.0
175	Progressive	14,686.8	1,182.5
176	United Services Automobile Assn.	14,417.9	1,855.5
177	Centex	14,292.7	268.4
178	Continental Airlines	14,232.0	459.0
179	Health Net	14,108.3	193.7
180	Chubb	14,107.0	2,807.0
181	CBS	14,072.9	1,247.0
182	L-3 Communications	13,960.5	756.1
183	AES	13,896.0	-95.0
184	Sun Microsystems	13,873.0	473.0
185	Texas Instruments	13,835.0	2,657.0
186	Colgate-Palmolive	13,789.7	1,737.4
187	Qwest Communications	13,778.0	2,917.0
188	World Fuel Services	13,729.6	64.8
189	Toys 'R' Us	13,646.0	65.0
190	Pepsi Bottling	13,591.0	532.0
191	Viacom	13,495.5	1,838.1
192	Oneok	13,477.4	304.9

Rank	Company	Revenues ($ millions)	Profits ($ millions)
193	SunTrust Banks	13,464.6	1,634.0
194	Penske Automotive Group	13,448.6	127.7
195	Consolidated Edison	13,388.0	929.0
196	American Electric Power	13,380.0	1,089.0
197	Marriott International	13,342.0	696.0
198	Public Service Enterprise Group	13,336.0	1,335.0
199	Waste Management	13,310.0	1,163.0
200	PG&E Corp.	13,237.0	1,006.0
201	EMC	13,230.2	1,665.7
202	Textron	13,225.0	917.0
203	Sara Lee	13,179.0	504.0
204	Duke Energy	13,134.0	1,500.0
205	Edison International	13,113.0	1,098.0
206	Cummins	13,048.0	739.0
207	Eaton	13,033.0	994.0
208	Williams	12,994.0	990.0
209	FirstEnergy	12,802.0	1,309.0
210	ConAgra Foods	12,755.8	764.6
211	Omnicom Group	12,694.0	975.7
212	Schering-Plough	12,690.0	-1,473.0
213	Northwest Airlines	12,528.0	2,093.0
214	General Mills	12,442.0	1,144.0
215	Circuit City Stores	12,429.8	-8.3
216	Aramark	12,384.3	30.9
217	Medtronic	12,299.0	2,802.0
217	PPG Industries	12,299.0	834.0
219	Jabil Circuit	12,290.6	73.2
220	Marsh & McLennan	12,148.0	2,475.0
221	Devon Energy	12,143.0	3,606.0
222	Smithfield Foods	11,932.6	166.8
223	Masco	11,833.0	386.0
224	Dean Foods	11,821.9	131.4
225	State Street Corp.	11,818.0	1,261.0
226	National City Corp.	11,791.3	314.0
227	Kellogg	11,776.0	1,103.0
228	US Airways Group	11,700.0	427.0
229	R.R. Donnelley & Sons	11,587.1	-48.9
230	Knight	11,505.7	312.9
231	Entergy	11,484.4	1,134.8

Rank	Company	Revenues ($ millions)	Profits ($ millions)
232	Sempra Energy	11,448.0	1,099.0
233	Genworth Financial	11,443.0	1,220.0
234	Visteon	11,316.0	-372.0
235	D.R. Horton	11,296.5	-712.5
236	Baxter International	11,263.0	1,707.0
237	Reliant Energy	11,208.7	365.1
238	Eastman Kodak	11,203.0	676.0
239	Danaher	11,107.1	1,369.9
240	DISH Network	11,090.4	756.1
241	Trane	10,915.1	286.3
242	Principal Financial	10,906.8	860.3
243	Genuine Parts	10,843.2	506.3
244	Harrah's Entertainment	10,825.4	619.4
245	Regions Financial	10,753.8	1,251.1
246	Lincoln National	10,738.0	1,215.0
247	Parker Hannifin	10,718.1	830.0
248	Progress Energy	10,714.0	504.0
249	Huntsman	10,713.4	-172.1
250	BB&T Corp.	10,668.0	1,734.0
251	Unum Group	10,567.1	679.3
252	Baker Hughes	10,428.2	1,513.9
253	Yum Brands	10,416.0	909.0
254	Integrys Energy Group	10,408.1	251.3
255	Sanmina-SCI	10,384.3	-1,134.7
256	Lennar	10,186.8	-1,941.1
257	Limited Brands	10,134.2	718.0
258	Air Products & Chemicals	10,125.0	1,035.6
259	Guardian Life Ins. Co. of America	10,070.7	386.8
260	Xcel Energy	10,034.2	577.3
261	CSX	10,030.0	1,336.0
262	Apache	9,977.9	2,812.4
263	Aon	9,973.0	864.0
264	PNC Financial Services Group	9,956.0	1,467.0
265	Avon Products	9,938.7	530.7
266	Coventry Health Care	9,879.5	626.1
267	Southwest Airlines	9,861.0	645.0
268	National Oilwell Varco	9,789.0	1,337.1
269	Thermo Fisher Scientific	9,746.4	761.1
270	Applied Materials	9,734.9	1,710.2

Rank	Company	Revenues ($ millions)	Profits ($ millions)
271	CenterPoint Energy	9,623.0	399.0
272	YRC Worldwide	9,621.3	-638.4
273	DTE Energy	9,575.0	971.0
274	Dollar General	9,495.2	-12.8
275	Liberty Media	9,482.0	2,114.0
276	Norfolk Southern	9,432.0	1,464.0
277	Starbucks	9,411.5	672.6
278	Praxair	9,402.0	1,177.0
279	Pepco Holdings	9,366.4	334.2
280	Tenet Healthcare	9,358.0	-89.0
281	Automatic Data Processing	9,318.7	1,138.7
282	Pulte Homes	9,263.1	-2,255.8
283	Dana Holding	9,216.0	-551.0
284	KBR	9,194.0	302.0
285	ITT	9,181.1	742.1
286	SLM	9,171.1	-896.4
287	Terex	9,137.7	613.9
288	OfficeMax	9,082.0	207.4
289	SAIC	9,041.0	415.0
290	Reynolds American	9,023.0	1,308.0
291	BJ's Wholesale Club	9,005.0	122.9
292	Liberty Global	9,003.3	-422.6
293	H.J. Heinz	9,001.6	785.7
294	Land O'Lakes	8,924.9	162.1
295	Rohm & Haas	8,911.0	661.0
296	Ameriprise Financial	8,909.0	814.0
297	Qualcomm	8,871.0	3,303.0
298	Sonic Automotive	8,849.1	95.5
299	Nordstrom	8,828.0	715.0
300	Alltel	8,811.3	183.2
301	ArvinMeritor	8,778.0	-219.0
302	Smith International	8,764.3	647.1
303	Commercial Metals	8,751.2	355.4
304	Hertz Global Holdings	8,685.6	264.6
305	Monsanto	8,607.0	993.0
306	CIT Group	8,605.0	-81.0
307	Fifth Third Bancorp	8,494.0	1,076.0
308	Jacobs Engineering Group	8,474.0	287.1
309	Assurant	8,453.5	653.7

Rank	Company	Revenues ($ millions)	Profits ($ millions)
310	Boston Scientific	8,357.0	-495.0
311	Fortune Brands	8,291.4	762.6
312	First American Corp.	8,195.6	-3.1
313	Virgin Media	8,152.5	-927.6
314	Owens-Illinois	8,134.1	1,340.6
315	First Data	8,051.4	158.9
316	Sherwin-Williams	8,005.3	615.6
317	Energy Future Holdings	7,992.0	-637.0
318	Calpine	7,970.0	2,693.0
319	NiSource	7,941.5	321.4
320	Campbell Soup	7,883.0	854.0
321	KeyCorp	7,873.0	919.0
322	Ashland	7,834.0	230.0
323	MGM Mirage	7,820.3	1,584.4
324	Chesapeake Energy	7,800.0	1,451.2
325	Crown Holdings	7,727.0	528.0
326	eBay	7,672.3	348.3
327	Pilgrim's Pride	7,598.6	47.0
328	Mohawk Industries	7,586.0	706.8
329	Ameren	7,546.0	618.0
330	Community Health Systems	7,545.2	30.3
331	Dover	7,487.2	661.1
332	Gannett	7,480.5	1,055.6
333	CarMax	7,465.7	198.6
334	Smurfit-Stone Container	7,420.0	-103.0
335	VF	7,415.5	591.6
336	Ball	7,389.7	281.3
337	Eastman Chemical	7,372.0	300.0
338	Dillard's	7,370.8	53.8
339	Clear Channel Communications	7,363.5	938.5
340	KB Home	7,328.4	-929.4
341	C.H. Robinson Worldwide	7,316.2	324.3
342	Western Refining	7,305.0	238.6
343	Enbridge Energy Partners	7,282.6	249.5
344	Targa Resources	7,269.7	68.6
345	Reliance Steel & Aluminum	7,265.6	408.0
346	PPL	7,245.0	1,288.0
347	Winn-Dixie Stores	7,225.3	300.6
348	GameStop	7,094.0	288.3

Rank	Company	Revenues ($ millions)	Profits ($ millions)
349	Estee Lauder	7,037.5	449.2
350	Synnex	7,004.1	63.1
351	AK Steel Holding	7,003.0	387.7
352	American Family Insurance Group	6,969.4	82.4
353	Yahoo	6,969.3	660.0
354	Dole Food	6,944.6	-57.5
355	Federal-Mogul	6,913.9	1,412.3
356	MeadWestvaco	6,906.0	285.0
357	Great Atlantic & Pacific Tea	6,850.3	26.9
358	Family Dollar Stores	6,834.3	242.9
359	AGCO	6,828.1	246.3
360	Owens & Minor	6,800.5	72.7
361	Energy Transfer Equity	6,792.0	319.4
362	McGraw-Hill	6,772.3	1,013.6
363	Autoliv	6,769.0	287.9
364	Global Partners	6,757.8	47.0
365	Quest Diagnostics	6,704.9	339.9
366	CMS Energy	6,699.0	-215.0
367	Celanese	6,641.0	426.0
368	Bed Bath & Beyond	6,617.4	594.2
369	Whole Foods Market	6,591.8	182.7
370	IAC/InterActiveCorp	6,566.1	-144.1
371	Ryder System	6,566.0	253.9
372	Black & Decker	6,563.2	518.1
373	Interpublic Group	6,554.2	167.6
374	Cablevision Systems	6,538.4	218.5
375	Goodrich	6,535.8	482.6
376	Aleris International	6,528.5	-125.6
377	W.W. Grainger	6,418.0	420.1
378	Newell Rubbermaid	6,410.9	467.1
379	Group 1 Automotive	6,393.0	68.0
380	Becton Dickinson	6,392.8	890.0
381	Embarq	6,365.0	683.0
382	Avery Dennison	6,307.8	303.5
383	Oshkosh	6,307.3	268.1
384	Performance Food Group	6,304.9	50.9
385	Peter Kiewit Sons'	6,237.0	400.0
386	Omnicare	6,220.0	114.1
387	ProLogis	6,216.8	1,074.3

Rank	Company	Revenues ($ millions)	Profits ($ millions)
388	Safeco	6,208.8	707.8
389	Franklin Resources	6,205.8	1,772.9
390	Hormel Foods	6,193.0	301.9
391	NCR	6,193.0	274.0
392	Molson Coors Brewing	6,190.6	497.2
393	Tenneco	6,184.0	-5.0
394	AutoZone	6,169.8	595.7
395	TravelCenters of America	6,166.2	-123.4
396	Starwood Hotels & Resorts	6,153.0	542.0
397	Harley-Davidson	6,143.0	933.8
398	Thrivent Financial for Lutherans	6,132.6	424.2
399	Pitney Bowes	6,129.8	366.8
400	Allied Waste Industries	6,118.1	273.6
401	Stryker	6,107.9	1,017.4
402	Charles Schwab	6,063.0	2,407.0
403	NRG Energy	6,039.0	586.0
404	CB Richard Ellis Group	6,036.4	390.5
405	Pantry	6,015.1	26.7
406	Advanced Micro Devices	6,013.0	-3,379.0
407	Emcor Group	6,006.2	126.8
408	Wesco International	6,003.5	240.6
409	Charter Communications	6,002.0	-1,616.0
410	Henry Schein	6,001.3	215.2
411	Avis Budget Group	5,986.0	-916.0
412	Ross Stores	5,975.2	261.1
413	Mattel	5,970.1	600.0
414	Realogy	5,967.0	-841.0
415	Darden Restaurants	5,925.0	201.4
416	Atmos Energy	5,898.4	168.5
417	Corning	5,860.0	2,150.0
418	Anixter International	5,852.9	253.5
419	Northeast Utilities	5,823.5	246.5
420	Hexion Specialty Chemicals	5,810.0	-65.0
421	Asbury Automotive Group	5,775.9	51.0
422	Mosaic	5,773.7	419.7
423	Affiliated Computer Services	5,772.5	253.1
424	Brunswick	5,770.9	111.6
425	Marshall & Ilsley Corp.	5,745.2	1,150.9
426	Shaw Group	5,723.7	-19.0

Rank	Company	Revenues ($ millions)	Profits ($ millions)
427	Micron Technology	5,688.0	-320.0
428	Kelly Services	5,682.4	61.0
429	Unisys	5,652.5	-79.1
430	Newmont Mining	5,645.0	-1,886.0
431	Owens Corning	5,604.0	96.0
432	Peabody Energy	5,599.2	264.3
433	W.R. Berkley	5,553.6	743.6
434	Blockbuster	5,544.4	-73.8
435	Fidelity National Financial	5,524.0	129.8
436	XTO Energy	5,513.0	1,691.0
437	UGI	5,476.9	204.3
438	Ecolab	5,469.6	427.2
439	Western Digital	5,468.0	564.0
440	Host Hotels & Resorts	5,461.0	727.0
441	Allegheny Technologies	5,452.5	747.1
442	Foot Locker	5,437.0	51.0
443	Agilent Technologies	5,420.0	638.0
444	Precision Castparts	5,414.1	633.1
445	Boise Cascade Holdings	5,413.5	127.7
446	Barnes & Noble	5,410.8	135.8
447	Northern Trust Corp.	5,395.1	726.9
448	Wm. Wrigley Jr.	5,389.1	632.0
449	URS	5,383.0	132.2
450	Rockwell Automation	5,344.6	1,487.8
451	BorgWarner	5,328.6	288.5
452	Pacific Life	5,325.0	647.0
453	Longs Drug Stores	5,297.9	96.2
454	DaVita	5,264.2	381.8
455	Graybar Electric	5,258.3	83.4
456	Leggett & Platt	5,248.9	-11.2
457	Timken	5,236.0	220.1
458	Expeditors International of Washington	5,235.2	269.2
459	Constellation Brands	5,216.4	331.9
460	USG	5,202.0	76.0
461	Symantec	5,199.4	404.4
462	Frontier Oil	5,188.7	499.1
463	Energy East	5,178.1	251.3
464	NVR	5,156.4	334.0
465	Auto-Owners Insurance	5,129.1	466.9

Rank	Company	Revenues ($ millions)	Profits ($ millions)
466	SPX	5,118.1	294.2
467	Tribune	5,112.4	86.9
468	Fiserv	5,021.7	439.3
469	Sovereign Bancorp	5,010.7	-1,349.3
470	Lexmark International	4,973.9	300.8
471	Hershey	4,946.7	214.2
472	SunGard Data Systems	4,901.0	-60.0
473	Western Union	4,900.2	857.3
474	Clorox	4,847.0	501.0
475	BlackRock	4,844.7	995.3
476	Advance Auto Parts	4,844.4	238.3
477	Insight Enterprises	4,830.6	77.8
478	Telephone & Data Systems	4,829.0	386.1
479	Liz Claiborne	4,824.5	-372.8
480	Western & Southern Financial Group	4,810.7	355.4
481	Fidelity National Information Services	4,810.6	561.2
482	BJ Services	4,802.4	753.6
483	Hovnanian Enterprises	4,798.9	-627.1
484	Holly	4,791.7	334.1
485	Universal Health Services	4,751.0	170.4
486	El Paso	4,749.0	1,110.0
487	Spectra Energy	4,742.0	957.0
488	Erie Insurance Group	4,736.5	212.9
489	PetSmart	4,672.7	258.7
490	Cameron International	4,666.4	500.9
491	Chiquita Brands International	4,662.8	-49.0
492	Jarden	4,660.1	28.1
493	Big Lots	4,656.3	158.5
494	Sealed Air	4,651.2	353.0
495	Toll Brothers	4,647.0	35.7
496	United Stationers	4,646.4	107.2
497	Robert Half International	4,645.7	296.2
498	FMC Technologies	4,638.6	302.8
499	Perini	4,628.4	97.1
500	Scana	4,621.0	320.0
501	Comerica	4,618.0	686.0
502	General Cable	4,614.8	208.6
503	Conseco	4,572.3	-179.9
504	Nash-Finch	4,532.6	38.8

Rank	Company	Revenues ($ millions)	Profits ($ millions)
505	Lubrizol	4,499.0	283.4
506	Stanley Works	4,483.8	336.6
507	Health Management Associates	4,483.3	119.9
508	PepsiAmericas	4,479.5	212.1
509	M&T Bank Corp.	4,477.8	654.3
510	Hanesbrands	4,474.5	126.1
511	Synovus Financial Corp.	4,462.8	526.3
512	International Assets Holding	4,460.3	-4.5
513	Neiman Marcus	4,419.7	111.9
514	Rockwell Collins	4,415.0	585.0
515	American Financial Group	4,404.7	383.2
516	Con-way	4,387.4	152.9
517	Steel Dynamics	4,384.5	394.6
518	Kindred Healthcare	4,378.2	-46.9
519	Brinker International	4,376.9	230.0
520	CH2M Hill	4,376.2	66.0
521	MDU Resources Group	4,375.5	432.1
522	Levi Strauss	4,360.9	460.4
523	Wyndham Worldwide	4,360.0	403.0
524	Legg Mason	4,343.7	646.8
525	Mutual of Omaha Insurance	4,337.4	140.9
526	Jones Apparel Group	4,300.6	311.1
527	Brightpoint	4,300.3	47.4
528	Polo Ralph Lauren	4,295.4	400.9
529	Level 3 Communications	4,269.0	-1,114.0
530	Cincinnati Financial	4,259.3	855.5
531	RadioShack	4,251.7	236.8
532	Harris	4,243.0	480.4
533	Dollar Tree	4,242.6	201.3
534	Wisconsin Energy	4,237.8	335.6
535	AECOM Technology	4,237.3	100.3
536	Gilead Sciences	4,230.0	1,615.3
537	Core-Mark Holding	4,211.5	24.1
538	EOG Resources	4,190.8	1,089.9
539	Live Nation	4,185.0	-11.9
540	Washington Post	4,180.4	288.6
541	Ikon Office Solutions	4,168.3	114.5
542	NYSE Euronext	4,158.0	643.0
543	Nvidia	4,097.9	797.6

Rank	Company	Revenues ($ millions)	Profits ($ millions)
544	H&R Block	4,095.8	-433.7
545	Old Republic International	4,091.0	272.4
546	Harsco	4,073.1	299.5
547	Laboratory Corp. of America	4,068.2	476.8
548	MasterCard	4,067.6	1,085.9
549	Borders Group	4,053.0	-157.4
550	Sonoco Products	4,040.0	214.2
551	Manitowoc	4,005.0	336.7
552	Sirva	3,969.9	-412.7
553	CA	3,964.0	118.0
554	Allergan	3,958.9	499.3
555	Amerigroup	3,945.5	116.5
556	Williams-Sonoma	3,944.9	195.8
557	Chemtura	3,926.0	-3.0
557	Temple-Inland	3,926.0	1,305.0
559	Nalco Holding	3,912.5	129.0
560	Zimmer Holdings	3,897.5	773.2
561	SanDisk	3,896.4	218.4
562	Dick's Sporting Goods	3,888.4	155.0
563	AbitibiBowater	3,876.0	-490.0
564	Michaels Stores	3,862.0	-32.0
565	Crosstex Energy	3,860.4	12.2
566	CUNA Mutual Group	3,849.6	166.2
567	Hasbro	3,837.6	333.0
568	BlueLinx Holdings	3,833.9	-27.9
569	Trinity Industries	3,832.8	293.1
570	Belk	3,824.8	95.7
571	Popular	3,822.5	-64.5
572	Genzyme	3,813.5	480.2
573	OGE Energy	3,797.6	244.2
574	St. Jude Medical	3,779.3	559.0
575	Broadcom	3,776.4	213.3
576	Flowserve	3,762.7	255.8
577	Consol Energy	3,762.2	267.8
578	Abercrombie & Fitch	3,749.8	475.7
579	Lennox International	3,749.7	169.0
580	United Rentals	3,731.0	362.0
581	Cintas	3,706.9	334.5
582	LandAmerica Financial Group	3,705.8	-54.1

Rank	Company	Revenues ($ millions)	Profits ($ millions)
583	FM Global	3,692.2	927.8
584	Stater Bros. Holdings	3,674.4	49.4
585	Simon Property Group	3,650.8	491.2
586	Bemis	3,649.3	181.6
587	Ruddick	3,639.2	80.7
588	Casey's General Stores	3,624.1	61.9
589	Zions Bancorp.	3,617.7	493.7
590	Armstrong World Industries	3,609.5	145.3
591	Nacco Industries	3,602.7	89.3
592	Sierra Pacific Resources	3,601.0	197.3
593	Solutia	3,578.0	-208.0
594	Alliant Techsystems	3,564.9	184.1
595	Harman International Industries	3,551.1	314.0
596	TECO Energy	3,536.1	413.2
597	Pinnacle West Capital	3,527.6	307.1
598	VWR Funding	3,522.0	-74.6
599	Alaska Air Group	3,506.0	125.0
600	Cytec Industries	3,503.8	206.5
601	J.B. Hunt Transport Services	3,489.9	213.1
602	Torchmark	3,486.7	527.5
603	Bon-Ton Stores	3,467.7	11.6
604	BearingPoint	3,455.6	-362.7
605	Forest Laboratories	3,441.8	454.1
606	Burlington Coat Factory	3,441.6	-47.2
607	Alliant Energy	3,437.6	425.3
608	Hospira	3,436.2	136.8
609	ServiceMaster	3,431.2	-42.4
610	Huntington Bancshares	3,419.6	75.2
611	Del Monte Foods	3,415.9	112.6
612	Dynegy	3,410.0	264.0
613	Pentair	3,398.7	210.9
614	Corn Products International	3,390.9	197.8
615	Warner Music Group	3,385.0	-21.0
616	SkyWest	3,374.3	159.2
617	Energizer Holdings	3,365.1	321.4
618	Rockwood Holdings	3,347.2	317.1
619	RPM International	3,338.8	208.3
620	Vulcan Materials	3,327.8	450.9
621	Greif	3,322.3	156.4

Rank	Company	Revenues ($ millions)	Profits ($ millions)
622	Lithia Motors	3,320.1	21.5
623	Allegheny Energy	3,307.0	412.2
624	NII Holdings	3,296.3	378.4
625	Saks	3,282.6	47.5
626	Vornado Realty Trust	3,272.5	568.9
627	Noble Energy	3,272.0	943.9
628	Great Plains Energy	3,267.1	159.2
629	Molex	3,265.9	240.8
630	General Growth Properties	3,261.8	288.0
631	NSTAR	3,261.8	221.5
632	Windstream	3,260.8	917.1
633	Pactiv	3,253.0	245.0
634	Valspar	3,249.3	172.1
635	American Axle & Manufacturing	3,248.2	37.0
636	Brink's	3,247.9	137.3
637	New York Times	3,241.8	208.7
638	Puget Energy	3,220.1	184.5
639	Seaboard	3,213.3	181.3
640	Airgas	3,205.1	154.4
641	Westlake Chemical	3,192.2	114.7
642	Idearc	3,189.0	429.0
643	Commerce Bancorp	3,179.7	140.3
644	Mercury General	3,178.8	237.8
645	Georgia Gulf	3,176.3	-266.0
646	Nicor	3,176.3	135.2
647	Republic Services	3,176.2	290.2
648	Biogen Idec	3,171.6	638.2
649	Olin	3,168.5	-9.2
650	First Horizon National Corp.	3,165.9	-170.1
651	Adobe Systems	3,157.9	723.8
652	Country Insurance & Fin. Svcs.	3,135.0	196.4
653	Unified Western Grocers	3,133.4	14.4
654	JohnsonDiversey	3,130.0	-86.6
655	A.G. Edwards	3,126.1	331.4
656	Unitrin	3,116.6	217.8
657	W.R. Grace	3,115.2	80.3
658	Raymond James Financial	3,109.6	250.4
659	Steelcase	3,097.4	106.9
660	Electronic Arts	3,091.0	76.0

Rank	Company	Revenues ($ millions)	Profits ($ millions)
661	Standard Pacific	3,087.6	-767.3
662	American National Insurance	3,071.1	240.8
663	American Eagle Outfitters	3,055.4	400.0
664	Berry Plastics Group	3,055.0	-116.2
665	Protective Life	3,051.7	289.6
666	Blackstone Group	3,050.1	1,623.2
667	Retail Ventures	3,044.6	141.3
668	Collective Brands	3,035.4	42.7
669	Universal American	3,034.6	84.1
670	Ryland Group	3,032.6	-333.5
671	New Jersey Resources	3,021.8	65.3
672	Charming Shoppes	3,010.0	-83.4
673	US Oncology Holdings	3,000.8	-35.0
674	Cooper Tire & Rubber	2,994.9	119.6
675	Superior Essex	2,993.1	63.7
676	Tiffany	2,991.6	303.8
677	Hewitt Associates	2,990.3	-175.1
678	Icahn Enterprises	2,985.3	308.3
679	Worthington Industries	2,971.8	113.9
680	CVR Energy	2,966.9	-56.8
681	Las Vegas Sands	2,950.6	116.7
682	Exide Technologies	2,939.8	-105.9
683	Universal	2,937.1	44.4
684	MDC Holdings	2,933.2	-636.9
685	Centene	2,926.0	73.4
686	Silgan Holdings	2,923.0	122.8
687	PHH	2,920.0	-12.0
688	Interstate Bakeries	2,917.3	-112.8
689	McCormick	2,916.2	230.1
690	Benchmark Electronics	2,915.9	93.3
691	Snap-On	2,914.1	181.2
692	Rent A Center	2,906.1	76.3
693	Carlisle	2,889.0	215.6
694	Jack in the Box	2,876.0	126.3
695	Vishay Intertechnology	2,875.0	130.8
696	Scotts Miracle-Gro	2,871.8	113.4
697	Teleflex	2,866.5	146.5
698	Thor Industries	2,856.3	134.7
699	UAP Holding	2,854.1	33.5

Rank	Company	Revenues ($ millions)	Profits ($ millions)
700	Securian Financial Group	2,852.2	206.5
701	Ingles Markets	2,851.6	58.6
702	Amphenol2,851.0	353.2	
703	Convergys	2,844.3	169.5
704	ABM Industries	2,842.8	52.4
705	JetBlue Airways	2,842.0	18.0
706	Juniper Networks	2,836.1	360.8
707	DRS Technologies	2,821.1	127.1
708	Mirant	2,815.0	1,995.0
709	NetApp	2,804.3	297.7
710	Patterson	2,798.4	208.3
711	Linens Holding	2,794.8	-242.1
712	Hanover Insurance Group	2,786.8	253.1
713	Systemax	2,779.9	69.5
714	Beckman Coulter	2,761.3	211.3
715	Pride International	2,760.3	784.3
716	CF Industries Holdings	2,756.7	372.7
717	United Natural Foods	2,754.3	50.2
718	Analog Devices	2,739.8	496.9
719	Amkor Technology	2,739.4	219.9
720	Granite Construction	2,737.9	112.1
721	Kla-Tencor	2,731.2	528.1
722	Iron Mountain	2,730.0	153.1
723	Questar	2,726.6	507.4
724	Intuit	2,724.9	440.0
725	Apollo Group	2,723.8	408.8
726	Jefferies Group	2,718.9	144.7
727	StanCorp Financial	2,709.2	227.5
728	Tractor Supply	2,703.2	96.2
729	Mueller Industries	2,697.8	115.5
730	LifePoint Hospitals	2,689.0	102.0
731	Wynn Resorts	2,687.5	258.1
732	R.H. Donnelley	2,680.3	46.9
733	Coach	2,678.9	663.7
734	Vanguard Health Systems	2,672.4	-132.7
735	Quanta Services	2,670.7	136.0
736	Mylan	2,666.0	-1,225.3
737	Expedia	2,665.3	295.9
738	Regal Entertainment Group	2,661.2	363.0

Rank	Company	Revenues ($ millions)	Profits ($ millions)
739	CenturyTel	2,656.2	418.4
740	Spectrum Brands	2,653.4	-596.7
741	Jones Lang LaSalle	2,652.1	257.8
742	WGL Holdings	2,646.0	107.9
743	PolyOne	2,642.7	11.4
744	Adams Resources & Energy	2,636.2	17.1
745	FMC	2,632.9	132.4
746	TD Ameritrade	2,632.4	645.9
747	Regis	2,626.6	83.2
748	International Game Technology	2,621.4	508.2
749	Crane	2,619.2	-62.3
750	Southern Union	2,616.7	228.7
751	Cabot	2,616.0	129.0
752	Perot Systems	2,612.0	115.0
753	LSI	2,603.6	-2,486.8
754	Quiksilver	2,588.2	-121.1
755	Sentry Insurance Group	2,587.8	305.5
756	Phoenix	2,572.8	123.9
757	Schnitzer Steel Industries	2,572.3	131.3
758	HNI	2,570.5	120.4
759	Lam Research	2,566.6	685.8
760	Barr Pharmaceuticals	2,557.6	128.4
761	Joy Global	2,547.3	279.8
762	Exterran Holdings	2,540.5	34.6
763	Susser Holdings	2,539.2	16.3
764	Hawaiian Electric Industries	2,536.4	84.8
765	Hubbell	2,533.9	208.3
766	Acuity Brands	2,530.7	148.1
767	O'Reilly Automotive	2,522.3	194.0
768	E.W. Scripps	2,518.5	-1.6
769	Sally Beauty Holdings	2,513.8	44.5
770	Universal Forest Products	2,513.2	21.0
771	Cooper-Standard Holdings	2,511.2	-151.0
772	CBRL Group	2,506.1	162.1
773	Graphic Packaging	2,504.6	-74.6
774	Spansion	2,500.8	-263.5
775	Watson Pharmaceuticals	2,496.7	141.0
776	AGL Resources	2,494.0	211.0
777	Graham Packaging	2,493.5	-206.1

Rank	Company	Revenues ($ millions)	Profits ($ millions)
778	Molina Healthcare	2,492.5	58.3
779	Landstar System	2,487.3	109.7
780	Markel	2,483.3	405.7
781	Wendy's International	2,469.9	87.9
782	UTStarcom	2,467.0	-195.6
783	AMC Entertainment	2,466.9	134.1
784	Zale	2,437.1	59.3
785	Penn National Gaming	2,436.8	160.1
786	Nasdaq OMX Group	2,436.6	518.4
787	Phillips-Van Heusen	2,425.2	183.3
788	PNM Resources	2,422.6	74.9
789	Annaly Capital Management	2,416.7	414.4
790	Arch Coal	2,413.6	174.9
791	Massey Energy	2,413.5	94.1
792	Kennametal	2,400.5	174.2
793	AnnTaylor Stores	2,396.5	97.2
794	HCC Insurance Holdings	2,388.4	395.4
795	Andersons	2,379.1	68.8
796	HealthSouth	2,377.6	653.4
797	Spartan Stores	2,370.4	25.2
798	Terra Industries	2,360.1	201.9
799	Brown Shoe	2,359.9	60.4
800	Solo Cup	2,353.3	68.2
801	Volt Information Sciences	2,353.1	39.3
802	Cabela's	2,349.6	87.9
803	Meritage Homes	2,343.6	-288.9
804	Nortek	2,340.1	29.6
805	AmeriCredit	2,339.9	360.2
806	Albemarle	2,336.2	229.7
807	Medical Mutual of Ohio	2,334.5	89.7
808	Service Corp. International	2,327.9	247.7
809	Weis Markets	2,318.6	51.0
810	Packaging Corp. of America	2,316.0	170.1
811	Rock-Tenn	2,315.8	81.7
812	Building Materials Holding	2,314.7	-312.7
813	McClatchy	2,313.3	-2,736.0
814	A.O. Smith	2,312.1	88.2
815	Airtran Holdings	2,310.0	52.7
816	DST Systems	2,302.5	874.7

Rank	Company	Revenues ($ millions)	Profits ($ millions)
817	Alliance Data Systems	2,291.2	164.1
818	Citizens Communications	2,288.0	214.7
819	Vectren	2,281.9	143.1
820	Lincoln Electric Holdings	2,280.8	202.7
821	International Flavors & Fragrances	2,276.6	247.1
822	Cleveland-Cliffs	2,275.2	270.0
823	Brown-Forman	2,268.0	389.0
824	Moody's	2,259.0	701.5
825	National Life Group	2,253.0	108.5
826	Pall	2,249.9	127.5
827	Valassis Communications	2,242.2	58.0
828	MetroPCS Communications	2,235.7	100.4
829	Burger King Holdings	2,234.0	148.0
830	Ralcorp Holdings	2,233.4	31.9
831	T. Rowe Price	2,233.1	670.6
832	Metal Management	2,229.0	116.4
833	E*Trade Financial	2,222.6	-1,441.8
834	Church & Dwight	2,220.9	169.0
835	Martin Marietta Materials	2,213.4	262.7
836	Ferro	2,204.8	-94.5
837	C.R. Bard	2,202.0	406.4
838	Univision Communications	2,196.0	-314.9
839	Andrew	2,195.1	-162.8
840	IMS Health	2,192.6	234.0
841	Scholastic	2,179.1	60.9
842	Autodesk	2,171.9	356.2
843	MPS Group	2,171.8	87.1
844	Thomas & Betts	2,168.9	183.2
845	NewPage Holding	2,168.0	-22.0
846	Pep Boys-Manny, Moe & Jack	2,162.6	-41.0
847	Children's Place Retail Stores	2,162.6	-59.6
848	Briggs & Stratton	2,157.2	0.1
849	Magellan Health Services	2,156.0	94.2
850	Nelnet	2,155.2	32.9
851	Southwest Gas	2,152.1	83.2
852	J.M. Smucker	2,148.0	157.2
853	Equity Residential	2,147.2	989.6
854	Furniture Brands International	2,145.7	-45.6
855	ENSCO International	2,143.8	992.0

Rank	Company	Revenues ($ millions)	Profits ($ millions)
856	Ametek	2,136.9	228.0
857	King Pharmaceuticals	2,136.5	183.0
858	Hercules	2,136.2	178.9
859	Cognizant Technology Solutions	2,135.6	350.1
860	Hudson City Bancorp	2,134.8	295.9
861	Applera	2,132.5	159.3
862	Affinia Group Intermediate Holdings	2,132.0	-30.0
863	Grant Prideco	2,118.7	519.2
864	Patterson-UTI Energy	2,114.2	438.6
865	Men's Wearhouse	2,112.6	147.0
866	Biomet	2,107.4	335.9
867	Stewart Information Services	2,106.7	-40.2
868	Roper Industries	2,102.0	250.0
869	West	2,099.5	5.4
870	Rowan	2,095.0	483.8
871	National Fuel Gas	2,090.1	337.5
872	Oil States International	2,088.2	203.4
873	Amerco	2,085.6	90.6
874	DynCorp International	2,082.3	27.0
875	Pioneer Natural Resources	2,071.3	372.7
876	Werner Enterprises	2,071.2	75.4
877	Imation	2,062.0	-50.4
878	Fastenal	2,061.8	232.6
879	Hayes Lemmerz	2,052.2	-227.9
880	Quanex	2,049.0	134.6
881	Cenveo	2,046.7	40.8
882	Sigma-Aldrich	2,038.7	311.1
883	Flowers Foods	2,036.7	94.6
884	Belden	2,032.8	137.1
885	Source Interlink	2,031.7	-37.3
886	Rush Enterprises	2,030.8	51.5
887	IDT	2,030.6	58.6
888	Warnaco Group	2,030.5	79.1
889	Hill-Rom Holdings	2,023.7	190.6
890	Interactive Brokers Group	2,023.4	300.5
891	Spherion	2,021.7	25.3
892	Laclede Group	2,021.6	49.8
893	IndyMac Bancorp	2,020.1	-614.8
894	NBTY	2,014.5	207.9

Rank	Company	Revenues ($ millions)	Profits ($ millions)
895	Applied Industrial Technologies	2,014.1	86.0
896	Dentsply International	2,009.8	259.7
897	Fleetwood Enterprises	2,007.9	-90.0
898	Boyd Gaming	2,007.3	303.0
899	Alliance One International	2,004.1	-21.6
900	Ferrellgas Partners	1,992.4	34.8
901	ScanSource	1,986.9	42.6
902	Commerce Group	1,982.4	190.9
903	Tupperware Brands	1,981.4	116.9
904	Sauer-Danfoss	1,972.5	47.2
905	Pacer International	1,969.4	54.3
906	Carpenter Technology	1,944.8	227.2
907	ACCO Brands	1,938.9	-0.9
908	CACI International	1,938.0	78.5
909	CommScope	1,930.8	204.8
910	National Semiconductor	1,929.9	375.3
911	Pool	1,928.4	69.4
912	USEC	1,928.0	96.6
913	MEMC Electronic Materials	1,921.8	826.2
914	Herman Miller	1,918.9	129.1
915	Donaldson	1,918.8	150.7
916	Tellabs	1,913.4	65.0
917	Sierra Health Services	1,909.7	94.1
918	CSK Auto	1,896.8	-0.1
919	UST	1,893.2	520.3
920	AptarGroup	1,892.2	141.7
921	Paychex	1,887.0	515.4
922	Jo Ann Stores	1,878.8	15.4
923	Alpha Natural Resources	1,877.6	27.7
924	Toro	1,876.9	142.4
925	Gardner Denver	1,868.8	205.1
926	HealthExtras	1,857.7	39.3
927	Iasis Healthcare	1,850.0	41.6
928	Mueller Water Products	1,849.0	48.2
929	Selective Insurance Group	1,846.2	146.5
930	Metals USA Holdings	1,845.3	13.9
931	Equifax	1,843.0	272.7
932	Xilinx	1,842.7	350.7
933	Brookdale Senior Living	1,839.3	-162.0

Rank	Company	Revenues ($ millions)	Profits ($ millions)
934	Arkansas Best	1,836.9	56.8
935	Baldor Electric	1,824.9	94.1
936	Public Storage	1,818.0	457.5
937	Mutual of America Life	1,810.2	7.5
938	Regal-Beloit	1,802.5	118.3
939	Century Aluminum	1,798.2	-101.2
940	Career Education	1,795.7	59.6
941	Mettler-Toledo International	1,793.7	178.5
942	Newfield Exploration	1,791.0	450.0
943	PerkinElmer	1,787.3	131.7
944	A. Schulman	1,787.1	22.6
945	PC Connection	1,785.4	23.0
946	Alexander & Baldwin	1,782.0	142.0
947	Fred's	1,780.9	10.7
948	Polaris Industries	1,780.0	111.7
949	Varian Medical Systems	1,776.6	239.5
950	Agilysys	1,774.6	232.9
951	AIMCO	1,773.6	29.9
952	Cephalon	1,772.6	-191.7
953	Watsco	1,770.5	65.6
954	RSC Holdings	1,769.2	123.3
955	Helix Energy Solutions Group	1,767.4	320.5
956	Dollar Thrifty Automotive	1,760.8	1.2
957	American Greetings	1,759.4	42.4
958	Modine Manufacturing	1,757.5	42.3
959	CME Group	1,756.1	658.5
960	Guess	1,749.9	186.5
961	Oceaneering International	1,743.1	180.4
962	Portland General Electric	1,743.0	145.0
963	Kansas City Southern	1,742.8	153.8
964	Colonial Bancgroup	1,742.7	180.9
965	PSS World Medical	1,741.6	50.5
966	La-Z-Boy	1,740.0	4.1
967	Knights of Columbus	1,739.9	88.4
968	Louisiana-Pacific	1,733.2	-179.9
969	Westar Energy	1,726.8	168.4
970	Chaparral Steel	1,722.9	269.3
971	Chico's FAS	1,716.0	88.9
972	Piedmont Natural Gas	1,711.3	104.4

Rank	Company	Revenues ($ millions)	Profits ($ millions)
973	Sealy	1,702.1	79.4
974	MGIC Investment	1,693.2	-1,670.0
975	MSC Industrial Direct	1,688.2	173.9
976	Duane Reade Holdings	1,686.8	-87.8
977	ExpressJet Holdings	1,685.5	-70.2
978	Cinemark Holdings	1,682.8	88.9
979	New York Community Bancorp	1,677.8	279.1
980	BE Aerospace	1,677.7	147.3
981	Arthur J. Gallagher	1,675.1	138.8
982	Plum Creek Timber	1,675.0	282.0
983	Central Garden & Pet	1,671.1	32.3
984	Fairchild Semiconductor Intl.	1,670.2	64.0
985	Dresser-Rand Group	1,665.0	106.7
986	Key Energy Services	1,662.0	169.3
987	Dun & Bradstreet	1,659.7	298.1
988	Sun Healthcare Group	1,658.9	57.5
989	Hub Group	1,658.2	59.8
990	Potlatch	1,656.5	56.4
991	Complete Production Services	1,655.2	161.6
992	Bob Evans Farms	1,654.5	60.5
993	Meredith	1,645.8	162.3
994	Beacon Roofing Supply	1,645.8	25.3
995	Atmel	1,639.2	47.9
996	Calumet Specialty Products	1,637.8	82.9
997	Apria Healthcare Group	1,631.8	86.0
998	Covance	1,631.5	175.9
999	Leap Wireless International	1,630.8	-75.9
1000	Helmerich & Payne	1,629.7	449.3

Solution Summary

14: 1, 2, 3 QUALIFY ME: GRANTS

- Grants provide money that usually does not have to be paid back.

- Grants do not put you in debt and you don't have to pay government grants back.

- The U.S. Government gives away billions of dollars a year to businesses and individuals.

- Grants provide a multitude of funding for school supplies, personal improvement, musical lessons, painting, art lessons, to purchase a home, purchase equipment, cover salaries, purchase wardrobe, etc.

- Search out options for grants.

- Check your state's websites for information about the grants they provide.

- Perform local research in your county, community or city to find what local grants may be available to you.

- Make phone calls to city and county government offices when seeking information on grant offerings.

- Three ways to apply for a government grant - phone, electronically or processed by certified application assistant.

- Don't give up - be tenacious with pursuing information.

- Writing a winning proposal is essential when applying for grants.

- A grant application should include a cover letter, outline or summary, personal project outline or description, personal statement of need, description of the project, and detailed information about the budget.

- Every state offers healthcare assistance for families.

- As a single parent, to obtain government funding you need to check with the city hall in the city where you live.

- Make sure you fill out the forms accurately, following instructions very closely. Specific attention to detail may make the difference of approval or denial of your request.

- Grants are available through corporations, foundations and trusts.

- Decide whether to pursue a grant individually or with the assistance of a professional.

The Future So Bright

INVESTING AND SAVING

Congratulations you have made it to the start of your bright financial future! If you are like most who get to this point, you have already experienced some great success from the previous chapters. Most people start implementing the techniques as soon as they read them, before they even get to the end of the book. My intention in writing this book is to help move you in the right direction towards success, getting you out of debt and building wealth. Considering all the money saving techniques you've learned, you can now apply that saved money to your investments and savings. As you start eliminating your higher interest debt you will have that money to apply to other debt. Before you know it you are reducing all debt until you have become debt free!

This final chapter is about the feeling of gaining some momentum and gaining some success. When you're setting your goals you can review all of the chapters. The Chapter, "Ducks In A Row" is very important because it keeps you organized and will help you stay that way. This is a chapter that I recommend you visit regularly. To continue to keep up with your finances check your debt eliminator chart on a regular basis, along with your wealth creation chart. These simple tasks will keep your finances at the forefront of your mind. When your finances are out of control the credit industry takes advantage of you, keeping you buried in debt! Do not let this happen to yourself, ever again.

With the tools and skills you've acquired you will no longer be overcharged. You will no longer be wasting away your valuable time and hard-earned money. You can now find the best areas and the best investments to utilize your income and grow the money you are saving. Once you are doing that you will be building momentum and moving forward. It's going to feel fabulous, you will see results and when you see those results it makes you want to keep going. You can then raise the bar on your goals, so that you can reach higher goals and this will keep inspiring you to excel.

Now it's time to take action to build your wealth. One thing I don't want is for this book to be sitting on your nightstand collecting dust. This does not do either one of us any good. What I want you to do is to utilize this information. I need your help doing that, which means you need to take action. I have laid everything out, making it very simple and easy for you. I suggest you keep a record or journal of the successes you have from the different techniques you have learned in this book, whether it is in the medical industry, mortgage industry, credit card companies, your banks, or building your credit. A journal or a log will keep you on the right track and help you gain the momentum of building your wealth. You can do this by simply getting a binder with section dividers and keeping your records in there with different topics. You're on the road to getting out of debt, reducing debt, eliminating debt and from there, building your wealth. It is possible for most of you to do this. You simply have to believe you can do it and apply the action steps. Setting goals that help you concentrate on where you can build wealth is the perfect place to start.

I appreciate all that you do to better yourself and I want to congratulate you. Remember to review the solution summary after each chapter and revisit the book as often as possible. Your credit and the financial world will often change and you can find new applications that will assist you. I have clients who have come to me and said, "Wow, Michelle, I can't believe I was able to save $2,400 a year in interest. All I had to do was contact the credit card company, and within five minutes I lowered my interest rates." Months later I received another e-mail from the same client letting me know she had successfully used my debt eliminator chart. Not only did she save money instantly, now she has gone back to review the debt eliminator chart and has eliminated $12,000 worth of debt! She said she is going to revisit her debt eliminator chart often. She and her husband can't wait till next year to see what is going to happen because they have had so many great results in such a short period of time. This can be you; it can happen to anyone, you simply need to utilize these tools.

When you organize, analyze, reduce and eliminate as many debt payments as possible, you can now invest that money. Let's use an example: if someone has $3,000 a month in bills and by using my techniques they can cut them in half, they would save $1,500 a month. Imagine taking just half of that money, $750 a month, and putting it into a five percent interest retirement account. In only 20 years you would have more then a quarter of a million dollars.

You can also apply the Rule of 72 to see how your money can double. The Rule of 72 is a mathematical equation. Rumor has it that it came from Einstein, however, there is no definite proof of this. The Rule of 72 equates the number of years that it will take for your investment to double from the interest. The way this works is that you take the number of the percentage rate that you would be receiving on any given investment and divide that number into 72. What it equals is the amount of years it would take for your money to double. So using the Rule of 72 is a good way to see if the interest rate you are getting on a prospective investment is going to provide an adequate return. For example, if you invest at 7% it would take roughly 10 years and 3 months to double your money.

With the money you have saved from the techniques in this book, you can now invest to build wealth. First, apply the principles in the book and on my website to eliminate your high interest and all consuming or bad debt. Then you can start investing. I have listed some descriptions of investments so you will start thinking in this direction. Then you can get started with investing for your retirement and building your wealth. The following list is not a personal recommendation from me for investing, it is simply a list for you to begin to explore. I do recommend hiring professional advisors. Be sure to interview them thoroughly before hiring them. Some advisors that may be helpful to you are: Certified Public Accountants (CPA's), Tax Advisors, Enrolled Agents (EA's), Attorneys, Stock Brokers, Financial Planners, and Financial Advisors. There are many different types of specialists available in all areas from this list of professionals.

Also, to give you some further insight and help you feel knowledgeable when addressing your finances, I have listed some fundamental investment terminology. This way, when you are researching or hiring professionals you will have some basic understanding of the vocabulary used.

ASSET: Is something of value. An asset can be in the form of cash at the bank; money is an obvious asset or even amounts owed to you that would be considered an asset.

FIXED ASSETS: Known as (PP&E) or property, plant, and equipment, fixed assets are items that are physical items that can actually be touched. They are tangible.

HARD ASSETS: Hard assets are assets that include real estate, physical plant of your building or facility, the office equipment, operational machinery, computers, vehicles, fixtures, etc. They will usually have a life expectancy of several years.

Most of the items that I just listed above have depreciation associated with them. Real estate is usually the exception. If you own the plant or the facility outright, the land will usually go up in value as opposed to depreciating. In real estate, please note that I said it "usually" goes up in value. Sometimes, if you buy high it can go down in value. This is the exception, not the rule. However, let us say, for instance, we were looking at the equipment, the machinery, the vehicles and fixtures; those items will have depreciation because they will have a life span.

INTANGIBLE ASSETS: Are another form of a fixed asset that could be considered your company's goodwill, such as, but not limited to intellectual property, services provided by your company, trademarks, or brand names; these are considered types of intangibles.

LIQUID ASSETS: Cash is considered a liquid asset. Also considered liquid assets: savings accounts, the cash value of insurance, collectibles, or other investments, checking accounts, certificates of deposit (CD's), IRA's, mutual funds, retirement accounts, stocks, bonds and securities, etc. Basically, anything you could liquidate quickly that has a cash value.

LIABILITY: A liability is a debt or an amount owed to an organization, company, or individual person. This could include the funds that are owed to the bank. Examples of liabilities are mortgages, different types of loans, personal and business taxes owed, credit card debt, medical bills, any type of household debts, child support, and alimony are all considered liabilities. Other examples of liabilities are auto loans, student loans, recreational vehicle loans, etc.

NET ASSETS: Is the amount remaining after you subtract the liabilities. A Liability is what is owed, and when you take that number and subtract it from the total assets, what you own, then, that amount is your net asset.

TYPES OF INVESTMENTS:

CD: A CD is a certificate of deposit. It is a savings certificate, which allows the holder to receive interest on the money they have put in to purchase the CD. A CD will always have a maturity date and an interest rate. The interest rate can be a varied amount, depending on who is offering the CD. They are often competitive. You should do your research and look into who is offering the best interest, maturity rates and maturity dates. What you want is a shorter maturity date with a higher interest rate. That will be your best investment for a CD from commercial banks, which is where you will purchase a CD. When a CD is valued under $100,000 it is called a small CD. Of course, if they are over a $100,000 they are called large or jumbo CD'S. Investing in a CD is a great option for a person who is looking for a guarantee. You are looking at a very specific amount, it doesn't vary, and it is exactly what it says it's going to be. It has a maturity date, you know when you are going to be getting the money, and you know the exact amount of interest. It is not volatile and it is a secure sound investment for a person that does not want any risk. There is no risk when purchasing a CD or a certificate of deposit.

BOND: A bond would be considered something you are going to be getting as an investment. For example, if large organizations or companies are looking to make improvements, they need to borrow large amounts of money. They will raise funds by offering bonds that are sold in a public market in set increments. Fees and interest are accrued, raising the value of the bond, which is where the investor makes the profit on the investment. So basically, when you are investing in a bond, you're loaning your money in order to get a return from an organization. Your return on that bond (loan to the company) is the fees and interest that accrue.

TREASURY BOND: There are several different types of government bonds such as Treasury Bonds. They are called Treasury Bonds because they are sold by the Treasury Department. Treasury Bonds have different maturity dates and different attachments associated with the length of time it takes for them to mature. Typically they can range anywhere from three months to thirty years, they are guaranteed by the US Treasury and are free of local and state taxes on the interest. As I mentioned above, there are corporate bonds, which usually are offered by large companies in need of selling their debt through the public securities markets. Just as they would sell stock this is how they can gain income to expand and grow. Corporate bonds are offered with very enticing interest rates to recruit investors. Typically, you will find that a corporate bond will yield a higher interest rate than treasury bonds because there is a risk attached to a corporate bond, which translates to a higher risk of the company possibly going out of business, bankrupt, or even defaulting on the bond. So, there is more of a risk, however, you get a higher return. Usually the government will have the money so there is less risk in Treasury bonds.

I do want to inform you that state and local governments can also go bankrupt. In fact, there is an example in Orange County, California where that happened recently. One of the advantages to state and local government and those types of bonds is that they can wave the state and local income taxes on the bonds, for instance. If that bond is paying a lower interest rate sometimes it's more valuable to purchase this type investment if, for instance, you are in a higher tax bracket. Then this would be a value for you to invest and you would have a higher after tax yield than possibly some other fixed income investment. There are also the tax-free municipal bonds known as

MUNIS. Now the par value of a bond is the amount of money that you will receive once the bond matures. After the maturity date the interest is accrued and added to the value of the bond.

MUTUAL FUNDS: Mutual funds are considered a pool of money or group of monies that is professionally managed for a group of shareholders to benefit. It is a managed firm of collective investments. Typically, what a mutual fund will do is put the money in several areas, such as, money markets, short-term bonds, stocks or other types of securities. Mutual funds are very popular because they have quite a few advantages. They are diversified, professionally managed, fairly liquid, and have a cost deficiency that makes them popular.

The reason why people love to invest in mutual funds is that they have a lower risk factor of losing any money. The reason why is because of the diversification. Mutual funds have a lower volatility because they are invested into several different areas. So, if something is not doing as well and another is doing better, you have a lesser chance of losing money because it's diversified. For example, if the fund is invested into five different arenas, whether it's invested internationally or within the United States, it's very rare where a situation would arise that all five areas the mutual fund is invested in would be losing money. It's a much lower risk, especially if you have a manager that is good or has a good track record. Mutual fund investment managers are experts at finding investments and are trained in researching the best returns. They have a strategy in place for the funds to have a higher chance of profiting. The reason why we say they are cost efficient is because when you look at putting a pool of money or collective monies together with many different people, it gives them more power to purchase the mutual funds. This is why it's helping you to achieve more of a return than you could as an individual investor. Now when you look at putting a pool of money together, you have more of a large variety with the diversification and you can buy in larger amounts. Which again, is going to give you a better return.

Mutual funds are also liquid, and most of them you can sell or turn in the funds for cash. This is why mutual funds are desirable to people.

INDEX FUND: An index fund is a mutual fund, which has a goal of copying the performance of the stock market index. Index funds typically will have lower fees to invest. The reason why is that they are managed by a very small percentage of people versus a larger mutual fund or managed fund. Typically, they use computers and the computers are doing most of the research. They don't have a manager or management team to do the research and analysis.

S&P500 (STANDARD & POOR'S 500 INDEX): In 1860, Henry Varnum Poor published, "History of the Railroads and Canals of the United States." This was a comprehensive compilation of financial and operational details of the U.S. railroads. During this time in the U.S. there was a rise of private capital markets in the railroad industry through private and public financing. In 1906, Luther Lee Blake formed the Standard Statistic Bureau that provided corporate news beyond railroads. Poor's Publishing and Standard Statistics merged in 1941, forming Standard and Poor's. S&P publishes the "Bond Guide" which published a list of about 7,000 bond ratings. The bond guide focused on corporate bonds, giving you statistics and quality ratings. This has evolved to what we know today as the S&P 500.

THE DOW JONES INDUSTRIAL AVERAGE (DJIA): The Dow Jones Industrial Average (DJIA) was at one time considered the best index for U.S. stocks. However, considering the DJIA has only 30 companies, the S&P 500 has surpassed the DJIA for its representation of the U.S. market. The S&P 500 is most often considered the meter for the market.

NYSE: The New York Stock Exchange (NYSE) was first created on May 17, 1792. It all started with 24 stockbrokers signing the Buttonwood Agreement. It got its name because it was signed under a buttonwood tree at the curb of 68 Wall Street in New York. On March 18, 1817, the New York Stock and Exchange Board was founded. In 1863, it adopted its current name, the New York Stock Exchange. Originally, before being called Wall Street it consisted of a group of brokers called Curbstone Brokers. Eventually, they moved from the curb outside under the buttonwood tree to the Tontine Coffeehouse to trade. Still, other brokers continued trading on the street. In 1930, the Curb Exchange was known as the leader in the International Stock Market. In 1953, the New York Curb Exchange changed its name to the American Stock Exchange (AMEX).

STOCKS: Stocks are a share or a piece of investment into a particular company. What that is giving you is a claim to a portion of the company's assets or earnings. Stocks can be a great investment, however, they can also be volatile. Even if you do your research and have a great advisor, a stock can still turn on you. There is no guarantee. So, when you are investing in stocks you need to do your due diligence or hire a professional that you have interviewed thoroughly. You want to make sure they are knowledgeable in that particular arena so that they can get you the best return on your investment. Make sure they give you a risk measure for the stock investment you are looking into. Across the board, when you are investing in stocks the risk can go from a small risk stock to a very high risk stock, depending upon the liability and depending on the history. Doing your research with a good advisor is going to allow you to make the best decisions based on the projected outcome for that stock. Stocks are very risky and there are no guarantees.

A stock is usually represented by a stock certificate and this is proof that you have ownership in that stock. Usually if you are working with a brokerage firm you won't actually see the stock certificate because they keep all the records. This is called holding the shares. The reason why they do this is because it makes it much easier. If that broker would like to trade the shares it makes the trade easier and quicker. Note: if you are a shareholder in a public company you have to realize that it does not mean that you will have a say in any portion of running the business.

RETIREMENT ACCOUNTS:

IRA (Individual Retirement Accounts)
There are 5 different types of IRA's:
> Traditional IRA
> Roth IRA
> Education IRA
> SEP IRA
> Simple IRA

The 2 most common IRA's are:

TRADITIONAL IRA: This IRA's contributions are made with pre-tax money. Only when your money is withdrawn are taxes assessed.

There are requirements to receive all benefits. Your contribution may be deductible depending on your income, tax-filing status, and whether or not you are covered by another retirement plan. The Traditional IRA may help lower your taxable income.

ROTH IRA: The Roth IRA contributions are made with post-tax money. When your money is withdrawn you are not assessed taxes. You will not have a tax deduction with a Roth IRA. There are income and other requirements to participate in a Roth IRA.

OTHER RETIREMENT ACCOUNTS:

401k: A 401k is offered by an employer. The employer will sponsor this type of plan and is usually used for different investment options, typically, mutual funds. As an employee you can make pre-tax contributions. Employer contributions are optional and can be considered a good benefit to a job, as it is not uncommon to have employers match your contribution. However, this is not required. There are also contribution limits and requirements.

PENSION PLANS: A pension plan is a guaranteed annuity for retirement. An employer can create a pension plan. There are many different types of plans that will guarantee an income for life. Some plans will also offer other options for withdrawal in varying amounts.

If you are still skeptical after learning some basic investing principles, thinking you do not have enough money to make a difference, so why bother saving and investing...try using the double a penny a day investing analogy and see what happens to your pennies each day, as illustrated by the chart on the following page...

DOUBLE A PENNY A DAY

.01	Day 1
.02	Day 2
.04	Day 3
.08	Day 4
.16	Day 5
.32	Day 6
.64	Day 7
1.28	Day 8
2.56	Day 9
5.12	Day 10
10.24	Day 11
20.48	Day 12
40.96	Day 13
81.92	Day 14
164.00	Day 15
328.00	Day 16
655.00	Day 17
1311.00	Day 18
2621.00	Day 19
5243.00	Day 20
10,486.00	Day 21
20,972.00	Day 22
41,943.00	Day 23
83,886.00	Day 24
167,772.00	Day 25
335,544.00	Day 26
671,089.00	Day 27
1,342,177.00	Day 28
2,684,355.00	Day 29
5,368,709.00	Day 30

You can see how by doubling a penny a day you could have over 5 million dollars by day 30. This is an example of how it is well worth the time and effort with any amount of money that you are investing.

My goal is for you to never have to worry or have any stress regarding your finances. I want you to be armed with the knowledge and guidance that you can move through any financially stressful time, knowing you can handle it. Life sometimes is unpredictable, and things come up that can take you off course financially. The great news is you can be prepared and you can be the person who can move through tough times. You purchased this book to begin with, and you are reading it to the end. This is a great step in the right direction, do not stop here. You have started the ball rolling and you will continue to gain information and knowledge. This book will take you forward in your life and on your path. It will help you going up the hill and getting to the top of your wealth creation. Good for you! Congratulations!

As our country is facing one of the worst financial crises in its history, we must have hope. As Americans are coping with adversity and hardship with job loss, economic crashing, wall street tumbling, and consumer spending down, we have to know we can make it through these though times.

This is a time to get back to core values, sense of community and go deep inside working on our own depth of relationships. I know Americans have big hearts and are generous. In these tough times we must band together and reach out to our neighbors who are going through tough times. Those who have more need to reach out to those who are struggling. This certainly is not a free ride for anyone who does not show up and try to contribute to life, having a good work ethic. This help is for those who are fighting the good fight and need a hand on the way back up.

The point is many wealthy people have had to face adversity at some point in their lives. In fact, if you talk to any successful person I am sure they have a story or two about living through adversity and coming out to the other side. This type of struggle can build character and lead to great things in life. Many of my greatest successes have evolved from the ashes of adversity.

The most beneficial action we can move towards right now for ourselves and our country is to educate ourselves in the area of finances.

The next step, while you're reducing or eliminating debt and building wealth, is to share the good news! It has always been my philosophy to share the knowledge and gifts I have been given. This is why this book came to life; it came from a desire to share information that I have been fortunate enough to learn. I believe in the law of circulation. When you give you receive. Maybe you can help someone by sharing what you have learned.

I also believe in giving back, so when you can, give to someone in need or a charity. Share the wealth. As you are getting out of debt, share your time with less fortunate people. There is always someone in need that is less fortunate than you. This will not only help them, it will also help you to see that your problems are not so bad and they are manageable. I thank you for your trust with Debt Rescue. So, here is to the wealth you gain, and may you always give in return! Make your life bountiful and blessed.

Solution Summary

15: THE FUTURE SO BRIGHT: INVESTING AND SAVING

- Organization and knowledge are crucial to healthy finances! The credit industry takes advantage of you when your finances are out of control.

- Positive action and momentum is key in order for you to benefit.

- Set goals and concentrate on building wealth.

- Create a binder or journal with your goals and achievements - document your progress.

- Review the solution summary for each chapter, often.

- Visit my website for assistance.

- Analyze, reduce and eliminate debt payments using the techniques in this program - invest that money.

- Thoroughly research any investment opportunities.

- Hire professional advisors - interview them very carefully before hiring them.

- Helpful advisors: Certified Public Accountants (CPA's), Tax Advisors, Enrolled Agents (EA's), Attorneys, Stock Brokers, Financial Planners, Financial Advisors.

- Continue to regularly seek financial knowledge.

- Share what you've learned.

- Give to charity and be generous.

- Practice the law of circulation - give and you will receive.

NOTES

NOTES

NOTES

NOTES

NOTES

NOTES